GRANTA

A Literature for Politics

6

Editor: Bill Buford
Assistant Editor: Diane Speakman
German Editor: Michael Hofmann
Executive Editor: Pete de Bolla
Design: Chris Hyde
Administration and Production: Jane Nellist
Editorial Assistants: Graham Coster, Francis Spufford
Editorial Board: Malcolm Bradbury, Elaine Feinstein, Ian Hamilton, Leonard Michaels
U.S. Editor: Jonathan Levi, 6WR, West 104th St, New York, New York 10025

Editorial Correspondence: Granta,

Granta, 12 Addison Avenue, London w11 4qr | email: editorial@granta.com

Subscriptions:

To subscribe go to granta.com, or call 020 8955 7011 in the United Kingdom

Granta is photoset by A-Line Services and Goodfellow & Egan, Cambridge.

Granta acknowledges the assistance of the Eastern Arts Association.

Cover design by Chris Hyde

ISBN: 978-0-14-014580-9

Pablo Picasso, *Guernica*, Madrid, Prado (photo: The Bridgeman Art Library).

Eugene Delacroix, *Liberty leading the People*. The Louvre, Paris (photo: The Bridgeman Art Library).

Gericault, *The Raft of the Medusa*. Paris, the Louvre (photo: the Phaidon Picture Archive).

Goya, *The Third of May 1808: The Execution of the Defenders of Madrid*. Madrid, Prado (photo: the Phaidon Picture Library).

CONTENTS

The Other Argentina

Daniel Kon Interviews of the Boys of the War   8

Andrew Graham-Yooll The Joys of Journalists and Dictators   29

Jeremy Seabrook and Trevor Blackwell
Mrs Thatcher's Religious Pilgrimage   39

The Holocaust Reinterpreted

Boaz Evron The Holocaust Reinterpreted: An Indictment of Israel   53

Jurek Becker The Wall   75

Gregor von Rezzori Memoirs of an Anti-Semite   107

The Transcripts of Eichmann Interrogated   153

Peter Weiss The Aesthetics of Resistance   205

Milan Kundera The Story of a Variation   229

Ariel Dorfman How to Read the Comics   241

Uwe Johnson An Unfathomable Ship   261

Nadime Gordimer City of the Dead, City of the Living   277

Antonio Lobo Antunes South of Nowhere   295

Contributors   323

Basil Blackwell

Fiction and Repetition
Seven English Novels
J. HILLIS MILLER
'As interesting for the light it casts on current literary criticism as for the individual studies it contains.' Times Higher Education Supplement
'Easily the most important book on fiction in a decade . . . It is not too much to claim that Fiction and Repetition will join the select few of seminal works on the novel . . .' British Book News
260 pages, **£12.50** (0 631 13032 6)

The Rape of Clarissa
Writing, Sexuality and Class Struggle in Samuel Richardson
TERRY EAGLETON
In this remarkable and arresting study, Terry Eagleton seeks to reclaim Richardson for our own time, as one of the most pioneering and revolutionary authors of English literature. He shows how the concern of **Clarissa** with the oppression of women graphically prefigures the feminism of today, and examines Richardson's obsession with the act of writing, his role as an aggressive spokesman for the middle class and his unparalleled insights into sexual politics.
120 pages, hardback **£12.00** (0 631 13029 2)
paperback **£4.50** (0 631 13031 4)

The Writings of Evelyn Waugh
IAN LITTLEWOOD
Outside his house Waugh set a plaque inscribed with the words 'No Admittance on Business'. To fend against the intrusions of an uncongenial world was a lifelong campaign in which his writing played a crucial part. His literary strategies are the subject of this book.
256 pages, c.**£12.50** (0 631 13211 2)

Thomas More: History and Providence
ALISTAIR FOX
The first comprehensive account of Thomas More's intellectual career, this book counterpoints his inner spiritual life, his writings and his public life with his evolving world view. Alistair Fox shows that one intellectual preoccupation links all More's writings: an attempt to find the nature of divine providence by which he believed the world must be ruled.
284 pages, **£17.50** (0 631 13094 2)

Basil Blackwell Publisher, 108 Cowley Road, Oxford OX4 1JF

Introduction

This special, double issue of *Granta* is, for us, the most representative statement about what we are trying to express in contemporary writing. It is organized to fill a gap, a felt emptiness in current literary achievement. For the last twenty to twenty-five years—from the advent of the *nouveau roman* to the desiccated, pyrotechnical elaborations on footnotes that John Barth insists on calling literature—so much of what is regarded as the 'avant-garde' has been noteworthy only for its insignificance. At a time when it is imperative that we have a literature *and* a language that are responsible, accountable, and instrumental to the lives we are having to lead—a literature that is an adversary of oppression and not an accomplice to it—we have instead a writing that is remarkable only for its dubious feats of technical virtuosity, its relentless self-referentiality, and its deliberate retreat from experience. The 'literary' writing since the Second World War—the great postmodern experiments that assume not readers but tenured explicators—is a literature of no importance, dedicated to telling us how little it means.

A Literature for Politics is dedicated to a different set of possibilities—the possibilities of political engagement. In this, however, we are also dedicated to a different understanding of what constitutes political literature.

One of the most pervasive commonplaces of the twentieth century is that literature and politics don't mix. Leftist politics—with its dogmatism, its inflexibility, and its often simplistic notions of social change—goes against the predominant romantic notion of the artist. Artistic creation, this notion has always assumed, proceeds not from political convictions or the dictates of a party line but from the independent, volatile, creative imagination. Artistic creation is, in every possible way, an art of the individual. Leftist literature, however, while obviously inspired by collectivist principles, has rarely offered much of an alternative, and—most often associated with the great proletarian heroes or the over-wrought socialist realism of the thirties—has quite rightly been seen as heavy, tedious, unbearably predictable, betraying a wilful ignorance of the important aesthetic breakthroughs of this century.

It should be apparent from surveying the contents of this issue that the political writing we present is of a different order. Part of this difference is in the almost universal treatment of all facts as fictions—as ideological fabrications that require debunking and dissecting. In this regard, Daniel Kon's and Andrew Graham-Yooll's demystifying of the notions of patriotism,

Jeremy Seabrook's and Trevor Blackwell's scrutiny of Margaret Thatcher's fantasy of the empire, and Ariel Dorfman's analysis of the propagandist fictions of the regime in Chile are important not merely as literary essays but as investigations of the world of political fictions in which we live and from which we must create our own beliefs.

Part of this difference, however, is of even greater significance. In 'A Story of a Variation'—an essay that could serve not only as an introduction to this issue but to most of the fiction published in *Granta*—Milan Kundera argues that, far from having exhausted its possibilities, the novel has merely failed to explore the real possibilities in it. Kundera invites us to see that there are two kinds of fiction: the psychological realism of Richardson (and, for that matter, most British authors writing today) and the irreverent, doubting, debunking fiction of Cervantes, Sterne, and Diderot. There is of course nothing new in this division, but the division has implications today that are different from what they were forty or fifty years ago. For the alternative to Richardson's psychological realism is not postmodern experimentation, but a political writing of the most general and important sort. The division is perhaps evident in a survey of the genuinely exciting and revolutionary novelists of the last two decades—and in this group I would include not only Milan Kundera, Gabriel García Marquez, Günther Grass, and John Berger, but newer writers like Christa Wolf, Jorge Ibarguengoitia, and Salman Rushdie. The difference should also be evident in a number of pieces published here: Gregor von Rezzori's disturbing account of the society that made him a Nazi and an anti-semite, Uwe Johnson's documentation of the ideologically determined notions of liberty, Antonio Lobo Antunes' treatment of the patriarchal society that sent him to war, and—perhaps the fiction of the most disturbing consequences—Adolf Eichmann's horrific self-deception. It is clear that we are witnessing a literature that is confident enough to take on contemporary issues and political concerns. But, more important, it is a literature no longer of the individual, no longer about the just or unjust fate of character: it is a literature of social and economic relations. Or, to put it another way: our hero is no longer the individual; our hero is the community.

The current issue of *Granta* is put together from the observation that we are living in a world that we are on the verge of destroying. And with issues so serious, it seems right that we demand a literature that is also serious: a literature of engagement, a literature for politics.

Bill Buford

THE OTHER
ARGENTINA

The Boys from the War

The war in the Falklands was a politician's war. Whether it is seen from Argentina's viewpoint—as an act of decolonization—or from Britain's—as a defence of the principle of self-determination—the idea is still the same: how we think and talk of the war is largely determined by what politicians have to say about it.

A very different understanding is provided by the soldiers who were asked to fight, and it is their viewpoint that Daniel Kon, a journalist from Buenos Aires, sought from among members of the returning Argentine army. Kon's aim was hardly impartial. He did not speak to generals or politicians. He couldn't be bothered with dates or battles or even the reasons that accounted for why Argentina found itself in the 'Malvinas' in the first place. He was interested in only one thing: what the 'chicos'—the eighteen and nineteen-year-olds of Argentina's infantry—had to say about their experience. Many of the young soldiers Kon interviewed had already fulfilled the one year military service required by the government, and were called back at the time of the invasion. Others, however, were 'volunteers' who went for different reasons: to defend the honour of their country, or—inspired by visions from Hollywood—to participate in what they believed would be the glory of battle, or else merely to be certain that they were not going to miss out on anything that their friends had already left to experience. None of these reasons sounded very convincing at the end of the war.

Most of the soldiers interviewed asked that their names not be printed in full.

Guillermo

Guillermo comes from a middle-class family. His father is an engineer, and his elder brother is at the Faculty of Architecture, where Guillermo is now studying. He completed his national service in 1981, and about six months later, received orders to join his army unit again. On April 14, he was transferred with the rest of his

*company to the town of Rio Gallegos. The next day, they set off for the
Falklands.*

Kon: The war in the Malvinas began amid tremendous popular
support. Were you able to share it?

Guillermo: Yes, in a way. But when it comes to the crunch, it's a
different matter. In the Plaza de Mayo, there were a lot of people
shouting: 'We'll kill them, we'll kill them.' But I knew that they
weren't going to kill anybody. I also knew that I'd be going to war,
and I think war's horrible. Killing a human being is horrible. For that
matter, killing a dog is horrible. And the moment you really have to
go to war, you start to wonder whether it's really necessary. I
suppose nobody wanted to go to war—even the volunteers.
But you had to be on the islands to know what it was really all
about. On April 14th the wireless message reached our regiment
ordering us to move southwards. But no one actually told us where
they were taking us. Most of the soldiers had absolutely no idea
even where we were. I don't know if this was a military tactic or not,
but it didn't help me. Where are we going? Nobody knew. You
know how I felt? Like a machine. I should add that some didn't
even know why we were fighting. But that wasn't the end of it. In my
company, the lads at least had some level of education. But in
other companies, like those near the front, some of the boys had
no idea what the islands actually meant. They were stuck there,
with a gun, without a clue where they were.

Daniel Kon

Kon: How did you feel about the prospect of war?

Guillermo: It was strange. I liked it, and I didn't like it. I quite liked the idea of living through an adventure, something I might never get another chance to experience. At the same time, I realized that something terrible was going to happen. I knew that it wouldn't just be a matter of travelling to the islands, and staying there while the English twiddled their thumbs. A lot of the boys thought nothing would happen, and so did quite a few of the officers. Nobody seemed to be aware of the possibility of war. I don't know what they imagined it would be like. Perhaps they expected the English to turn round and say: 'All right, the islands are all yours.' Or maybe they thought they'd find some kind of diplomatic solution. To me, the world looked in too much of a mess to solve the situation peacefully.

The day after we arrived, we set out for our assigned positions. We surrounded Puerto Argentino* and reached Moody Brook, which used to be the barracks of the Royal Marines. General Jofré's Tenth Brigade set up camp there. The rest of us scattered in the mountains. My company was on a little hill, about three hundred to four hundred yards up, just in front of Moody Brook. Other companies were scattered about six miles further west, on Mount Longdon. I can give you all these details now, but at the time I didn't have a clue where I was. Coming back on the Canberra as a prisoner, I talked to some of the English who showed me a tiny pocket map with coloured dots marking our positions. They weren't officers, just ordinary soldiers. But the moment they had gone ashore, they knew where they were and which mountain they were on, whereas I had no idea at all. I knew I was two or three miles from Puerto Argentino because you could see the town from my position. But that was all I knew. If you took me to the Kent mountains or the Longdon mountains at night, and asked me where Puerto Argentino was, or which way was north, I couldn't tell you. If I had been told to withdraw I'm sure I would have run in the

*After the invasion, Port Stanley was renamed Puerto Argentino.

10

opposite direction. We just weren't prepared. If you arrive in a new town, you want a map to see where you are. Now imagine a war . . . .

Kon: What were those first days like, from your arrival on the Islands to the attack on May 1?

Guillermo: We were still eating fairly well. They brought up the food from a depot that was set up in Moody Brook, and it wasn't bad. A little watery, but, really, not too bad given the circumstances. But it was when the food started to run a little short that we began to go down to get a few things . . . . Well, in fact, we 'stole' them—that's actually the right word for it. We had to steal from the food depot at Moody Brook which was guarded by one hundred and fifty well fed soldiers.

So between one thing and another, it was May 1. That night I first saw the shots from our anti-aircraft batteries, and the next morning I saw the Harrier jets passing overhead. We hit two. I saw them disappearing in smoke. One fell into the sea, and the other one behind a mountain further off.

Kon: Were you under attack at that time?

Guillermo: No, up until then, I was like someone in the front row of a cinema, watching.

Kon: And how did you feel watching the show?

Guillermo: I loved it, and why shouldn't I admit it? It was just like a film. Reality had been made into cinema . . . .

Kon: So you were fascinated?

Guillermo: I remember that when we shot down the first English plane that day, everybody went crazy, shouting and cheering the anti-aircraft guns like football fans. About half an hour after that first attack, I wrote in my diary that a mine went off. But it wasn't the English yet; it turned out to be only a sheep that had stepped on the mine and was killed. We had been told at the outset that we were absolutely forbidden to touch the sheep. Then food started to run short, and we took our guns ready to shoot, and started to eat the sheep we killed.

Kon: Did you kill sheep yourself?

Guillermo: More than 50. I had a very good gun. I don't know whether I was a good shot or not, but I killed quite a few. And we skinned them on the spot so we didn't have to carry them around with us. Some boys killed the sheep for fun, but they soon realized that their lives depended on it.

Kon: You, like everyone from the city, were used to cooked meat served at a table, and now you found yourself having to skin an animal?

Guillermo: Yes, I'd never skinned an animal before, or seen anybody else do it. In fact, I hadn't even killed a fly before then.

Kon: Did it seem a natural thing to do, when it came down to it? Had you changed so much that it seemed normal?

Guillermo: At first, it was a new experience, and I enjoyed it. I knew that I was going to learn something when I killed and skinned the sheep. It was also a way of passing the time of day. Later, it became vital for our survival. We organized ourselves into a group of six. We were all closely united, and shared all our jobs, including going down to Moody Brook or, later, the town to steal food. When the heavy shelling started, the Tenth Brigade moved from Moody Brook to the town, taking the food depot with them. They left nothing behind, not even a single tin of sweet potatoes. Our cheese supplies were beginning to run out and so was the bread. The food in the mess was getting worse and worse—when it arrived at all, that is, which it often didn't. The boys in my group began to move around, because otherwise we would have died of starvation. We started looking for food in the town's depots, which were guarded by the military police. We would slip away from our regiment, walk the two or three miles to the town, and steal food from the depots while the police weren't looking. Just like pick-pockets. We were a small gang, but without a leader. There were, all together, seven of us, and we were completely organized.

Kon: Did you make these journeys into the town quite frequently? Didn't anybody ask any questions?

Guillermo: Normally, nobody asked anything. People from other lines crossed our position too. We were a very mixed bunch, but the seven of us always stuck together. Each person in the group had a special job: one day it was fetching firewood, the next day cooking, and the day after stealing food. It was just like getting up to go to work. In the end, we were interested only in completing that day's job. You could see the Harriers attacking, but they weren't important: what mattered was that it was still your turn to go and steal food from the town. It was a tremendously satisfying thing to return with a load of stolen food that you could then share with the rest of the group. We often had lamb or rice, but the onions, potatoes, and salt we had to get from the town every two or three days. In the town we had to find the depots, slip through the police guard, and get the stuff out. Sometimes you were caught and asked what you were doing there. You told a few lies and got away with it. Other groups found a way of getting hold of sugar and veal.

Kon: Is it true that food was also being sold?

Guillermo: I think so, at first. But later, everyone realized that the money was useless. One of the punishments for stealing was to be sent to the front line (after the English came ashore, we knew where the front line was). But we had become a gang of highly skilled bandits by that time, and were never caught.

Kon: And when the military police saw you loaded down with food, didn't they question you?

Guillermo: It was a large area, and we took some short cuts. Apart from that, there were so many people around, that they never asked you anything.

13

Kon: One of the things that saved you was learning to live together?

Guillermo: Yes, of course. At first, sure, we had fights, bickering— there was a lot of selfishness. But later, being made to share the same worries, the same uncertainties about when we would get back home and who was going to die, we realized that we had to live together. We split into groups, small at first and cut off from one another. When the groups became closer knit, they mingled with the others and made friends.

Kon: So a whole social structure was set up, groups like families within a larger group to which they all belonged.

Guillermo: That's right, we split into clans, each clan in its own cave, living like tramps.

Kon: From your description, you make yourselves out to be primitives, trying to form clans, living with the absolute minimum requirements.

Guillermo: Yes, as you say, we were primitives. We made fires with tiny bits of wood, we used empty sweet tins for cooking, and we went around with our hands and faces blackened with the smoke (later we built a chimney in the cave with a piece of a pipe). We were tramps. I suppose we must have been a pitiful, frightening sight. I went two months without having a bath. And, most incredibly, you resign yourself to that way of life; you get used to it.

Kon: You mention resignation and habit. Did that mean that you gradually lost track of how you were before, even if you didn't completely forget it?

Guillermo: Yes. Obviously you don't forget your past, how it feels to live in a city, eat well. You can't forget the society and culture you've been brought up in, but you still get used to living like a tramp; you accept it as the new way you're going to have to live.

You had to eat filth, steal, kill animals, but you had to do it if you didn't want to suffer. It was really what you had to do, otherwise, well, you were surviving but not much more: existing.

Kon: Tell me about the moment you arrived at Puerto Argentino.

Guillermo: It was complete chaos. We had no idea who had died and who had survived, and there were a lot of people missing. But it was then that we started discovering storehouses stuffed absolutely full with food. When we went down to steal food, we found three or four depots, but it now turned out that there were about forty and they were enormous, filled to the ceiling, so full that we couldn't even get into some of them. But what most annoyed me was that it was the English who gave us the food. It was the first time that I had seen the 'official' boxes of food rations, and it just had to be an English soldier who gave it to me. We felt terribly indignant! Why wasn't it all being distributed? I still can't understand that. I don't think it was out of malice. The only explanation I can think of is total disorganization. This disorganization turned out to be very costly. I hope that this war has the effect of maturing our army.

15

Kon: Guillermo, you say, now that some time has passed, that you are able to see everything more clearly. Does this include the dangers you were exposed to and the friends you lost?

Guillermo: I think so. I lost several friends, and what really hurts most is that those boys died in a war in which they were hopelessly ill-trained to fight. We were simple targets for the English artillery. I often felt like a duck in water, being shot at from all directions. I felt terribly helpless. We didn't feel like soldiers. We didn't want to go to war. And that's why we felt like prisoners, condemned to hard labour.

Kon: How do you feel the epithet of hero suits you?

Guillermo: Everyone's calling us heroes now, but I don't feel like a hero. I don't feel any stronger or more heroic than anyone else just because I was there. I was a conscript carrying out my duty. I'm not going to go around saying 'You missed the Falklands'.

Kon: I've heard that expression on several occasions. I've been told that some of the Falklands soldiers say it to those who stayed behind.

Guillermo: 'You missed the Falklands.' It's a joke. We said it out there as a joke. To tell someone that he was an innocent, a little inexperienced, say, you said: 'You missed the Falklands.' But it was just a joke.

Fabián

Fabián is a guitarist in a rock group. He lives with his parents and a younger sister in a simple, but spacious house, with a beautiful garden. He completed his national service on March 8 1982. On April 9, they called him up again, and, on the 13th, he was moved to the Falklands. His platoon, on Mount Longdon, was in the most advanced position of the whole regiment, and it suffered the heaviest losses.

Kon: How did you feel when you were called up again?

Fabián: We were called up right away, but we still didn't know if we were to be sent to the Malvinas. I remember it was midday—I was already in the regiment—and we were sitting together, watching a news program on television. One of the reporters was talking about the soldiers—that is, *us*—how bravely we went to war. He said that all soldiers must be ready to defend the Malvinas. 'Oy, am I going to hate you if they come and take me there?' I remember thinking. That chap on the news bulletin even had an Argentine flag, and he was interviewing the mother of a soldier already on the islands. 'What would he think if he or his son were taken off to the Malvinas?' we wondered. And I continued to remember him even when I was in the Malvinas. We also remembered the demonstration in the Plaza de Mayo. 'I wish I had a large crane,' I told one of my friends, 'so that I could pick up one—any one—of those screaming demonstrators in the Plaza de Mayo, and bring him here to the conditions in which we're living. Then I would return him to the Plaza de Mayo, and see if he felt like screaming.' We were already called up and were watching the people shouting on television: they looked just like football fans, and were oblivious to the danger—that is, our danger. Meanwhile, we were living through the anguish of not knowing whether we would be taken to the islands or not. It was terrible.

The tremendous English attack on the night of June 11 surprised Fabián as he was doing guard duty. He heard voices, distant at first, but soon much closer. He woke his colleagues just at the moment that hundreds of tracer bullets began raining down on them. They tried, in vain, to reach the cannon for which they were responsible. Alone, with no orders, without even the most elementary of weapons, there was nothing they could do. Except scramble back to their trench. And wait. They spent the whole night in hiding. Miraculously, the advancing English actually trod on the roofing of the trench, but did not discover them. The next morning, they came out into the open. They were taken prisoners.

Kon: How did you feel as you hid that night?

Fabián: It was the worst night of my life. I spent the whole night trembling, praying that we wouldn't be found, that a grenade wouldn't hit us. At first, grenades were exploding all around us, and then, by the sound of the voices that grew louder, we could tell that the English army was moving off. I was lying on the ground, clinging to my helmet, as if that would give me more protection. I had Carlos and Gustavo on either side of me. There was complete silence. No one wanted to breathe too deeply in case they discovered us. It was a terrifying moment. We didn't know how they'd react if they found us. Our guns were all broken, and so, unarmed, we had no way of defending ourselves. We heard voices on all sides of our position. It was still dark, and, surrounded by rocks, we weren't easy to find. The hours went by. We were still flat out on the ground, and we didn't say a single word. There was one moment when we almost died of fright: some English, running past and shouting, passed right over our heads. They trod on the roof of our position but, somehow, didn't discover us. I thought I was going to die; my heart felt like it was going to explode. 'Why can't they find us?' I thought. They had passed directly over our heads and we heard the crunch of their boots on the metal sheet we had put up as a roof. It was a miracle that they didn't find us.

Dawn came. We thought we were the only survivors from the whole company. We had no idea what had happened to the rest. We began to talk in whispers. 'What do we do now?' we asked each other. 'If we get out, maybe they'll kill us.' We eventually decided that we couldn't hide for ever. It would soon be nine o'clock in the morning. We heard a few English talking near by. I suppose they didn't even consider looking inside our position because they thought that there couldn't be anyone left at that time of day. Suddenly we heard the familiar voice of one of our officers. 'They've taken him prisoner,' we said. 'Let's take our chance while we can and get out.' Carlos was closest to the exit. 'I'll go first,' he said. He took everything off—his helmet, his belt, and left only his 9mm pistol. 'Cover me,' said Carlos. 'If they shoot kill at least one of them.' He left. Gustavo and I held our breath in the trench. Carlos stepped out right in front of an Englishman. I think the chap asked him how many there were of us and Carlos signalled three with his fingers. We got out of the trench, with our hands above our heads. I saw the light again: it was a sunny day.

Kon: Did you feel that it was over?

Fabián: Yes, I thought that I had lived through the worst that could possibly happen to me in a war. But I was wrong. A little while later, I was going to be subjected to something even more terrible.

The English front line was by now well advanced. Here, the Argentine soldiers still left were either prisoners, like us, or already dead. That's why I tried not to look around me too often, because I guessed that if I did I would come on a horrible sight. We were made to walk a few yards, and were then brought together with other prisoners. There must have been about thirty of us in all. Amid the general despair, this was a joyful moment. We weren't alone. We met the soldiers from both our platoon and others. We talked for a while. Everyone had roughly the same story: the surprise of the attack, with so many more men than we had. At that moment, none of us knew who had died and who had managed to escape. But we assumed that there must be a lot of dead Argentinians in the area. After a while, we were separated from the group and made to walk for several yards. We passed a pile of corpses of English soldiers, most of them covered in blankets. I tried not to look. 'Luckily,' I thought while I was walking, 'I am not forced to look at my dead companions.' Things were scattered everywhere: food, weapons, clothes. That's why we thought the battle had moved in closer to Puerto Argentino. They told us to halt, and, when I saw where we had been taken, my heart nearly stopped. They had marked out a large square in the ground, and beside it was a pile of Argentine bodies. We had to dig the grave and bury them.* They gave me a spade and I, along with the other boys, began digging. It was horrible: I would dig and then cry, dig and then cry. I tried to calm down, to think about something else, to

---

*By asking captured prisoners to bury their own soldiers, the English were in violation of the Geneva Convention.

consider what I was doing as work. But it was impossible. We then gathered the bodies so as to put them in the mass grave, without coffins, shrouds, plastic bags, or anything. Some of the bodies were half burned from grenades. Others had bullet wounds. A boy helped us to lift one body that was face down. It was Corporal N.— poor chap. When I saw him, I started crying all over again. He had won a bottle of whisky from me in a bet, but now I would never give it to him. Then we buried Second Lieutenant Baldini. He had fought bravely with his soldiers up to the last moment. Another body belonged to a boy in my platoon, Carlos Alberto, with whom I had been talking just the day before. I don't know. It's very difficult to describe this. I don't think anyone will understand what I lived through in those moments. If I had been forced to go through this before the war, I think I would have fainted; I couldn't have stood it. War does make you colder. But the pain inside me is still the same—that doesn't change. Some of the lads with me had to bury their best friends. It was pitiful. I never imagined you could suffer so much. We filled the grave with about eight or nine bodies, including some youngsters whom we didn't know. We tried to take some belongings from our friends, even if only their identity papers, to give to their families, but the English wouldn't let us. They had very little time, because the Argentine artillery was raking the area more heavily than ever by now. Every now and then, while we were digging, bombs fell very near by, and the English signalled to us to get down. They did as well. 'I wonder if I'll end up getting killed by an Argentine bomb,' was what I thought to myself.

Santiago

Santiago was born into a humble family, in a province in north-eastern Argentina. His father is a police officer and his mother a housewife. In 1981 he completed his national service, and exactly a month and a day later was called up again. At 7 p.m. on April 11, his company arrived on the Falklands. They spent two days in a position about a mile away from the airport at Puerto Argentino and then moved to the end of the great canal that stretches south of Puerto Argentino, turning its back on one of the slopes of the Kent and Dos

---

Hermanas mountains. There he dug his trench, and there he remained until the final battle.

Kon: What was your time like in the Malvinas?

Santiago: It was a nice experience for me, but at the same time very sad.

Kon: Nice?

Santiago: Well, I mean, it was interesting. I'm from the north, and, out there, the land's not the same.

Kon: When you say 'land' you're talking about the landscape?

Santiago: Yes, everything was very different for me. It was also a sad experience. It was almost always raining; it snowed sometimes; there was a strong wind, and our heads, ears, and toes all ached. And, as everyone knows, we were very hungry, and some of the officers treated us very badly. They took our food away and ate it themselves. If some lad stole food in the village and was caught he was stretched and pegged out on the ground. Later, when we were fighting, we also suffered a lot, because we saw other boys die, very close.

Kon: What were some of the problems you experienced?

Santiago: We ate terribly. Hardly any food ever reached us. Many of the lads started escaping to the village to steal food from the depots. Others went to the mess, which was quite a long way away, and persuaded the kids in charge to give them a few onions or carrots. They showed their hunger by lifting their hands to their mouths, or else they pointed to the houses' back gardens, where the Kelpers [the Falklanders] grew potatoes, carrots, and onions. Some let them have something, others didn't. I know some who, when stealing food, went armed with their pistols. They were almost always caught. Word got around that the boys were escaping from the regiments, so a constant roll-call was started.

One or two would always be missing, and, when they returned, they were punished. They were made to take off their long socks and walk bare-foot in cold water, covered in frost. In another platoon, they were stripped from the waist down and were told to rest their balls on a plank and were then hit hard from behind. In my platoon, they were put in the camp prison. They were made to remove their caps and gloves, and, with their feet and hands tied to a tentpole, they were left out overnight. When the lads began to freeze, they went all stiff. They couldn't even shout for help. They could do no more than cry. Eventually they were untied, and, after being beaten to warm up their bodies, put next to a fire to recover. It was terrible seeing the lads there, tied up, freezing, and thrown on the ground. Once, I got so angry, seeing a lad stretched and pegged, that I untied him.

Kon: Did anyone see you do it?

Santiago: Yes, and I was asked why I did it. I answered what I felt: that I couldn't see why I had to watch one of our soldiers suffering like that when we were at war. I didn't shout, of course, but just said what had to be said. 'What are we going to fight the English with if we freeze our own soldiers?' The corporal agreed, but he said it wasn't up to him. He told the head of the platoon, a sergeant, who threatened to have me stretched and pegged. But no one was going to stretch me because I didn't do anything wrong. I only saved a soldier who was freezing.

We got practically nothing to eat. Some of us had a little maté and a few drops of milk made a boiled maté, except it was nothing like maté, just water.* I went two-and-a-half days without eating, without even tasting a single thing. When a little food did arrive, it was cold and watery; the other lads looked so desperate that I took only a couple of spoonfuls and gave the rest to them. Some of the kids were so hungry that they sucked the rotten bones of cows that had been dead for over a month. It made me sick. The cows had died a long time before, just after we arrived. They had been killed treading on the mines.

---

*Maté is a South American tea.

Kon: In the face of such suffering, were there boys who simply resigned themselves to the situation?

Santiago: Yes, some said 'May God's will be done: if God wants to take me away, He'll take me away.' Others shot themselves in the foot and had to be taken to hospital. There, at least, they weren't cold and hungry. One lad I know shot himself in the right foot, but the bullet passed between his toes, and only grazed them. He was put on trial. Others got hold of totally rotten onions and ate them until they were ill, so that they would be taken to hospital. There was always some kid of misfortune. On one occasion, a piece of meat a sergeant had hung up was stolen. When he found out who did it, the sergeant beat him and stretched and pegged him to the ground. He did everything to him, and after not feeding him for two to three days, sent him to the front line, where he then fell asleep on guard duty. That lad had given up, and when asked by the corporal why he was behaving so irresponsibly, he answered: 'I don't want to know another thing. Do you know what I want? I want a plane to come and blow me into shitty little bits. I've already asked the sergeant to kill me.'

Ariel

Ariel was so sure of an Argentine victory that he thought he would be returning from the war with an English red beret as a trophy. He was born in a working-class family and lived, until he was twelve, in the provinces. At the age of eleven, he contracted rheumatic fever and required medical treatment for the next thirteen years. He completed his military service on November 12, and on April 9 was telephoned and told to re-join the army. He arrived in the Falklands on the 15th. Once there, he was part of a group that moved among possible fronts of enemy attacks. He was later transferred to Stanley House, the school building that was transformed into the command and information centre for the Argentine army. Once there, his bones began to ache from the constant cold and the damp, and his fever returned. His knees became inflamed, and he found it difficult to remain standing. A little later, he collapsed while on guard duty, and was returned during the last days of May to Argentina among a group of the injured and the sick.

Ariel is still suffering from tremendous pain—to such an extent that he can hardly walk. He mentioned to me that, even though he had 'nerves of steel' during the war, once he left his rifle and his trench behind him, he has been undergoing some kind of psychological collapse.

Kon: Do you sleep well?

Ariel: Yes, I sleep enough.   At first, in hospital, I hardly slept at all. I was wide awake even though I was taking Valium. Now I'm starting to sleep seven or eight hours a night again. Unfortunately, I still have very bad dreams. They started shortly after I left the Malvinas. It's always the same dream. I see my trench, and then I'm fighting hand to hand combat. I see that my companions are also fighting. Then they begin falling—wounded or dead. And I also dream about the return flight when they took me out of the Malvinas along with other ill and wounded people.

Kon: Ariel, what words would you use to describe what war is like?

Ariel: That's difficult! It's very tricky to define war. All I can say is that it shouldn't exist.   You know why I think that? Because I can't accept or understand how people who reach such important positions in the government are not capable of sitting down at a table—even if it means missing two or three nights' sleep—to reach an agreement. Instead each takes his own side and leads thousands of people to kill one another.

Kon: When you learned about the diplomatic failures, did it make you feel very indignant?

Ariel: Of course. When you're at the bottom of a trench with bombs exploding on all sides of you, night and day, you just can't understand how it's not possible to come to some agreement. You feel as though the whole world's gone mad. I came to believe that for the leaders of countries, it's easier to order their people to fight

25

than to make peace. Sometimes I imagined that if the leaders of the two countries were brought to my trench, the war would end at once: they wouldn't want it to go on a minute longer. That's why, after all I've been through, there are things that I wouldn't change for anything in the world. For example, this peace we have at the moment, here, in my home, the songs of my birds: you can't replace all that, and especially not with a gun and a trench.

Kon: And yet you seem to have taken on this war as a just cause which you decided to defend?

Ariel: Yes, but that's different. I knew that it was all for a cause—call it a just cause, if you like. It was something that belonged to me, you see, and that's why I went off to the Malvinas full of pride. I would go again today, but only under two conditions: first, I would ask those who decide whether to send us to our deaths, if they are not capable of missing two or three nights' sleep and food, as we did, in order to reach an agreement, and if it is really inevitable that I must go to war to defend my country, then I'll go, but only if those who are sending me there learn to lead and organize a war, and only if the gun they give me is not a 1956 model, as I had in the Malvinas.

W hat I have written here represents, after many hours of recorded interviews, some of the thoughts of the boys from the war. But these are the thoughts of only those boys who could speak. Some will never be able to. There are others who can still speak, but, for one reason or another, their stories do not appear in this book. Their stories will have to be heard some other time. They would include the following:

The story of M, the soldier who watched the enemy's bullets kill his best friend standing beside him, and who then immediately fainted in the middle of the battle. When the English advanced, he was found still unconscious and was taken prisoner. Today, M spends his time at his house in Castelar, in bed, in silence. Everything his parents know about the war (including the death of his friend and his fainting)

U.N. Peace Proposal

1 Immediate cessation of all hostilities

2 Withdrawal of Argentine troops

3 Withdrawal of British fleet

4 Beginning of negotiations

5 Suspension of economic sanctions against Argentina

6 "Transitory measures"* by the United Nations

*The sending of a U.N. administrator to govern the South Atlantic islands during negotiations was told to them by another soldier.

The story of Jimmy, the Jewish boy, from an Orthodox religious background, punished by an officer for stealing food. He is still in hospital recovering from frost-bite.

The story of H, who, also because of frost-bite, had to have his testicles amputated. At the moment, he travels from his house south of Buenos Aires to see a psychologist in the city. H denies completely that he has been castrated, and refuses to talk about it. To all my questions he just repeats proudly that he fought in the Falklands War.

The story of T, the lad from Córdoba who is currently undergoing a medical examination that will decide his future. T is the son of a retired Army officer and a school-teacher. His father taught him, while still a child, how to handle a Fal gun. His mother taught him to play the piano. And by the age of eight, T was a virtuoso at both gun and piano. At that age he gave his first concert in a theatre in Córdoba. Along with five other soldiers from Córdoba, he was part of an artillery group who, for their shooting skill, were included among the troops who took the Malvinas on April 2 1982. Two of these five boys returned from the war before it ended. One had a foot and an arm amputated. The other was T, who had two fingers missing from one hand, and whose other hand was covered with multiple burns and injuries.

When T arrived in Buenos Aires, in the middle of May, he underwent surgery to remove the splinters from his hands. His main worry then was that he wouldn't be able to go on playing the piano. Amalia Fortabat visited him, along with the rest of the injured, and later brought him presents. She persuaded the pianist Bruno Gelber to pay a visit. That meeting calmed T down considerably. Gelber convinced T that he would go on playing the piano, that nothing was impossible. Another frequent visitor was the wife of General Galtieri, who had grown very fond of T, and helped him in everyday activities like eating and washing his hair. 'Luckily,' T told his mother many times, 'all five of us are alive today. When the other three boys finally return from the war, we're going to work together, all five of us. I'm going to ask Papa to help us start a business. You know what, Mama?

We're like brothers now. We spent our worst moments together, nearly dying of hunger, with our heads buried in the mud to avoid getting killed.'

In the final battle, however, T's three friends from Córdoba were killed. 'From that moment,' his mother told me later, 'my son has been inconsolable. He doesn't want to speak to anybody, he shouts at Mrs Fortabat, he tells her that all the presents in the world can't bring his three friends back. When an officer passes his bed, he shouts insults at him. 'Cowards, failures,' he calls them. The other day, an officer got fed up and told T to shut up, because if he didn't, he would be court-martialled. 'Oh no, not a court-martial,' my son shouted, opening his shirt and revealing his chest. 'Be a man, shoot me now, come on, shoot me.' The officer looked down and left.'

Like T, many of the adolescents who were in the Falklands, have many questions that need to be answered. T now lives completely obsessed by the deaths of his three friends. 'I just can't bear the thought that they're buried out there—like dogs, worse than dogs—beneath that disgusting mud.' The last time Mrs Galtieri tried to visit T, he burst out shouting: 'You, again! What are you doing here? Get out of here! Get out of here and ask your husband if he's going to give me back my friends. Ask him what he thinks about that now. What does anybody think about that now? Why won't anyone answer me?'

Translated from the Spanish by Adam Feinstein

The Joys of Journalists and Dictators

April 19: Peace failed. It would have been a rotten deal. And, besides, nobody wanted it. It's war that everyone appears to need. Argentina hasn't had one since 1870, and the government slogan—broadcast on the radio to the exclusion of the usual admonitions about paying taxes and vaccinating dogs—states that a country reaches maturity only by war. There is euphoria, rejoicing, and a clamour for battle. Perhaps, this time, there really will be a war, and the chance to write real stories on the realities of a war that is not really here.

General Haig arrives to spend Easter in Buenos Aires. He is welcomed by crowds of men, dressed in sweat-shirts and pajamas, and women, wearing aprons over their skirts—a gathering that stretches all along the motorway between the airport and the city. The United States is cheered. General Haig is cheered. He has come, the people think, to help Argentina.

On Saturday, a crowd gathers in front of Government House and fills the Plaza de Mayo. It is showing General Haig the strength of popular support. It is a curious display if only because it assumes that the United States Secretary of State—or anyone else from Washington—understands popular support. General Haig, looking out from the balcony of Government House, must have thought that the people assembled there were a bunch of nuts.

The crowd then cheers the military. This, too, is a curious display. A few days earlier it had wished every uniformed man a cancer in his mother's liver. But the dispute for the Islands has wrought many changes in the Argentine population. People come from all over the country. Some arrive in cars, with bumper stickers ridiculing 'La Tacher': a 'band-aid' covers her mouth in one; another shows her being buggered by Galtieri. One shows the Argentine blue and white colours raised above a Union Jack. Others arrive marching in a column formed behind the Argentine flag. Some come clustered behind a union banner. Many appear dressed in the native costumes of the countries of their immigrant parents: the support for Argentina, the point seems to be, comes from all over the world, transcending borders, memories, and the limits of the imagination.

Many carry signs, often in English, for the benefit of foreign television cameras:

We are the people of peace,
Death to Margaret's army.

Or:

Good-bye Queen,
God save Argentina.

The more severe nationalists carry a placard that reads: *'Ingleses, piratas, masones, herejes,* go home.' And one particularly un-compromising patriot has inspired the crowd to jump and chant:

No cabe duda,
no cabe duda,
la Reina de Inglaterra
es la Reina mas boluda.

A foreign correspondent for a British paper asked for a translation, and when I told him, he was ('I say, that is a bit off') slightly offended:

There is no doubt,
There is no doubt,
The Queen of England
Is the biggest twat of all.

Nevertheless, the journalists are happy and well taken care of. The press have been given the roof of Government House—where a helicopter awaits General Haig's urgent departure—and the journalists enjoy the security-agents' view of the crowd below. The text of the 'March of the Malvinas' is distributed by representatives from Government House. A jingle, that begins 'Come on, Argentines, Come on and win', punctuates what passes for news-reels. Everywhere there is excitement and anticipation. Surely the war will put an end to the imitations of the chronicles of Gabriel García Marquez. Now at last we might write like Ernest Hemingway.

There are, however, some feelings that are difficult to reconcile. In 1976, after the military coup and the murders that followed it, thousands of Argentines left the country and went into exile. But now they are returning. They arrive like rich amnesiacs: the exiles seem unable to recall why they were exiles in the first place, and, with their pockets filled with strong foreign currencies, they are having the times of their lives. By virtue of their presence the exiles offer tacit support to the military rulers who caused the 'disappearance' and death of twenty thousand men and women. Galtieri, like 'La Tacher', could put a war to good use; he has a few memories that he needs to bury—murders that might now be judged heroism—and by returning the exiles seem to be offering Galtieri a hand. What do they think has been happening during the six years they were away? Roque Daltón wrote of the survivors in El Salvador that they were the 'half dead';

these returning exiles are the half living, a chunk missing from their lives: it is the six years that they were not here to witness.

The Falkland invasion has become an amnesty of the damned. At the annual book fair, new titles by Gabriel García Marquez, Mario Benedetti, and every other banned Latin American author, are displayed by nervous publishers. There is also the new novel by Mario Vargas Llosa—who is currently popular in Argentina for his dramatic work *La Señorita de Tacna* that plays every night to full houses not because it is one of the only entertainments in town that does not mention the Malvinas, but because of an exciting nude scene by actress Katja Alemann, a relative of the economy minister, whose role is that of a temptress in an old man's memories. People might be better advised to look at the novel. *La guerra del fin del mundo* tells the story of a nineteenth-century rebellion in Brazil led by a holy man who entered history with the same zeal and energy with which, under normal circumstances, he would have entered a lunatic asylum. The book's five hundred and thirty-one pages perhaps makes it accessible only to convalescents and Fleet Street sub-editors (or others with time to spare) but should be required reading for this band of 'psychological war correspondents' writing of this war at the end of the world.

Perhaps the current hysteria derives from an uneasy awareness of the past and the future. Everybody ignores the memories of the old tragedies, while anxiously adjusting to the possibility of new ones. Euphoria and apprehension mix maniacally.

The Argentine papers quote Paul Groussac, the critic and historian who immigrated here from France in the nineteenth century and who claimed in 1910—to his own mind and to the delight of subsequent generations of Argentines—that there was no doubt that the Malvinas belong to Buenos Aires. Groussac has been dead for years. And so have many others who might have best advised Argentina. Leopoldo Torre Nilsson, the film-maker who spent his life defying the censors, died of cancer in September 1978. Victoria Ocampo died in February 1979. Jorge Luis Borges—who once wrote that 'Defeat has a dignity that victory lacks'—has gone to New Orleans. Others are also abroad or cowed by the noise of triumph into acquiescing in the policies of the government. One did not. Mario

Paoletti, an Argentine short-story writer in exile in Spain, writes:
I saw on television the Plaza de Mayo filled with people, and I was overcome with shame. I suppose the British nationalistic hysteria is equally indigestible. Something similar occurred during the World Cup in 1978. That was the day of the Cup Final between Argentina and Holland, when the country went 'mad' with joy, and rushed to the Plaza de Mayo to cheer President Videla. At that time Videla's people were torturing me . . . . If they really want to reconquer their land, the Argentines could start in the Rojas, the province of Buenos Aires, where one hundred thousand families live on the land that belongs to three families.

Mario Paoletti was obviously not sympathetic enough to the government to caution it against changing the name of Port Stanley to Puerto Rivero, after Antonio Rivero, who is said to have led the rebellion against the British usurper in the Falklands in 1833. This week the Port was renamed again—this time, Puerto Argentino—after it was discovered that Rivero was in fact no libertarian but a scoundrel on a rampage of murder, arson, and robbery.

Few flags fly over Ranelagh, the most English of the Anglo-Argentine suburbs of Buenos Aires. Although only twenty miles south of the capital it is not easily accessible from the motorways and its train service is unreliable. As a result, Ranelagh has developed into a nearly autonomous British island in the midst of the Argentine countryside.

The British-owned Southern Land Company founded Ranelagh in 1913 with ten English-style suburban detached houses. By 1930, Ranelagh showed all the promise of a growing and prosperous colonial town, and was able to support its first taxi—it is still driven today by Harold Welbourn, known to some as 'Well worn'—but there hasn't been a new taxi added to the one-man fleet yet. The village's two railway crossings still have no gates, and many of its dirt streets bear the wooden municipal notice boards that read: 'No traffic within seventy-two hours after rains.'

Ranelagh has never shown much interest in politics—especially the politics of the Falklands. The village veterinarian is, in this, a little extraordinary in wondering if the new moon in three days' time will have the same unsettling effect on the government that it is bound to have on the horses he has been treating for worms. Apparently, a few engineers on the British railways—nationalized in 1848—had visited Port Stanley, but no one else has gone, or , if they have, they aren't admitting it: the British did not welcome travellers from Argentina and Argentina found it difficult to tolerate Argentines visiting a British colony. There were, however, three exceptions. One, a young Scot who worked in the travel business, informed his neighbours that Ranelagh was not as big as Port Stanley, but said no more. The other two were not among Ranelagh's more reputable residents. One was Gregorio, a Polish anarchist whose liver was in an advanced state of decomposition. He always advocated occupation of the Falklands on the grounds that it would secure large stocks of duty-free gin for Argentina; the British, he said, could be prevailed upon later not to discontinue supplies. The other was Ivan, a grossly overweight Russian, whose three daughters wanted to visit the Islands on learning that there was a shortage of women. In Port Stanley they were eager to extend the lucrative service already available in Ranelagh to the many men who travelled to the village every week to use the local golf club.

In Ranelagh—as in Hurlingham, City Bell, and the other outposts of the British Empire in Argentina—the Falklands were always referred to as the Malvinas out of deference to the host country. But they were colonized by the British, of course, which was what mattered.

May 17: Today's communiqué was the sixty-second since hostilities began with the Harrier bombing of Stanley airport on May 1; Communiqué Number Sixty-two refuted news-agency reports from London that Argentine planes had strafed the aircraft carrier HMS *Hermes.* The communiqué was not unusual. These telegraphic communiqués, whose veracity has been surprising and their honesty often baffling, will surely represent Argentine's official record of the conflict. Their message has been something in the order of: 'We are not winning yet; we are defending ourselves; but they keep on coming.' The communiqués served as antidotes to the official statements that were always embellished with rumours—Argentina's only growth industry—even though Communiqué Number Thirty-six banned rumours.

Example: an Air Force officer in the President's office at the Casa Rosada told local reporters from the *Gente* and *La Semana* magazines that the HMS *Hermes* had been destroyed, that the HMS *Invincible* had been damaged, that five Task Force ships had been sunk, that an unknown number damaged, and that thirteen Harrier jets had been shot down. The local reporters went to the Sheraton Hotel and told the foreign hacks—who welcomed a good rumour because then they did not have to invent their own—and the hacks paid the locals for the rumours in dollars, beer, or pleasantries. The foreign hacks then telephoned Paris or Chicago or London or Moscow. Tass responded first, reporting the *Hermes* sunk. In London the Ministry of Defence wheeled out spokesmen who said they could not comment, thereby creating doubt. The newspapers then published the rumour and the spokesmen's inability to comment, and by doing so gave credibility to the possibility of a disaster. The news-agencies cribbed the story that was then picked up in Buenos Aires, where the official news-agency Telam claimed it came from the Telam correspondents in London (though it had no correspondents in London), and Argentine papers ran the sinkings and hits on their front pages, which were then refuted by Communiqué Number Sixty-two. The official communiqués were astounding for their veracity.

Every day was like that. Where did it all start? Perhaps in magazines such as *Gente*, which ran an artist's impression of what the *Hermes* would look like sinking after a hit by a French Exocet missile, and Venezuelan television reproduced the picture which the papers in Caracas picked up and which people then said was true because they had read it in the foreign papers. Or perhaps the stories began in the Argentine naval newspaper *Noticias*, which ran the sinkings of British ships in the form of a score-card in a game of battleships on its front page. Or perhaps it was *Revista 10*, which reproduced on its cover a photograph of the HMS *Invincible* with a cloud of smoke engulfing its deck. The English news-agency Reuters then reported the publication of the photograph, thereby acknowledging another sinking as a possibility, and thus the circuit began once again.

The problems did not, of course, originate only in Argentina. 'All set for the invasion,' the *Sun* glowed on May 15. Why should that rag be the only British paper received in Buenos Aires? Travellers brought it as a curiosity that the news-agencies then used for front pages. The bottom of the front page on that particular day read 'Death of the Argy Sub' (which occasioned a complaint from a man who said that it should be spelled Argie because his name was Argy and he did not like to be mentioned every day). The submarine was Argentina's *Sante Fé*, sunk in South Georgia, which, once again, started up the rumour machine. In Buenos Aires the papers said that the battle for South Georgia raged on, even though the man who commanded its defence—promoted to Captain for the torture of some of the *desaparecidos* whom he helped to make disappear—had surrendered three weeks ago. The rumour, of course, was ruined a little later when the Captain-Torturer's one hundred and fifty troops were returned to Buenos Aires, acknowledging that they had been well treated but complaining about British food: it was abominable. They were ordered to say no more. Their embarrassing return meant that an officer at the Joint Chiefs of Staff had to admit that the loss of South Georgia was actually a tactical surrender, because Argentina knew that it could not be defended and had used it to distract British attention. The officer quoted somebody, Charlemagne perhaps, to explain statements that meant the British were losing and the Argentines were winning.

Then the cruiser *Belgrano* was sunk by a torpedo, killing three hundred and fifty people. The commander, Captain Bonzo—a very unfortunate name to have in any propaganda war—held a press conference at the Sheraton Hotel and called the sinking a crime against humanity. But he talked too long: the journalists got bored, the staff got bored, and the crews from the television networks from abroad said it was impossible to extract good quotes, and his dramatic story was dropped. 'Gotcha' shone the *Sun*—oh, when will it ever be eclipsed? Everybody was crying until the HMS *Sheffield* was sunk and then everyone was laughing, saying how good the Argentine pilots were: they must have trained in the Buenos Aires traffic.

The BBC then reiterated a broadcast first made in April that any British who had nothing to do in Argentina should get out. A few packed their bags, but they were the privileged class of men and women, short-term residents called 'contract staff'. They did not have much to pack, and their wives and children were merely moved across the River Plate for a company-paid holiday. The others, the forty thousand or more Anglo-Argentines, showed no intention of leaving. They had too much to pack. Their way of life was too special to fit any packing case.

They did not want to leave, and neither did the journalists. At the end of the day, after they had fired off their reports loaded with imagination or rumours or figures of real fatalities, the journalists went to supper in elegant restaurants and drank good wine and ate huge steaks, and later laid an air hostess at the Sheraton or went dancing at Régine's, Mau Mau, or the Hippopotamus—already booked by a man from ITN for the office Christmas party. Or late at night, the drunkest of the correspondents gathered at Sedon's bar and sometimes sang 'Galtieri, who do you think you are?' to the tune of the theme from *Dad's Army* or the *River Kwai* or with no tune at all. No was beaten up. It was not violence the journalists feared: it was the prospect that the war would end or their visas would expire, and then the fun would be over.

But eventually the fun had to end. The city, the Paris of South America, was blacked out almost completely—by military decree. Restaurants started to close early. Even some of the foreign films— the only entertainment that did not mention the Malvinas—were taken off the market. *Coming Home*, about Vietnam veterans returning to the United States, lost its exhibition certificate. And so did Costa Grivas's *Z*, recently restored after ten years: 'the circumstances in the country' made their exhibition inadvisable.

And the night got blacker. At the Organization of American States, diplomats from Argentina got the most they could have hoped to achieve from their Latin American allies: a vote of sympathy. And the most they could expect to achieve from Communist Cuba: a vote of sympathy.

June 17: An eerie hush falls over the city. After an unseasonably long summer and a warm autumn, winter arrives suddenly. The people who had cheered Galtieri just one week before as he lowered the flag at sunset from the pole outside Government

House gather again in the Plaza de Mayo: this time to call him a bastard. Galtieri has fallen—not in shame for the defeat of Port Stanley—but under the weight of the medals received for good conduct or under the pressure of his generals. He is replaced by a man with a Greek name who immediately advises newspaper editors, who have already been humiliated by the military's manipulation of the news, to stop printing war-horror stories. The papers begin to shorten and ultimately abandon the accounts of the boys, recently repatriated from Port Stanley by a British liner, who had been castrated because their testicles had been frost-bitten from sitting for so long in the trenches. The newspaper editors ignore the stories of incompetence and cowardice shown by the army officers. They decide it is better not to mention that the supply commanders had bungled: that, because of them, the front line had starved; that the second line had received only an occasional meal; and that the officers at the rear had been able to munch away until they returned embarrassingly overweight. The newspaper editors will not notice that some of the soldiers had not bathed for three months, that their guns had jammed, that their feet, their food, and their fuel had frozen. There will be no feature stories about amputations, starvation, the psychiatric treatment now required for the returning infantry, or the suicides of bereaved parents who had not known what war meant. There will be no estimates of the total number killed.

What the papers do say is that the economy is in ruins. Not even the auction for the Patriotic Fund is able to raise money. The patriotic fervour seems to have vanished. A soup kitchen is set up outside the Regina Martyrum Church, near the Congress, where women queue to fill a bowl to feed a family. Middle-class women answer advertisements in the papers to work as maids in Madrid for a year so that they can send money back to their husbands, their *machismo* crushed because they have no jobs. The irony is not lost on the Spanish who, years ago, once lost their women to the prosperous Paris of the New World.

In Britain victory is celebrated. On June 17, there are 3,061,229 people without jobs: perhaps some of them will turn up in the Falkland Islands to help clear the Argentine land mines. On June 17, a small crowd gathers and yells 'Pakis out' at a man on a street in

Kentish Town. There are isolated stories of cripples and death. But here, like Argentina, there are no stories about the soldiers. There are no interviews. Victory is too precious to spoil.

From the notes kept while in Argentina
Andrew Graham–Yooll

Mrs Thatcher's Religious Pilgrimage

It is only since Mrs Thatcher's Falklands triumph that her incredulous opponents have begun to understand the true extent of her ambition; and many of those who came to scoff now realize that they have been summoned to pray. An examination of the texts of her major speeches as Leader of the Conservative Party should have shown clearly, however, the nature of Mrs Thatcher's struggle. Her object is not simply to be the most successful politician since the Second World War; she is embarked on a more epic enterprise: a heroic pilgrimage, an odyssey through time towards a fabulous moment in which past and future meet in a new Victorian age purged of the impurities of Socialism. Her aim is the conquest of history.

In this tormented undertaking, Mrs Thatcher relies on a mangled rhetoric conjured up from the disparate elements of popular experience and tradition. Passing through and ransacking the different levels of the culture, she pieces together remnants and patches that become, in her skilful hands, a seamless robe of domestic, economic, political, and indeed cosmic moralism. First, perhaps, is the domestic imagery, to reassure and comfort: 'A nation is an extended family. Families go through their hard times; they have to postpone cherished ambitions until they have the means to satisfy them.'* The imagery enables her to move easily to more exalted levels, endowing each with domestic authority. Thus, for instance, the economy: 'Men must have confidence in the common currency of everyday life. Honest money is a mark of the kind of society we Conservatives seek. So the steady reduction of the rate of inflation is essential, not just to good house-keeping, but for the deepest philosophical reasons.' From the domestication of the economy, it is but one easy step to claims of grander significance, as when she conflates the natural evolution of capitalism—'our system, the free enterprise system which delivers goods to the mass of the people'—with not just biological evolution but the ways of our forefathers:

Industrial revolutions are painful. We know that from history. Adaptation is painful. It's a natural and sometimes a healthy human instinct to want to go on in the old way . . . . But the truth is, changes of this sort are part of real life. They are fundamental to our survival. If today people aren't willing to move as their fathers did, the economy can't thrive.

The moral aspects of her project, on the other hand, depend on resonances from a wide range of pirated primary religious culture—Methodist hymns, the Bible, and *Pilgrim's Progress*. Thus she addresses the Conservative Annual Conference as though they were an assembly of the elect: 'Throughout the long years of opposition, you have kept faith.' Wishing she could offer a 'less rugged road,' she calls on her hearers to 'resist the blandishments of

For our part we will resist the calls for easy options. Ulysses, you will remember, resisted the siren voices and came safely home to harbour.

the faint-hearts.' Even when she is not explicitly using the language of the Bible, it emerges in the most unlikely places to shape the rhythm of her speech. Thus 'We saved our living standards; our jobs we could not save' is given an irrefragable authority by the half-remembered cadence of Matthew 27.42: 'He saved others; himself he cannot save.' The impalpability of these references creates a powerful, implicit sub-text, which buoys up the banalities of her vision into something unaccountably profound; sense merges with a mysterious evocation of universal truth.

At the heart of Thatcherism is its great commandment, 'There is no alternative.' In this way, the development of capitalism is assimilated to the exigencies of an absolute religious creed. It is here we glimpse the full extent of Mrs Thatcher's intentions: to present the political necessities of capitalist evolution as to make of them

something both beneficent and inevitable. It is this benison upon necessity that gives Thatcherism both its strength and its claustrophobic circularity. It renders her political opponents' efforts to break out of it to appear not only ineffectual or ridiculous, but immoral.

This absolute moralism inhabits different levels of experience with the ease of some fabulous creature equally at home in all elements. The metamorphoses are dazzling, swift, and abrupt: 'There is no hard and fast line between economic and other forms of responsibility to self, family, firm, community, nation, God.' The individual is measured by how far he has followed these moral principles; and so is the destiny of the country as a whole. We have a

> **There were those who would not admit it—even perhaps some here today—people who would have strenuously denied the suggestion but—in their heart of hearts—they too had their secret fears that it was true: that Britain was no longer the nation that had built an Empire and ruled a quarter of the world. Well they were wrong. The lesson of the Falklands is that Britain has not changed.**

duty to set an example to less favoured nations ('Aggression must not be seen to pay'; 'We do not appease dictators'). We have an even greater duty to recover our once privileged position as the most perfect embodiment of capitalist ethics. So it is that the arbitrary necessities of capitalist self-expansion are written into the moral order of the universe, and are sanctified even by selective echoes of a Non-conformist provincial childhood and common-sense Christianity. 'I learned from childhood the dignity which comes from work, and by contrast the affront to self-esteem which comes from enforced idleness. For us, work was the only way of life we knew, and we were brought up to believe it was not only a necessity but a virtue.'

Mrs Thatcher's success is not only in her ability to plunder the chapel culture in which she was born—that fertile source of imagery and suasion—for she is also a story-teller to the nation, offering us easy and instant illustrations like those of the brightly coloured pop-up picture books of our childhood ('If this country's story is to change, we, the Conservatives, must re-kindle the spirit'). Leaving nothing to chance, she tells us an endless succession of fairy-tales and parables to lighten our darkness. Above all, she wishes us to understand that the monster which has plagued our childhood, the Minotaur of capital, is no such thing. Quite the contrary. Not only is it our best hope, our only ally and friend, it is our very salvation. Her business is transformations: the toad on the princess's pillow will turn out to be a handsome prince. There is therefore nothing to fear. Beauty embraces the Beast. See, it wishes us no harm. It is a gentle giant; if we treat it properly, its bounty will know no limits.

In this book of fairy-tales, Capitalism and Socialism are twins; but the evil twin has stolen his brother's birthright and besmirched his reputation. For many years, most of the unsuspecting villagers have believed the story that Capital stole things when they weren't looking, and was capable of all kinds of cruelties unless shackled and con-

---

And let our nation, as it has so often in the past,
remind itself and the world:
> **"Nought shall make us rue,**
> **If England to herself do rest but true."**

---

trolled. Fortunately the fairy godmother is at hand with her dreadful rhyming couplets to set this topsy-turvy world to rights. She urges us to awake from what is actually a nightmare, and face the reality of the long journey, the quest with its dream-like quality: 'This is the road I am resolved to follow. This is the path I must go. I ask all who have the spirit—the bold, the steadfast, and the young in heart—to stand and join me as we go forward. For there is no other company in which I would travel.' And so the myth, the return, the journey, the dream, all become interchangeable and mutually reinforcing metaphors; and in the pilgrim's progress the snares and delusions are the Socialist nightmare, 'one of the blind alleys of history.' Her vanity fair is Socialist utopianism, 'this recent creed'; and her ambition is nothing less than to extirpate it, to re-make history as though it had never been.

In her re-writing of history, Mrs Thatcher asks us to join her on a journey that is, above all, a journey home. More than this, it is a journey which should never have been necessary but for the folly

43

of mankind. Her story, then, is really the story of the Fall. Paradise was Victorian England, when the primal wisdom had its natural reward in Britain's respected and unrivalled position in the world. 'The Victorian Age has been badly treated in Socialist propaganda. It was an age of constant constructive endeavour, in which the desire to improve the lot of the ordinary man was a powerful factor.' The serpent Socialism insinuated itself into this Eden, however, and persuaded old Adam that God's economic commandments need not

But you, Mr President, are a sailor, and you know that the voyage to full competitiveness in today's world is a long and hard one. But I say to you the ship sails east; the ship sails west; whatever the wind that blows, 'tis the set of the sail, and not the gale that determines the way she goes.

be obeyed and that man could take control of his own destiny by eating of the tree of knowledge. But for Mrs Thatcher this will not do. The workings of the economic universe cannot be known or penetrated. The 'unseen hand' must govern our destiny. That mysterious process of wealth creation 'cannot be anticipated or simulated by politicians and their advisers however distinguished or decorated.' And it is this 'magic of the markets' that is the secret alchemy that transmutes individual selfishness into the public good. Deceived by the serpent's voice—the 'easy options' of Socialism—the people have been expelled from their earthly nineteenth-century paradise. And so we slip into the epic of the Israelites wandering in the wilderness in search of the promised land for which Mrs Thatcher is the new Moses, re-discovering the old, immutable laws.

In leading us to the promised land of the Victorians, Mrs Thatcher appears as not merely a prophet and a seer, but also a redemptress. It is for this reason that she does not believe that 'history is writ clear and unchallengeable.' It is also for this reason that she speaks with such authority—and not as one of the scribes: 'In the years to come, we shall re-establish, in a form appropriate to tomorrow's world, the foundations on which Britain has flourished in the past.' Her new Jerusalem consists of the convergence of past and future: it is, on the one hand, the topography of mid-Victorian England—the window over the grocer's shop in a market town—

and, on the other, the more modern terrain of today's successful capitalist nations—Japan, say, or the countries of Southeast Asia or even South Korea and Taiwan. The appeal to the future—her call for change—reverberates with echoes from the past. But it is, of course, a specific past. When she says 'If the victims of today's retrenchment become tomorrow's merchant venturers, we shall have laid the foundations of a far healthier and more prosperous future for our children than we can ever hope to offer them by clinging to the monuments of the past,' she is referring only to Socialist monuments, like trade unions, that blemish the idyll of her nineteenth-century merchants. And to reassure us, she resorts, once again, to homely domestic images:

> People are reluctant to move—even a comparatively small distance—to take new jobs. Well, it's a natural reaction. What woman welcomes the turmoil of moving house? Who wants to separate herself from friends and neighbours, to set about finding a school for the children and discovering by experiments who is the best local butcher?

And so labour's epic of migration, of violent and driven disturbance, the horrors of industrialized England, is firmly put in its place. It is nothing more than the usual little problems with tradespeople.

As a cultural entrepreneur, Mrs Thatcher exemplifies the market's basic imperative of buying cheap and selling dear: it should be apparent that her method is to retrieve and hoard discarded, half-forgotten fragments of the popular culture, that, while functional in their day, are now merely decorative, like chafing-dishes and

> **What has indeed happened is that now once again Britain is not prepared to be pushed around . . . . We have instead a new-found confidence—born in the economic battles at home and tested and found true 8,000 miles away.**

chamberpots and warming pans. As a merchant of memorabilia and nostalgic bric-à-brac, she lays out her wares in the Petticoat Lanes of fantasy: the slum districts emptied now by those who, from experience, would have spotted the shoddiness of her wares. The oakum pickers in the workhouse, the domestic slaves, and child prostitutes might have challenged her sanitized version of a Victorian England full of enterprise and charity, with their own account of cholera and stillborn children. Her words are like Victorian drapery, voluminous and all-concealing; and it is over all the inconsistencies that she drapes the seamless garment of her rhetoric, woven from odds and ends of her economic, moral, and religious rag-picking.

In his autobiography, Edwin Muir speaks of the difficulties of looking back through time. 'Time wakens a longing more poignant than all the longings caused by the division of lovers in space, for there is no road back into its country. Our bodies were not made for that journey; only the imagination can venture on it; and the setting out, the road, the arrival; all is imagination.' Not for Mrs Thatcher. Sustained by nursery stories and pieties, she is determined to realize those infant fantasies of omnipotence in the transformation of our society. In the magic make-believe world of the child, there *are* ways back into that country from which we have been exiled. The *temps perdu* can be regained; and to prove it, she demonstrates that the re-writing of history is not confined to theory. For the Falklands conflict is the living parable which exemplifies her power over time. Not only is it a re-creation of a nineteenth-century imperial splendour, it is also, by that same process of absorption and manipulation of popular memory, a re-play of the Second World War: but *this* stand against Fascist aggression is a revised version, with the meaning of the people's war squeezed out. She has re-created Churchill's triumph without the subsequent Socialist victory. The socialism has been eliminated, and only the patriotic charisma remains.

Mrs Thatcher's fathomless sub-text, however, does not stop here. She plunders the iconography of the home, the Bible, and the grandeur of the Victorian Empire. But her greatest theft is from Socialism itself, as she carries out lightning raids on first its idealism and then its language, with a view, no doubt, to eventual colonization. With the generosity reserved for one's defeated enemy, she proclaims that 'Socialism has tried—and in the early days, tried

> **I'm always being asked where the new jobs are going to come from; and whether we'll ever get back to full employment. The same questions must have been asked at the time of the first industrial revolution.**

genuinely and with true compassion—to care properly for those in real need. It failed because the system it operated couldn't create the wealth necessary to cure the very social ills that gave it birth.' To what territory is she laying claim, when she, as a Conservative Prime Minister, asserts that 'I remember the words written on an old Trade Union banner: United to Support, not Combine to Injure,' and then affirms 'That is the way we were'? She suggests, it seems, that Socialism is evil, but formerly was not quite so evil.

> I think of those members of the Labour Party and trade unions who see the movement they serve abandoning the ideals to which they have devoted their lives . . . . They do not share our Conservative ideals—at least they think they do not, but they do want free and responsible trade unions to play an honourable part in the life of a free and responsible society. So do we.

And it is with the same aggressively colonizing spirit that she announces to Conservative trade unionists, 'You Conservative trade unionists can rightly claim to represent the original ideas and aspiration of trade unionism. You are not something alien, something added, but part of the movement's conscience helping to restore it to its original purpose.'

It is, of course, worth recalling that this original purpose—this journey to the new Jerusalem—was once the Socialist's quest. But now the terms have been reversed. It is now 'the sour fruits of Socialism' that spread before us. We see 'not a crisis of capitalism,

> **Confidence comes from the re-discovery of ourselves, and grows with the recovery of our self-respect . . . . Britain found herself again in the South Atlantic and will not look back from the victory she has won.**

but of Socialism.' Appropriating the rhetoric of Labour, Mrs Thatcher has created a world in which nothing is any longer what it seems. Socialism is the true oppressor of the people; capital is what sets us free, comes as our deliverer. All the attempts to humanize the experience of labour—the resistance against poverty, exploitation, and dispossession—have now become the sources of tyranny and oppression. She speaks of the 'millions' who 'go in fear of union power.' 'Our people,' she argues, 'will not willingly return to the fettered life of Socialist dogma.' She flays what she calls 'Socialist landlords' as 'the last vestiges of feudalism in Britain,' and castigates 'the perpetuation of large council-owned fiefdoms' which 'means that millions of families are not masters in their own homes.' It is obvious what Mrs Thatcher has achieved. She has absorbed the heroic journey of Labour and all the potent images which sustained an outcast working class in its wretchedness, those to whom the Labour Party once offered its own combination of material and spiritual improvement. And when Mrs Thatcher refers to Labour's 'Orwellian nightmare of the Left', the transformation is complete: the resistance to the ravages of capital is presented as the obstacle to its 'beneficent' and 'inevitable' progress.

All this would never have occurred if the experience of Labour had not, over the course of the last thirty years or so, already been trivialized. It would not have been possible if the space once occupied by Labour's epic pilgrimage had not already been evacuated. Mrs Thatcher has invaded these trampled ruins, and, in

Socialism's holy of holies, the heart of the working class itself, has set up altars to her alien gods. Since the 1950s, it is the Socialist promise that has been shrinking. The triteness of its imagery has been a measure of its desertion of the dream: in place of the confident reliance on the religious sub-text of millennial hope and a new awakening, we have been offered the mean and diminished metaphors of Labour politicians—a touch on the tiller, a fine tuning of the economy, a tinkering with the nuts and bolts of capitalism. The conditions for Mrs Thatcher's success have been created for her by the shrivelling of Socialist vision into Labour government. We would

Failure? Do you remember what Queen Victoria once said? "Failure: the possibilities do not exist".

not wish to see this as a story of betrayal by individuals or groups (that false epic which seems to give comfort to so many on the Left, as though that could redeem the calamity or offer any sort of renewal), so much as the exhaustion of the will, energy, and imagination of the Party and the working class after the 1945 settlement. It is that exhaustion which has revealed both the ambiguous nature of the Labour Party (that marriage of convenience between the ideals of the early Socialists and the practical needs of the trade unions) and the deep secular changes of the post-war working class. It is as though Labour had believed that history ceased in 1945; or perhaps, to use Mrs Thatcher's metaphors of sleep, fell into its own Socialist dream. Mrs Thatcher has been under no such illusion: her dream has been on a grander scale altogether. Not only did history not stop in 1945, but it can be reversed. That her plan involved the conquest of time has been apparent in her statements and speeches since she became leader of the Conservatives. Thus in 1977:

> Ian Macleod and the 'One Nation' group set the tone for much of post-war Conservative thought and action. That was a generation back. We now stand before the new challenges: how to restore the economy, how to enlarge our liberties, how to restore the balance between trade unions and the community, how to regain an underlying sense of nationhood and purpose . . . . Circumstances in the late seventies are different from those of thirty years ago. We shall prevail. We did and we shall.

In shattering the consensus, Mrs Thatcher has called the bluff of a

Labour movement which had become accustomed to boast of its own power. When she says 'We are living off the Victorians' moral and physical capital,' she senses that Labour has been living off its less securely invested moral capital of 1945—and in a far more spendthrift and extravagant way. It may be that she has even something to teach Labour about the Victorians, perhaps that the Labour Party should have been slower to distance itself from those prophetic Victorian socialists who warned that the efficient management of a mixed economy was not the sum of the Socialist dream. William Morris in the 1880s:

> What is it that you want from the present Labour movement? Higher wages, more regular employment? Shorter working hours—better education for your children, old-age pensions, libraries, parks, and the rest? Are these things and things like them what you want? They are, of course. But what else do you want? If you cannot answer the question straightforwardly I must say you are wandering on a road the outcome of which you cannot tell . . . . If you *can* answer it and say Yes, that is all we want, then I say Here is the real advice to give you: Don't meddle with Socialism.

It is possible to admire the skill and agility with which Mrs Thatcher moves between the different levels of rhetoric, soaring from the domestic to the cosmic within a few breaths. It is perhaps less easy to admire the ideological totalitarianism that this rhetoric assumes. For what she repeatedly declares is not only that capitalism is the best of all possible worlds, but that it is the only possible world. 'We Conservatives did not invent these ideas, nor did we find them in books. This is the sense of the people, which we simply accept and try to clothe in laws and policies. There are difficulties. But we are strengthened by the knowledge that there is no other way.' All argument is futile, if not pernicious, by the impacting of the *ought* and the *is*. Few prophets have claimed the certainty of Mrs Thatcher when she proclaims, as she does in an interview with her biographer, Patricia Murray: 'This is what one is desperately trying to preach, and IT IS GOING TO COME TRUE.'*

In the sixties, Marcuse argued that it was by its 'repressive tolerance' that capitalism would retain its hold over people and create a one-dimensional society. In the eighties, a similar one-dimensionality draws a cruder strength from Mrs Thatcher's curious

We have seen the birth of the permissive society. Has that benefited women? Far from it. Women know that society is founded on dignity, reticence, and discipline.

insistence that freedom can only lie in the recognition of historical necessity. Those who steal other people's clothes—especially from Marxist washing-lines—run the risk of finding themselves cross-dressing; and by no means only in that more obviously penetrable disguise of a transvestism of patriarchy. When she states that 'After several years we shall have a different kind of irreversibility from the socialist kind,' and that 'there are some economic, physical, and moral laws which just cannot be repealed,' she is saying that people will, under her guidance, become mature enough, not only to repine no longer for vain alternatives, but even to forget that they were ever possible. 'Tories became Tories well before the modern concept of a free-market economy meant anything, well before it became a matter of political controversy. Conservatism will, I believe, continue to be a living, growing creed long after economic controversy gives way to

---

*Margaret Thatcher, 1980.

other issues, long after socialism comes to be seen as one of the many blind alleys of history, of interest to the historian alone.' We, who do not share her historical prescience, may be given leave to wonder what kind of a world it will be in which economic issues have withered away. We may wonder at the means that may prove

> **Don't expect me to imitate one of my namesakes, You'll remember that when Becky Thatcher got lost in the caves with Tom Sawyer, she didn't behave at all like me. She kept on saying things were only going to get worse and worse, and she wished she'd never left home.**

necessary to insure this happy state of affairs is indeed brought to pass. It may be that in a world in which there are no economic issues to be debated, there will be no issues to debate at all. It all suggests the politics not so much of the masque and the pantomime as of the final curtain.

Trevor Blackwell and Jeremy Seabrook

All the quotations are from Mrs Thatcher's major speeches from 1975 to 1982.

GRANTA

BOAZ EVRON
THE HOLOCAUST
REINTERPRETED:
AN INDICTMENT OF
ISRAEL

T wo catastrophes have hurt the Jewish people in the twentieth century: the Holocaust and the lessons drawn from it. And today, illogical and anti-historical interpretations of the genocide of the Jews are being used, either deliberately or out of ignorance, as propaganda—in the non-Jewish world, the Jewish Diaspora, and within Israel's own Jewish nation. This propaganda has now become one of the most serious threats to the Jewish people and the State of Israel.

Before beginning, I feel I must express reservations about the term 'Holocaust' itself, which, in its common rhetorical usage has taken on a strange and misleading power. Derived from its original sense of a *complete* sacrifice—a *whole* burnt offering—holocaust has come to signify any event characterized by the comprehensiveness and the unexpectedness of its destruction. A holocaust can be used to represent virtually any disaster—an earthquake, a fire, even a thunder storm on an otherwise sunny day—that strikes suddenly, without historical precedent or context; it is more evocative than specifying: its causes cannot be understood or analysed. In the context of World War Two, 'Holocaust' is a circumlocution that is semantically no different from the famous Nazi circumlocution, the 'Final Solution'. Both terms hide the truth behind another name. 'Final Solution' was used by the murderers to cover up their crime; 'Holocaust' neutralizes the crime for those who managed to survive it. 'The genocide of the European Jews', while obviously more cumbersome, is in fact a more accurate representation of what actually happened, and conveys that there were specific victims of specific murderers in a specific part of the world. Unlike the almost mystical 'Holocaust', the term 'the genocide of the European Jews' allows us to understand that this terrible crime was a particular historical event that can and—we now realize—must be understood in its historical context. That circumlocutions of this sort have been used for so long reveals how complex our feelings are when we approach this subject. They also point to the tremendous hypocrisy and pretence evident in all sides involved in understanding it.

L et us address, first, the erroneous and commonplace assumption that the Jews were the only victims of Nazi genocide. It is true that the Jews were the first and main victims; but it is also true they were hardly the only ones. In eastern Europe, the gypsies were equally slaughtered, and, as Hannah Arendt has rightly pointed out in *Eichmann in Jerusalem*, the same techniques of extermination used against both the Jews and the gypsies were also beginning to be implemented against the Poles. In their devastation of Poland, for instance, the Nazis murdered over three million non-Jews. Similarly, the Nazis started exterminating the Russians, including not only millions of prisoners-of-war and forced labourers but also a fair part of the civilian population. The same techniques were used, or ultimately were meant to be used, against other 'inferior races', the policy about which was invariably complex—determined by the 'race' in question. For instance, although no explicit order was given to exterminate the Slavs, the directive to do so was understood at the Wahnsee conference in 1942. But long before the Wahnsee conference or the advent of Hitler's Reich, pan-Germanic ideologists considered the Slavs an inferior people, derived from the implications of the imperialist thinking known as 'Drag nach Osten'—the wish to go east—that has been apparent in German mythology for centuries. Within the context of the Reich, it is possible to argue that it was only a matter of time before the Slavs were enslaved and ultimately exterminated, and that this extermination was prevented only by the victory of the anti-Nazi alliance that ended the war. Moreover, in those final months, the internal logic of the Nazi ideology caused the same terror-and-murder methods to be used against the German population itself, to 'put an end to defeatism'. Anti-Semitism, I am arguing, was only a catalyst: it occasioned the development of the extermination system and refined its methodology. But it was only the beginning: the principle of endless selections was meant to be a permanent feature of the Nazi regime.

That this principle was meant to be a permanent feature is extremely important, and it must be faced if we are to understand the genocide of European Jews *historically*. And it must be faced if Jews wish not to cut themselves off from the rest of humankind. This was, after all, what the Nazis wished. It is also what our own ultra-nationalists appear to wish, who see the genocide of Europe's Jews as a typical and exclusive phenomenon of Jewish history, and, in so doing, fail to understand the full implications of an event that represented the breakdown of European society as a whole. For in making Jews the only victims of genocide, some Jewish interpreters of history—particularly those of the Zionist leadership—have erected in effect, a misleading memorial commemorating the sins of all nations against the Jews. A memorial of this sort serves a kind of twisted satisfaction, and is a distorted expression of the traditional Jewish concept of the 'Chosen People'. This kind of thinking can only be damaging. The Jews must not cut themselves out of history because, as the Nazis have demonstrated, any attempt to cut out a specific human group from the common human definition must surely lead to an attack on humankind as a whole. Moreover, this unhealthy ultra-nationalist and modern version of history is, ultimately, not unlike the anti-Semitic concept itself. It is hardly surprising that many people have pointed out the similarities between the clichéd rhetorics of both the Nazis and the Zionists —especially as regards the 'Diaspora Jew'.

This ultra-nationalist view of history has other important consequences as well, for it serves to substantiate the Zionist theorem that the Jews cannot exist while dispersed among many nations, with no territory of their own. The survival of the Jews, this theorem assumes, is only possible if they are secure in their own sovereign homeland supported by their own army, and that if during World War Two they had established their own homeland and army the Jews could not possibly have been slaughtered. Again, this view of history obscures the facts of what actually occurred during the war. It is, in this context, important to note that it was the Nazi objective to destroy the Poles and the Russians. Both were territorial nations living on their own homeland and, in the case of the Soviet Union, one of the great military powers of the world. The fact of sovereignty or military strength would not have been an obstacle, if the Nazis had succeeded, in the ultimate destruction of Poland and the Soviet Union. Moreover, their ultimate destruction would not have been exceptional in the context of world history: many, if not most, territorial nations of history have indeed been conquered at one time or another. Many were often exterminated. Many lost their national identity, having ceased to exist in the historical form we know them to have had. It is, I am suggesting, a historical fallacy to believe that the Jews now living in Israel 'were saved by Zionism'. They were saved by the fact that bears no relationship to Zionism: that the Nazi armies were defeated at El Alamein and at Stalingrad, and were thus prevented from conquering Palestine and exterminating the Jews living there.

One of the main arguments of Zionism is effectively groundless because entirely inappropriate. A guaranteed protection against 'ideological' genocide is not in military power or national sovereignty. It is in the ongoing struggle against all ideologies that exclude a specific human group from humankind. We need not division but a struggle for this aim: international co-operation intent on overcoming national differences and borders instead of strengthening them. And indeed this struggle is required especially of the strongest groups inside Israel and inside the Zionist movement.

An anti-historical understanding of the genocide of European Jews has been perpetuated by the Zionist leadership, but it is also an understanding that has been encouraged by virtually every other group that was involved in or touched by it. First there were the Germans themselves. It was in Germany's urgent self-interest to misrepresent the genocide of the war—to restrict its effects to one body of people—so as to limit the hatred, fear, suspicion, and demands for vengeance felt towards Germany by the rest of the world—especially the Slavs. By obscuring the fact that others, too, were meant for slavery and genocide and by keeping the memory of the Holocaust circumscribed to Jewish victims only, Germany has encouraged the world to view this historical episode as nothing more than an insane attack carried out not by the German people but a crazed Austrian dictator who ruled over Germany and who had acquired his anti-Semitic ideas in the slums of Vienna.

The western powers were also interested in limiting the memory of the Nazis' extermination policy to the 'Final Solution'. In the European-Christian tradition, the Jews are traditionally the 'outsiders'—the prejudice against them has a historical context—while Germany has always been central to western European civilization. It is no accident that Germany has assumed a leading role in the Atlantic Alliance that was established shortly after World War Two as the military and economic alignment meant to counter Soviet power. Germany had to be restored to the family of nations: its exclusion as an 'outsider' would have been historically unprecedented. Let us be frank: the genocide of the Jews—like that of the other 'outsiders', the gypsies—simply does not carry the same weight as the extermination of 'legitimate members' of the European family of nations. Imagine, if you like, our understanding of Germany today if it were the Dutch or the British who were exterminated. So, in dealing with genocide as if it were concentrated solely on the Jews and in making the point explicit by allowing for reparations to those Jews who survived, Germany has been able to re-enter the fold.

In eastern bloc countries, a similar distortion occurred. This is especially true in the Soviet Union which has not only not emphasized the fate of the Jews but at times obscured that fate by the authority of a history devoted to detailing the numbers of Soviet and Polish citizens murdered by the Germans. Some claim that this 'omission' is explained by the fact that anti-Semitism is still prevalent among parts of the Soviet population (as, for instance, in the Ukraine). A history emphasizing the murder of the Jews would therefore evoke little sympathy among the non-Jewish Soviet population whereas a history dedicated to depicting the murderous character of Nazism is far more useful in an education against Fascism. Regardless, in eastern countries, the stress of the representation of World War Two is on German Fascism which is carefully differentiated from the German people as a whole. Ideological principles are involved here, of course; but, more important, there is also the need to accept 'their own' Germany into the family of east European nations. There is no place for fear, hatred, and the desire for revenge. And, in the final analysis, a fruitful and economically healthy relationship is established between the victims of the German Third Reich and the German Federal Republic which is its historical successor: the same Republic that has achieved the great 'economic miracle' and has emerged as one of Europe's most important economic powers.

'Jewish monopolization of the Nazi phenomena' (if one dares to use such terms), presenting the Jews as almost the only victims of the Nazis, is unhealthy and unproductive for a number of reasons. For not only does it cut off Jews from the rest of the human race, but it breeds a kind of defensive self-awareness among the Jewish population that does in fact make them *feel* cut off from the human race and its laws. It could easily encourage certain Jews (provided they have the power) to treat non-Jews as sub-humans and thus to imitate, however inadvertently, the racism of the Nazis themselves. Other Jews, whom I shall describe later, react by interpreting the words and acts of the world in a totally irrational manner. On the other hand, this defensive self-awareness invites a completely misinformed understanding of Nazi fascism. By equating Nazism solely with anti-Semitism, it is possible, especially among those who are unsympathetic or indifferent to the Jews, to treat Nazism as merely 'a matter concerning Jews only'. Separated from its historical context, Nazism is distorted to the point of being unthreatening.

During the Fifties, awareness of the Holocaust began to fade, in Israel as elsewhere. Immigration from Islamic countries brought to Israel a population who was ignorant of the horrible reality of the genocide of European Jews and who tended to regard it as merely an '*Ashkenazi* matter'. The young, locally born generation understood Israel in a way that was completely independent from life in the Jewish diaspora: genocide was the affair of the European Jews, not of the Israelis. The survivors of that genocide—who had settled in Israel before becoming a part of its life—still had their terrible memories. But these memories were not, as yet, an organic part of Israeli public awareness. Even the ritual used to commemorate the Holocaust was yet to be developed. Although the 'Day of the Holocaust and of Heroism' was proclaimed soon after the founding of the State of Israel, the '*Yad Vashem*' Memorial Institute was not established until the end of the Fifties. Most of the Holocaust literature was still to be written. Much of this silence, no doubt, was evidence of a temporary phase, a sort of paralysis like that felt by a man after he receives a serious blow, just before the real pain sets in.

It was the trial of Adolf Eichmann that caused the decisive change in the awareness of the Nazi genocide, both for the Israelis and for world opinion. As far as I know, nothing has been published on the political background of the trial, but I believe I am not mistaken in assuming that, in addition to the wish and the need to judge and punish the 'main executant' of the 'Final Solution', there was a desire to inform the world that such crimes will not go unpunished any longer. Thus, Israel became the instrument that sought to apply higher principles of human justice, in spite of the legalist arguments raised by the kidnapping in Argentina. In any event, the initial aims of the trial were complex: but not nearly as complex or as important as the results.

I believe we can assume that one aim of the trial was to renew Germany's feeling of guilt, and, even more important, to strengthen awareness of Germany's guilt in the eyes of the rest of the world, in spite of the thinking characteristic of Germans at the time that, having paid compensation, they had already settled their debt to the Jewish people. The greatest political consequence of the trial was in Germany's three-part agreement with Israel that followed it: to establish diplomatic relations with the State of Israel, to increase reparation payments considerably, and to stop arguing about 'an end to payment of this debt'.

This concept of guilt without end is precisely what was wrong about the Eichmann trial. The trial thus was not merely a symbol of retribution against Nazi criminals (but nothing more than a symbol as the hanging of one Eichmann could never be considered adequate punishment for the murder of millions of Jews). It was not merely a reminder to the world of the extent of the Nazi horror. It was also a platform for practical gains. Konrad Adenauer's government had evaded until then open relations with the State of Israel because of obvious diplomatic considerations: he was afraid of letting his government jeopardize its relations with the Arab world. The reparations that had been made prior to the trial constituted, from Germany's point of view, the payments required by the equivalent of a legal imperative: they were related not to current politics but past problems, and could not be confused therefore with a formal acknowledgement of the State of Israel. The Eichmann trial forced Germany to make a commitment, to act against its natural interests, and to grant Israel special prerogatives, without Israel having to reciprocate in kind, to pay—as is the custom between states—in the hard coin of mutual interests. There is not—God forgive—a need to protect Germany. It is obvious that Germany cannot draw a line to delineate the past from the present so that it can start all over again. But it is necessary to point out the facts as they stand, and to examine their most serious consequences. For on the whole, it was Israel's own interests that were damaged most.

The pattern of relations with Germany is, in fact, the model of the relations between Israel and most countries of the Christian West, first and foremost the United States. These relations are not necessarily based on an objective affinity of interests, but on the generalized, and indeed justified, sense of guilt felt by the enlightened and leading groups of the Christian world towards the Jewish people. This pattern of relationships has yielded the following results:

> First: The special treatment accorded Israel, expressed in unconditional one-way economic and political support, has placed it in an economical and political hothouse, dissociating it from the world's economic and political realities. Since its establishment, Israel has hardly been called upon to face the real forces operating in the world—except in the military field—and to adjust to them.

> Second: As a result, Israel has developed an economy and a foreign policy divorced from reality; indeed it is moving further away from it, as detachment from a changing world means areas of activity in Israel have assumed a pathological aspect, producing a lopsided occupational structure, corruption, and cynicism, with an increased dependence on foreign support. Similarly, the detachment from reality renders it ever more difficult for Israel's supporters to continue their support.

> Third: The most paradoxical result is to be seen, from the Zionist point of view. Zionism aimed for the *normalization* of the Jewish people, establishing it as a sovereign political entity among other sovereign nations, a *political* nation acting within the world's political-economic framework. The hot-house conditions fostered

by outside support and the State's reliance on the moral guilt of the outside world—or, to put it bluntly—on moral blackmail, actually prevented normalization.

Fourth: In fact these conditions caused an acute aggravation of the diaspora syndromes. American or British Jews, for example, are not dependent on anyone's favour. They are equal citizens in their countries, may occupy senior positions, and enjoy satisfactory economic conditions, not due to any outside favours of benevolence, but thanks to their own industry, initiative, and intelligence. Israel, on the other hand, has become the perpetual beggar, a burden, and a nuisance, to the world. It survives not because of its own strength, not because of its own political, economic, or military authority within the network of world powers, but on *'the credit of the six million'*, on past sufferings and miseries—not the present and the future.

Fifth: The constant harping on the Holocaust, anti-Semitism, and Jew-hatred throughout history, has created in the Israeli public and its leadership a strange moral blindness. As Israel always conceives of 'the world' as a hater and persecutor, it tends to consider itself free of all moral obligations. While its main arguments rest on an appeal for justice and the world's obligation to *the remnants of the Holocaust*, it feels free to contract agreements with the world's darkest, most repressive regimes, to negotiate arms deals with the worst governments, and to oppress non-Jews subject to its rule.

The exploitation of the memory of the Holocaust for these purposes has been developed into a fine art. Almost any Israeli official appearance abroad involves an invocation of the Holocaust, in order to inculcate in the listeners the proper feelings of guilt. This is done even in a country like the United States, which has never engaged in the persecution of Jews, and where freedom of religion and the equality of the Jews before the law were taken for granted even in colonial times. The 'justification' for this inculcation of guilt is that the United States did not try to halt the process of extermination when it could. Similarly, every important non-Jewish visitor to Israel is taken as a matter of course to *Yad Vashem*, as part of his initiation, and is sometimes also sent to Kibbutz *Lohamei Hagetaot*, for good measure, in order to inject him with the proper mood and the ritual guilt expected of him.*

The Christian world does have a very bad conscience about the Jews, both because of past centuries and because it did indeed remain indifferent during the Nazi extermination (although it should be remembered that the Allies did not bomb the extermination camps while hundreds of thousands of non-Jews were also being murdered there, and it seems that the Soviet leadership was completely indifferent to the plight of Soviet prisoners-of-war). The Western powers therefore accepted the moral guilt and have to date supported Israel far beyond their legitimate national interests, sometimes even against them. Perhaps the only Western country which treats Israel according to its true interests, without the burden of guilt, is France. As a result it was subjected to a campaign of vituperative Israeli propaganda, but to no avail; our government finally learned that the French are not about to be browbeaten and, in this case, began to accustom itself to the facts of life.

Thus a most extraordinary diplomatic situation has been created: the foremost basis of Israel's policy towards the rest of the world is not one of mutual benefits derived from working with us, or one of threatened danger by working against us—as is normal among nations—but one involving the invocation of guilt and moral pressure. From this viewpoint, Mr Begin's Holocaust rhetoric is a faithful continuation of a tradition initiated by Labour governments. Incidentally, it is amusing to observe the difficulties our policy-makers have in finding a common language with countries where there are no guilt feelings regarding the Jews, as is the case among most Third World states. These nations experienced no pangs of conscience when they suspended diplomatic relations with

---

*'Kibbutz of the ghetto fighters'—a settlement in Galilee founded by those who escaped the Nazi concentration camps.

us, and one can hardly accuse the Chinese of anti-Semitism, when they have but the vaguest notion who the Jews are!

The result is that the State of Israel, established ostensibly to enable the Jews to *lead a normal existence as a nation-state among other nation-states*, deliberately adopts a policy which puts it outside the system of power relationships normal among nations. It insists on being treated as an abnormal state; it avoids direct economic and political involvement in a world of power and interests, in the *historical* world; and it tries to maintain a *non-historical* existence as a sect divorced from the historical process. Needless to say, such a policy, successful as it has been in the short run, is doomed to fail ultimately, having been based on nothing more than a sense of past guilt. This consciousness has its limits, and it may be compared to a bank account which is not replenished but steadily exhausted by heavy withdrawals. The reserves of guilt feelings are being steadily depleted—fewer and fewer people remember the Holocaust, in spite of the reiterated harping on it. For those who do not remember it, its monotonous invocation becomes a nuisance. It will be a hard day for Israel when it is called upon to perform in the real world, after the final exhaustion of its *moral credit*, and when its entire political structure and outlook have been formed under hot-house conditions.

I stated that 'Holocaust awareness' in Israel had been on the wane during the Fifties and re-emerged with the Eichmann trial, though doubtless it would have appeared again in one form or another. But there is a great difference between a spontaneous reawakening, derived from the need to understand the past as a key to the present, and an official, propagandistic indoctrination, churning out slogans and a false view of the world—the real aim of which is not an understanding of the past at all, but a manipulation of the present.

The memory of the Nazi extermination served as a powerful tool in the hands of the Jewish leadership both here and abroad. The Jewish leadership abroad is largely subservient to the Israelis, and their purpose is mainly to rally and regiment the Jewish Diaspora, above all in the United States. This regimentation has been achieved by the exploitation and cultivation of two main factors: first, the American Jews' feelings of guilt about not having done more to prevent the disaster; second, the insecurity of some Jews about their position in American society. The guilt feelings are utilized in the following manner: Israel is presented to United States Jews as being under a constant threat of annihilation by the surrounding Arab countries, in spite of the fact, rarely publicized, that Israel is several times stronger and that in the foreseeable future it is in no military danger. The presentation of this threat provides an opportunity for the Jews to assuage their guilt feelings through their economic and political mobilization *for the prevention of a second Holocaust.* Any war is therefore represented as a menace to the State's very existence, and the ensuing victory is then represented as a miracle, due among other things to Jewish support, thus providing Jews with a sense of achievement and participation in the heroic events. Israel is also presented in this light to the non-Jewish world, in an attempt to silence criticism of its policies with the unanswerable argument: 'You, who stood idly on the sidelines during the Holocaust, may not tell us what we should do to prevent another Holocaust.'

For this purpose, the Jews of Israel are represented as the 'surviving remnant', although in reality many of them either immigrated into Palestine before World War Two (or are their descendants) or came from Islamic countries. The illusion has been ably served in the past by the Arab statesmen and their talk of eliminating the Zionist entity, talk which only died down after the Six-Day War. From this point of view, the PLO's refusal to recognize Israel and to amend the Palestinian Covenant are the last straws clutched at by Israeli policy.

Here another significant factor enters the picture: the image of an Israel under threat of destruction is necessary and precious to *American* Jewry. One tries to explain to American Jews that, as a matter of fact, Israel is *not* in danger of annihilation; that Israel's cultural and organizational level, even in its currently demoralized state, is still far higher than those of the surrounding Arab nations; and also that this qualitative advantage, when all is said and done, constitutes its true military superiority: but the response of the American Jewry is one of resistance, resentment, and anger. Then one realizes that this image of Israel is a necessity to American

Jews, as it enables them to overcome their Holocaust guilt. Many react with displeasure when it is pointed out that Israel's proper national objective should be the independence from external factors, even from Jewish support. But Americans want this dependence to continue so that they feel that they are needed. In addition, support for Israel is necessary because Americans have no other focus for their identity as Jews. Apparently they are incapable of solving the problem on their own terms, within themselves, escaping it by way of their own vicarious solutions. The Israeli soldier, the *Israeli Hero*, is also needed to compensate for the fact that the Jew is not generally depicted in the United States as the tough virile warrior extolled by society. But it is, of course, curious that this 'warrior' is a dual, self-contradictory image: the virile superman and the hapless potential Holocaust victim.

Both images, of course, have little relation to reality. And the fact that Diaspora Jews, and mainly those in America, use Israel to view themselves as *vicarious heroes*, while they would not even dream of immigrating to participate in the *heroic battles,* intensifies their sense of guilt and enhances the moral control of the Israeli establishment. I would even hazard a guess that this establishment is not really interested in their immigration to Israel but prefers their guilty unstinting support from afar.

It should be noted further that this massive transfer of Jewish (and non-Jewish) American funds into the hands of the Israeli power elite takes place without the donors having any say or right to criticize the ways that the money is spent in Israel itself. Only the Israelis, who, it is said, are on the spot and are more familiar with the situation than foreign Jews—being after all in the very firing line, facing the threat of the new Holocaust—are entitled to express any opinion on the subject. If the danger of a new Holocaust were not invoked again and again, Diaspora Jews might have demanded more say and participation in such decisions. In effect, the Jews of the Diaspora have been converted into a kind of colonial possession of the Israeli power establishment, serving as an inexhaustible source of revenue, without the right to exercise any control over its expenditure—exactly the sort of situation which caused the British colonies in North America to revolt against the British Crown under the slogan 'No taxation without representation!' Any possible protest is silenced, of course, by playing on the insecurity felt among some American Jews, mainly of the first and second generation of immigrants, living in American society. Again, Israel is offered as a refuge in a storm, an insurance against the future: the same Israel which at the same time is pictured to them as a candidate for annihilation. It would be useless to argue that this is a contradiction in terms, for we deal here with utterly irrational attitudes.

One of these American survivors of Nazi Europe, a respected professional, told the author: 'We Jews are lucky to have so many other minorities here, like the Blacks, the Puerto Ricans, the Irish, the Italians, etc. Otherwise we would have been butchered long ago.' People to whom I quoted this statement said that it was utter nonsense; after all there were times when American society was made up almost entirely of white, Anglo-Saxon Protestants, yet Jews were never persecuted, and they always enjoyed equality before the law, even in the colonial era. (Though indeed, even today, there is some social discrimination against Jews in certain places, and not only against them.)

In England, too, which is ethnically more homogeneous than the United States, there has been no persecution of the Jews since they were re-admitted into the country under Cromwell, in the seventeenth century. But even though statements like the one quoted above are utterly fallacious, and merely reflect the essential distrust with which many survivors view the non-Jewish society in which they live, they do testify to a certain psychological reality which is ably utilized by Israeli propaganda. These insecure, former European Jews place a blind trust in Israel, and unlike the average American Jew, with whom the subject is more or less open to discussion, the European Jew cannot be argued with. Any Israeli action, however stupid or aggressive, wins instinctive agreement. Thus, whereas many American Jews experience an acute sense of discomfort, embarrassment, and even shame, at Mr Begin's behaviour and rhetoric (not unlike the feelings many Israelis have about him), the insecure European Jews identify with him completely, much more than they did with Mr Rabin before him. Begin is so thoroughly a Diaspora Jew, one of their own, a Holocaust survivor, that they say: 'To hell with what the Goyim think about his style and personality. Anyway, who are those Goyim, if not actual or potential murderers? Didn't they rejoice in their hearts while we were being gassed and burned? So why should we care what they think?'

I have tried to show how the invocation of the Holocaust is, in addition to its use as a means of pressuring the non-Jewish world, one of the main instruments by which the Israeli power establishment controls Diaspora Jewry and converts it into a tool of its economic policy. The funds collected in this manner, without being controlled by their donors, are distributed among the various institutions of the Israeli power elite according to an agreed ratio, and in their turn serve as a means of manipulating the Israeli public, which also has no say about their distribution, since it has not contributed to them. This process actually began in the Twenties, when the Labour Movement denied the Zionist organization any say about the allocation of the funds entrusted to its care. But only after the war and the founding of the State of Israel did the process reach its highest refinement. In reality this means that *it is a structural interest of this system to perpetuate Israel's dependence on outside help, since it enables the Israeli power elite to exploit Diaspora Jews, on the one hand, and maintain its control over the Israeli public, on the other, by means of the incoming contributions, without being obliged to render an account of these resources to anybody.* This may lead us to view with a certain scepticism talk about 'economic independence,' which has indeed almost disappeared since the Six-Day War.

The country's economic dependence benefits the power elite and helps perpetuate it in power. This is irrespective of whether the government is that of the Alignment, Mapam, Likud, or the NRP. They are all members of the system. Though the foregoing is a side issue of our theme, it deserves fuller elaboration and treatment.

I have stated before that the goal of Zionism was to put an end to Jewish dispersal and to turn the Jews into a sovereign territorial nation. And, indeed, in conformity with classical Zionist predictions—according to which establishing the Jew on his own land would create a new type of Jew and a new Jewish mentality—an independent national consciousness, distinct from the Jewish one but with an affinity to it, began to develop in Eretz Israel. Already in the Forties and the Fifties, the leadership became aware of a process begun in its own ranks; as for example, in Ben Gurion's transfer of emphasis to Eretz Israel, and his reversal of priorities: instead of the Hebrew *Yishuv* in Palestine serving the needs of the Jewish people, the Jewish people was to become an instrument in the hands of the *Yishuv*. If matters had been permitted to follow their natural course, the new Israeli nation would have developed independently of the Jewish Diaspora, and would eventually have formed a distinct and separate entity. The ties between this nation and the Diaspora would gradually have become more feeble and vague, thus attenuating the ideological and the power basis of the ruling establishment. This leadership therefore set out to block and reverse the process.

The most effective ideological tool for the achievement of this objective was the exploitation of Arab hatred, the drawing of an analogy between Nazis and Arabs, with the corollary that Jewish destiny is the same everywhere, in Israel or in the Diaspora, like a mark of Cain branded on Jewish brows from the beginning of time by mysterious, supernatural forces: we are always an object of hatred and there will always be the urge to annihilate, here and everywhere, now and always. The only difference between Israel and the Diaspora is that in Israel we can fight back, whereas in the Diaspora we have no alternative but '*to be led to slaughter like sheep*'. Inevitably this led to various historiographical theories and conclusions about the unique, mystical course and meaning of Jewish history, to Messianic illuminations and so on, conclusions which the nationalistic right wing was quick to embrace, though in the Labour movement, where some vestiges of its rationalistic origins still persisted, there was a reluctance to follow the inner logic of this argument. It need hardly be said that in the writings of the founders of Zionism there is virtually no trace of such an interpretation, as initially Zionism was an attempt to provide a rational solution to the frightful problems facing the Jewish people of Eastern and Central Europe during the crisis of the dynastic European systems. Had the founders of Zionism conceived the Jewish problem in this light, they would hardly have arrived at the

Zionist solution. Their main aim was *to put an end to* 'Jewish destiny', to the Jewish 'uniqueness as victims', and to create a more just society.

If the purpose of Zionism was merely the establishment of a more effective self-defence organization, they would not have considered the effort worthwhile. Thus the murder of Europe's Jews, which, as argued earlier, *should be understood mainly in the context of German and European history*, and of the social position occupied by the Jews in the European socio-economic structure, is conceived as a disembodied, meta-historical, eschatological phenomenon. There is continuing effort to blur the decisive differences between Arab hatred and Nazism, such as the fact that the Nazis invented the myth of the 'Jewish Conspiracy' for the purpose of inflaming an irrational, psychotic hatred of the Jews in the German people, whereas the Arabs are engaged in a struggle against a real enemy whose military might really threatens them, who has already caused the flight of more than a million of their brethren from their homes, and who is now subjugating another two million. Moreover, Arab hostility is directed, rationally enough, against the *Israelis*, and not against all Jews wherever they are (although the support most Jews extend to Israel does tend to spread the hostility to all Jews). We need not dwell on the vast differences between the Arabs and the Germans in social conditions, cultural and religious backgrounds, their economic, political, and national stages of development, differences which make it impossible to discuss the two phenomena in the same breath. But as most Israelis know little of the Arab world, and for so many of them 'all Goyim are alike', in their eyes there is no difference between a Palestinian peasant refugee and a member of the SS—heir to a technology and a perverted ideology, trained in the massacre of populations and nations. And as so many Israelis still bear the psychological scars of persecution and discrimination in their countries of origin, this shallow propagandistic analogy falls on fertile ground. This is true not only of the masses, not only of the immigrants, but also of many Israelis with pretensions to education and historical discrimination.

Thus, both on the eve of the Six-Day War and after the Yom Kippur War, serious people talked about these events as 'an expression of the Jewish fate which unites us all,' as if other nations had never fought, were never suddenly attacked, as if the danger of war were not an inseparable part of sovereign political existence, rather than 'a Jewish tragedy'.

Simultaneously Jews assert that *'the Jewish people is Israel's only loyal ally'*. Since the Jewish people is *not* a political power, nor is it a clearly defined and organized entity, no alliance is possible between it and a sovereign state. A state can contract alliances only with other states. This assertion, then, can mean only one of two things: either Israel is not a real state, or the Jews *can move states* (notably the United States) to contract alliances with Israel. In reality, when you try to examine the real content of the slogan *'an orientation of the Jewish People'*, you realize that Jews will always succeed in forcing the United States Government to support Israel; that is, it is an orientation on the USA. But the slogan also has another meaning: the evasion of realistic policies in the real world—where there are no 'loyal allies' but only shifting communities of interests—and a retreat to a status of non-historical dependence.

The identification of the Arabs in general, and the Palestinians in particular, with the Nazis, together with the constant reiteration of the danger of a Holocaust, which arouses panic in the average Israeli, as well as the doctrine of 'the Jewish people as Israel's only loyal ally', lead to the following consequences:

First: It freezes Israeli political consciousness in a prestate stage, to the point that it is incapable of relating to, or understanding, the real forces operating in the political arena. The country's foreign relations are shaped not according to the reciprocal interests of political bodies, but on the basis of American Jewry's lobbying strength, as if Israel were not a foreign country but part of the domestic American system. As a result, the public level of consciousness remains one of a sect, rather than of a sovereign political community, and is therefore incapable of judging the political leadership by realistic standards.

Second: These analogies have produced grave moral consequences. As the choices the Israelis believe they confront are not realistic, but either 'Holocaust' or 'victory' (or at least 'holding fast'), it relieves them of moral compunctions. Whoever believes himself to be in danger of annihilation can consider himself free of any moral qualm which might tie his hands in his efforts to save himself. The only thing that stops him is the utilitarian consideration that certain acts could hurt his image abroad. This is the logic guiding people like Moshe Shamir or Geulah Cohen and other founders of the *Tekhiah* ('Renaissance') party, who argue that we may do anything, because the world wants to destroy us. They are, therefore, uninhibited in advocating the most drastic steps against the non-Jewish population of the country. Such arguments remind us of the excuses made by the Soviets when they displaced populations on the grounds that they displayed 'chauvinist, counter revolutionary tendencies'. Also, although such comparisons may be shocking, we should remember that the Nazis justified the murder of the Jews with the basic argument that the Jews were planning the ruin and destruction of the German people: the choice was between the destruction of the Jews or the destruction of the Germans. Any argumentation based on claims that the other side harbours intentions of annihilation implies, in most cases, the presence of those very intentions towards the other side. An honest person should be extremely cautious before endorsing such a thesis, as he may in reality be endorsing the massacre of innocents (it goes without saying that there are cases in which exterminatory intentions do exist, so that a thorough examination of the facts is always in order).

The third result may be the gravest: A leadership cannot be divorced from its propaganda. Sooner or later it too begins to believe in the reality of the propaganda image. This is particularly true in the case of the present Israeli leadership, which is immeasurably more naive than its predecessors, and also more a captive of ideology and hallucination. Thus the leadership, too, operates in the world of myths and monsters, which it has created in order to maintain and perpetuate its power. It is no longer capable of understanding what is happening in the world, and the nature of the historical processes in which its country is involved. Such a leadership, in the deteriorating political and economic situation of Israel today, constitutes a grave danger to the very existence of the state.

Thus, paradoxically, the 'Holocaust consciousness' inculcated by propagandistic means, has produced a real danger of destruction. A precondition to the healing and revival of Israeli society is a realization of the country's true historical and political status. As in psycho-analytical therapy, a recognition of your real condition is the beginning of the cure.

Translated from Hebrew by New Outlook, Tel Aviv.

GRANTA

JUREK BECKER
THE WALL

H ere I am, at a time when we Jews are quietly minding our own business and our neighbour is called Olmo who spends half the day quarrelling with his wife, and if you have nothing better to do you can stand behind the door and hear every word. And the street still has its houses, in each of which something has happened to me. I'm not allowed to leave it, the street—Father has strictly forbidden me. Often I don't believe his reason for this, but sometimes I do: that there is a boundary, an invisible one, beyond which children are snatched away. No one knows where it runs, that's the sneaky part. It seems to be constantly changing, and before you know it you've crossed it. Only in our own street, it seems, are children relatively safe, safest of all outside their own house. My friends, with whom I discuss this enormous problem are of two opinions. The know-it-alls laugh, but there are others who have already heard about it too.

I ask: 'What'll happen to me if they catch me?'

Father replies: 'It's better for you not to know.'

I say: 'No, tell me—what will happen to me?' He merely makes a vague gesture and refuses to talk to me any more. Once I say: 'Who is it anyway who snatches away the children?'

He asks: 'Why do you have to know that too?'

I say: 'It's the German soldiers.'

He asks: 'The Germans, our own police—what's the difference if they catch you?'

I say: 'But there's a boy who plays with us every day who lives many streets away.'

He asks me: 'Is your father a liar?'

I'm five years old and can't keep still. The words tumble out of my mouth. I can't keep it shut, I've tried. The words push against my cheeks from the inside, multiplying at a fantastic rate and hurting my mouth until I have to open it. 'What a child!' says my Mother, who no longer has a face, only a voice. 'Just listen to that child, that crazy child.'

What happened must have been strange, unheard of, otherwise it wouldn't be worth telling. For all I know I may have killed Mr Tenzer the shopkeeper. I'll never find out. He lives in our street and wears a little black cap and has a little white beard. He is a tiny little man. When the weather is cold or wet you can go to his place. He tells stories. The toughest kids sit silently in front of him, not saying a word, never opening their mouths, perfectly quiet, even though later they make their jokes. But he never lets more than four come in at one time. I am his favourite: it makes me feel good believing that. Once when he picked me up and put me on top of the cupboard—he proved to be very strong. We were all surprised.

Father says: 'What kind of person would put a child on top of a cupboard? And anyway, why are you always hanging around old Tenzer? He must have a screw loose.'

I say: 'You have a screw loose.' He swings his arm back, but I run away, and when I return later he's forgotten all about it. Father often swings his arm back, but he never hits me.

One day I've quarrelled with everyone and go over to Tenzer's place. I've never been alone with him before. When he opens the door and sees only me outside he's surprised and says: 'Such a small gathering today?' He is busy doing his laundry, but he doesn't send me away. I am allowed to watch. He washes differently from my mother, who always splashes water all over the room. He handles the underpants and shirts gently, trying not to make even more holes, and sometimes he sighs over a specially big hole. He holds a shirt high above the bowl, and while it drips he tells me: 'It's thirty years old. Do you know what thirty years means for a shirt?'

I look round the room; there's not much to look at. There is only one thing that I've never noticed before. Behind the high head-board of the bed, on the floor beside the window, stands a pot. A large cloth hangs in front to hide it. I would never have made the discovery if I hadn't been lying on the floor and looking in that very direction out of boredom. I make a little detour over to the thing. I push aside the cloth, which would hide it from someone twice my size. In the pot there is a green plant, a strange one that pricks sharply as soon as you touch it. 'What are you doing back there?' shouts Mr Tenzer after hearing me cry out. There is a drop of blood on my forefinger—I show him my thick blood. I stick my finger in my mouth and suck it; then I see tears in his eyes and am more scared than ever.

I ask: 'What did I do?'

'Nothing,' he says, 'nothing at all, it's my fault.' He explains how the plant functions and how many animals would have eaten it if it weren't for the prickles. He says: 'You're not to tell anybody about it.'

I say: 'Of course I won't.'

He says: 'You know that no one's allowed to have a plant?'

I say: 'Of course I know that.'

He says: 'You know what happens to anyone who ignores a rule?'

I say: 'Of course.'

He asks me: 'Well, what do they do to him?' I don't answer. I just look at him because he's about to tell me. We look at each other for a while, then Tenzer picks a piece of washing out of the bowl and wrings it out violently. He says: 'That's what they do to him.' Of course I tell the story to millions of people, not to my parents but all my friends.

I pay another visit to Mr Tenzer because ever since that day he has allowed me to play with his plant as if we were brother and sister. The door is opened by an old woman, so fearfully ugly that anyone in my place would have been terrified. She asks in a nasty voice: 'What do you want here?' I know that Tenzer has always been alone and wouldn't have dreamed of letting such a person into the house, so the fact that she is in his home alarms me even more than her appearance. I run away from the witch and pay no attention to the curse she calls out after me. The street hardly sees me—I just fly along it. I ask my Mother where Mr Tenzer is. She starts to cry. Only a moment ago she had been embroidering the cloth to which she belongs. I ask: 'Where is he? Tell me!'

But I have to wait for Father to tell me when he comes home that evening: 'They've taken him away.'

By this time I'm no longer surprised, hours have passed since my question, and many times they have taken someone away who was suddenly no longer there. I ask: 'Whatever did he do?'

Father says: 'He was *meshugge*.'

I ask: 'What did he really do?'

Father rolls up his eyes and says to Mother: 'You tell him, if he really wants to know.' And at last she says, though very softly: 'He had a flowering plant. Just imagine, they found a flowering plant in his room.' It is rather quiet. I am suffering because I mustn't say that that plant and I are friends. Tears drip from my Mother's eyes onto her cloth. Never before has she had a good word to say for Tenzer.

Father cuts his chunk off the loaf as he does every evening after work. I am the real sufferer but no one takes any notice of me. Father says: 'I've said it all along, he has a screw loose. To be taken away for the sake of a flower—of all the ridiculous reasons!'

My Mother has stopped crying but says: 'Perhaps he loved that flower very much. Perhaps it reminded him of someone, how do we know?'

Father with his bread says loudly: 'That's no reason to put a pot of flowers in one's room. If someone insists on living dangerously he can plant tomatoes in a pot. You can remember a person a thousand times better with tomatoes.'

I can't contain myself any longer. I don't like my father very much at this moment. I shout: 'It wasn't a flower, it was a cactus!' Then I run outside and remember nothing more.

Father wakes me in the middle of the night; the curtain in front of my bed has been pulled aside. He says: 'Come along, my son.' He bends over me and strokes me. My mother is also fully dressed. There is movement in the house, footsteps and clattering sounds through the walls. He lifts me out of bed and sets me on my feet. To keep me from falling over with sleepiness, he supports my back with his hand. It's a good thing he's not hurrying the least bit. My Mother brings me my shirt, but I sit down on the bucket that is our toilet. The moon rests on the crossbar of the window; suddenly there are two bulging carry-alls in the room. If you look long enough at the moon its face doesn't stay still: it winks at you. Then my Mother pulls my shirt down over my head. 'Come along, my son,' says Father. They both try to think of what they might have forgotten; Father finds a pack of cards and stuffs it in the bag. I also have something to take along: I place the cloth ball my Mother made for me beside the bags, but I am told there's no more room. Then we walk down the pitch-dark stairs, across the whispering courtyard, out onto the street.

Many people are there already, but none of my friends. 'Where are the others?' I ask Father.

He lets go of my Mother's arm and says: 'It's only our side of the street. Don't ask what it all means, those are the orders.' This is a disaster, since my friends all live on the other side.

I ask: 'When are we coming back?' They stroke my head again but explain nothing. Then we tramp off in response to a command given by someone I can't see. The way becomes more boring with every step; we must be crossing the invisible boundary ten times over, but when you're given orders of course the ban is lifted.

A small section of the ghetto—and this has nothing to do with memory, it's the truth—a small section of the ghetto is like a camp. A few long barrack-like brick huts standing at random are surrounded by a wall. It's not so terribly high; from day to day its height seems to me to vary. Certainly if one man stood on the shoulders of another he could look over it. And if you stand back far enough you can see broken glass glinting on the top. But why have a camp in the middle of the ghetto, which is camp enough, you wonder? To which I can reply, though no one explained it to me at the time: people are assembled in this camp before being taken to a different one, or to a place where there is more need for them than in the ghetto. In other words: the idea is to be in readiness in the camp. Is it a good sign to be here, is it a bad one? This is debated day and night in the long brick huts. I'm sick of hearing it.

The three of us are allotted one bed, a hard affair made of wood. Though it is a bit wider than my former one, we are miserably cramped. There are also some empty beds in the hut. Right after the first night I lie down on one of them and announce that from now on this is where I'm going to sleep. Father shakes his head. I shake my head in reply and ask for his reasons, at which he swings his arm back again. I have to yield—it is a victory of unreason. We experiment with various positions: myself on the left, then on the right, then with my head between my parents' feet. 'That gives us the most room,' says Father, but my mother is afraid that one of the four feet might hurt me. 'Sometimes a person kicks out violently while dreaming. You don't realize it, but you do.'

Father can't deny this. 'All the same, it's a pity,' he says. I end up lying in the middle, not consulted, and must promise to move as little as possible.

Every morning there is 'inspection'—that's the first word I learn in the foreign language. We line up in a long row outside the hut. It all has to be done very quickly because a German is already standing there waiting. The tips of our toes mustn't be too far forward or too far back. Father straightens me out a bit. The first person in the row has to call out 'One', then we number off to the end of the row. The numbers roll along and pass over my head. My Mother calls out her number, then Father calls first his and then mine, and already it's the next person's turn. This annoys me—I ask: 'Why can't I call out my number myself?'

Father answers: 'Because you don't know how to count.'

'Then you can just whisper my number to me,' I say, 'and I'll call it out.'

He says: 'First of all there's no time for that, and second—we're not allowed to whisper.'

I say: 'Why don't we stand at the same spot every morning? That way we would always have the same number and I could learn it.'

He says: 'Listen, my son, this is not a game.'

There are two in my row who aren't much older than I am, one of them calls out his own number, the other one's number is called by his father. I ask one of them: 'How old are you?' He spits past my head and walks away. He must come from the upper end of our street—I rarely got that far. After the numbering the German shouts: 'Dismissed!' That's an inspection.

By the second day I'm already bored to death. There are a few smaller kids around, but when I approach them their leader tells me: 'Beat it, but *pronto*.' They all look at me angrily, those idiots, just because their leader wants to show off with that word. I ask my Mother what *pronto* means, she doesn't know. I say: 'It must mean something like quickly.'

Father says: 'Who cares?'

The camp is dead, and I can't bring it to life. I start to cry, but it doesn't help. In one corner of the camp I find a little grass. I mustn't go too far away, my mother says; Father says: 'Where can he possibly go to here?' I discover the gate, the only place where there is movement—sometimes a German comes in, sometimes one goes out. A soldier who is a sentry walks up and down until he sees me standing there. He raises his chin quickly. I can't say why I have so little fear of him. I take a few steps back, but when he starts walking up and down again I retrace my steps. Once more he moves his head like that—once more I do him the favour—then he ignores me.

That afternoon a different soldier is standing at the gate. He calls out something that sounds dangerous. I go into a hut that is not ours. Though I'm afraid, there's nothing else for me to do. The same beds are there, and there's a stench which isn't like anything I've ever smelled. I see a rat running by—it gets away from me—I crawl on my hands and knees and can't find its hiding place. Someone grabs me by the scruff of the neck. He asks me: 'What are you doing here?' He has one blind eye.

I say: 'I'm not doing anything.'

He stands with me in such a way that the others can see us. Then he says: 'Tell me the truth.'

I repeat: 'I am not doing anything. I'm just looking.'

But he says in a loud voice: 'He wanted to steal, the little bastard, but I caught him.'

I shout: 'That's not true!'

He says: 'It' true all right! I've been watching him all morning. He's been waiting for hours for a chance.'

One of them asks: 'What are you going to do with him?'

The liar says: 'Shall I beat him up?'

One man says: 'It would be better to boil him.'

I scream: 'I wasn't going to steal, really I wasn't!'

I can't get free of his grip, and the liar squeezes harder and harder. Luckily someone calls out: 'Let him go, he's the kid of someone I know.' But he holds onto me a bit longer and tells me not to let him catch me again. I don't tell Father anything about it; most likely he would punish the disgusting fellow—but then I'd have to stay in our own hut. It's not worth it.

Next day all is well again: early in the morning the other side of the street moves into the camp. I've hardly taken five steps outside when someone sounding like Julian calls me and hides. I needn't look very far, He's round the next corner, pressing himself against the wall and waiting for me to find him. Julian is my good friend. We haven't seen each other for a long time, maybe a week. His father was a doctor, that's why he's always well dressed, even now.

He says: 'Well, I'll be damned!'

I say: 'Julian.' I show him round the camp—there's not much to show—his hut is the farthest away from ours. We look for a spot that from now on is to be our special place: in the end he picks it, even though he has been here only a few minutes and I have probably been here for as long as a week.

He asks: 'D'you know Itzek is here too?'

He takes me over to Itzek's hut—Itzek is my good friend too. He is sitting on the bed and has to stay with his parents, so he can't be glad about me. We ask his father: 'May he at least go outside with us for a bit?'

His father says: 'No chance.' But when Itzek begins to cry he gets permission from his mother, who is normally very strict. We show Itzek our special place; we sit down on the stones. The wonderful thing about Itzek is his turnip watch—I look at his trouser pocket where it is always ticking away. Twice so far I've been allowed to hold it to my ear, and once he let me wind it, after I had won a bet. His grandfather gave it to him because he loved him, and told him to keep it well hidden or else it would get pinched by the first thief to come along. Julian also has something wonderful, a wonderfully beautiful girl friend. No one has ever seen her except him. She has fair hair and green eyes and loves him madly. Once he told us that they sometimes kiss. We didn't believe him so he showed us how she purses her lips. Only I own nothing wonderful. Father has a torch with a dynamo which has a handle you have to squeeze to make it light up. But if one day he can't find it we all know who'll be suspected first.

I say to Itzek: 'Show me your watch.' But his rotten parents found it and swapped it for potatoes. Julian still has his girl friend. Itzek is crying over the loss of his watch. I don't make fun of him. I would try to comfort him if I weren't too shy. Julian says: 'Stop crying, kid.' So Itzek runs away, and Julian says: 'Never mind him.' And the splendid turnip watch has been swapped for potatoes—it defies comprehension. I tell Julian what a day in this camp is like so he won't expect too much. Until Itzek comes back Julian tells me about his girl friend—her name is Marianka.

Since I left our street, nothing much has happened there. Only Muntek the cobbler has committed suicide. Whenever we sat on his steps he used to come out of his dirty shop and kick us. Now he's dead. It's a funny feeling because only the other day he was still alive.

I ask: 'How did he do it?'

Julian says he slashed his wrists with glass and bled to death. Itzek, on the other hand, who lived three houses nearer to the cobbler than Julian, knows that Muntek plunged his cobbler's knife into his heart and twisted it three times.

Julian says: 'I never heard such nonsense!'

They argue for a while until I say: 'What's the difference?' But the story also has a sad ending because Itzek's mother had left a pair of shoes with Muntek for repair. When she heard of his death she hurried over there, but the shoes were gone—the shop had already been stripped.

Still sitting down, Julian pees between me and Itzek in a beautiful arc. He can do that better than anybody. Then he has a plan and makes a solemn face. He wants us to put our heads together. He whispers: 'We have to go back to our street—at night would be best.' Julian has never made such a crazy suggestion before.

Itzek asks him: 'Why?'

Julian turns his eyes toward me, indicating that I should explain to this idiot, but I'm at a loss myself.

Julian says: 'The whole street is empty now, right?'

We answer: 'Yes.'

He asks: 'And what about the houses?'

We answer: 'They're empty too now.'

'The houses aren't empty at all,' he says, and all of a sudden he knows something we don't know.

We ask: 'Why aren't the houses empty?'

He says: 'Because they're full, stupid.' He despises us for a little while, then he has to explain, otherwise we would leave. So: the street was emptied, house by house, but as we know better than anybody, the people weren't allowed to take much with them, at most half their possessions. The other half is still inside the houses—by Julian's estimate there must be great piles of stuff still lying there. He tells us, for example, that he hadn't been able to take along his big toy motor-car because his fool of a mother had trampled on it and instead had given him a bag full of underwear to carry. I remember my grey cloth ball. Only Itzek didn't have to leave anything behind—he had nothing.

'You'll never get over the wall,' I say. Julian throws a stone at the wall—the stone passes so close to my head I can feel the wind.

He asks me: 'Over that one?'

I say: 'Yes, over that one.'

He asks: 'Why not?'

I say: 'The Germans are watching night and day.'

Julian looks round with wide eyes, then says: 'Where do you see any Germans here? Besides, they sleep at night. Didn't you hear what I said? That we have to try during the night?'

Itzek says: 'He's got wax in his ears.'

I say: 'Anyway, the wall's much too high.'

Itzek says to his friend Julian: 'You can tell how scared he is.'

All Julian says is: 'We'll have to look for a good place.' Julian says to me: 'Coward.'

We look for a place and of course Julian is right, there is one, where metal struts have been put in like steps. 'What did I tell you?' says Julian. My heart beats fast because now I have to go with them or be a coward. There is another advantage to the place: it is far away from the camp entrance and so it is also far from the sentry. Though there is another sentry who walks round and eventually passes every spot, most of the time he is in his little German guardhouse, sitting and smoking or lying down asleep.

Julian says: 'I will tell you again, the Germans all sleep at night.'

I ask: 'How do you know?'

He answers: 'Everybody knows that.'

And Itzek points at me and says: 'Only he doesn't.'

'Shall we go tonight?' Julian asks, looking at me.

I think how easy it would be to agree to everything now, and later simply not show up. I look at the struts and test the bottom one with my hand.

I say: 'The Germans must be crazy.'

'So what do you say?' Julian asks me again.

I say: 'Why don't you ask him too?'

Julian asks Itzek: 'Shall we go tonight?'

Itzek is silent for a moment, then says: 'Tomorrow night would be better.'

'Why wait until tomorrow night?'

Itzek says: 'One shouldn't rush matters.' This view is familiar from his father, a lawyer by profession (whatever that means).

My preparations begin that evening. If ever I am to succeed in getting out of bed at night unnoticed, I mustn't sleep between my parents—I must sleep at the edge. I start coughing, until my Father wants to know what's the matter. My Mother places her hand on my forehead. The coughing goes on and on. I can see them whispering together. As I lie down I say: 'I can't get any air in the middle. Don't worry, I won't fall out.' And I cough so violently that I really do have to gasp for air so that they have to give me a place at the side.

Every night someone shouts: 'Lights out!', then the light goes out; for a short while whispering continues. The elves fly in the dark—they are a secret that must never be spoken about. Once when I wanted to talk about elves with my Mother she merely put her finger to her lips, shook head, and said nothing. The roof of the hut opens up to the elves, the walls bend down to the ground, but you don't see anything—you just feel the waft of air. They float in and out, just as they please. Sometimes one of them brushes you with her veil or with the wind. Sometimes she even says something to you, but always in elfin language, which no human can understand; besides, elves speak incredibly softly. Everything about them is more delicate, more gentle, than with humans. They don't come every night, but not that seldom either—then there is a hidden, joyful movement in the air until you fall asleep, and probably even longer. At the first hint of light they vanish.

Tonight I intend to practise getting up, I've told myself: if I manage once to get out of bed without waking them, I'll also manage when it really matters. Only I must be sure they've fallen asleep.

Normally Father falls asleep so quickly that he is already snoring before the elves arrive. Sometimes I poke him deliberately in the ribs, and it doesn't disturb him. But tonight of all nights they whisper together and lie with their arms round each other like children and kiss, as if they hadn't had all day to do that. I'm stuck—they've never kissed like that before in the hut.

I hear Father whisper: 'Why are you crying?' Then I feel sleepy—I believe the first elves are already there. I roll my eyes to drive off my tiredness.

I hear my mother whisper: 'He's stopped coughing, do you hear?' Then Father wakes me and says: 'Come along now, inspection won't wait for you.'

My Mother says to Father: 'Let him be, he hasn't had enough sleep.' Such a disaster won't happen to me again, I swear, even if I have to prop open my eyelids with matchsticks. So tonight I'll have to leave the bed and the hut with no rehearsal; but the good thing is that I now know how easy it is to fall asleep against one's will.

Father nudges me in the row. I look up and hear him say under his breath: 'Twenty-five!' Though my mind is already on the coming night, my heart beats faster, now that I have a chance to show what I can do. The numbers come rushing along—the eyes of the German facing us always stay with the number. I'm scared; Father cannot know what kind of a moment he has chosen. I have to press my lips together not to call out too early, then I shout 'Twenty-five!' It must have been exactly the right moment, after the woman ahead of me and before Father—the numbers roll away from me without a hitch. It's a good feeling.

After inspection Father says: 'You did that splendidly. Only next time don't shout so loud.' I promise. He picks me up in his arms—that's not nice in front of all those people.

We meet—Julian, myself, and Itzek—and wait for the coming night. Julian has noticed that at our chosen place there is no glass on the wall, which is very lucky. Itzek says he noticed that too.

Julian says: 'I needn't bother to go to our old room. I'm going somewhere else right away. Are you going to your rooms?' I consider whether our room is worth while: the cloth ball is still there, maybe the torch too—it hasn't shown up yet in the camp.

Itzek says: 'Honestly now, who's scared?'

'Not me,' says Julian.

'Not me either,' says Itzek.

'Not me either,' I say. I ask Julian whether he wouldn't like to visit his girl-friend when we're outside.

He answers: 'Not at night, silly.'

A cold wind drives us away; only Julian knows where to go. He knows of an empty hut; we run there. Though I don't like to admit it: Julian is the leader among us. There is no door. We step into the dark room, which contains nothing; only some two-tiered bunks pushed against the walls such as I've never seen before. Itzek climbs around on them and jumps from one to the other, like a cat, and Julian looks at me as if everything here belonged to him. Then someone says: 'Clear out, and I mean now!' Itzek is so terrified that he falls off a bunk, picks himself up, and runs outside. Julian has already disappeared. I am left standing alone in the middle of the room. The voice, which sounds both tired yet as if coming from a strong person, says: 'What's the matter with you?' I stand there out of sheer curiosity; besides, Julian will see which of us is a coward.

I say: 'With me?' Then something white emerges slowly from a bunk, far back in the mountain of bunks. I've seen enough. I rush out into the open where Julian and Itzek stand at a safe distance, waiting and perhaps glad, perhaps disappointed, that I have emerged unscathed from the danger. I say: 'Phew, you should've seen what I saw!' But they don't want to hear my story. It's barely raining now.

We decide to meet at our special place and then go over to the wall together. Julian asks, why not meet at the wall right away, and I have a reason: If one of us is late, it wouldn't be such a good idea to wait for him at the wall.

After we have agreed, Julian says: 'We'd better meet at the wall.'

Without giving it much thought I ask: 'When are we going to meet anyway?'

We think about this for a bit, then Julian looks at me angrily as if with my question I had actually created the problem. He always needs to blame someone and says to Itzek: 'If you weren't so stupid and still had your watch, there'd be no problem.'

Not one of us can think of a sign in the night to tell the time by. Until Itzek says: 'Lights Out is the same time everywhere, isn't it?' That's the best idea yet, even Julian can't deny that, 'Lights Out' could be the kind of sign we need. 'Right after Lights Out,' says Itzek, 'then one more hour, then everybody will be asleep, then we can meet.'

'And how long is an hour?' asks Julian, but he has no better suggestion. We agree on the length of an hour: it is the time which even the last person in the hut needs to fall asleep, and a bit longer. We place our hands one on top of the other and are sworn conspirators and separate until night time.

Then I am back with my parents sitting on the bed. My Mother gets up from her sewing and says that I am wet through. She takes off my shirt and dries my head. Many people are walking round in the hut, their hands clasped behind them: one of them is Father. Someone sings a song about the cherries a pretty lass is always eating, about the bright dresses she is always wearing, and about the little tune she is always singing.

For the first time in my life I can hardly wait for night. The fear has gone. That's to say, it's really still there but it is not as great as the anticipation I feel. If only I don't oversleep, I think, if only I don't oversleep again, I mustn't oversleep.

I tell my Mother: 'I'm tired.' It is still afternoon. She lays her hand on my forehead, then she calls Father. 'Strange—he's tired and wants to sleep.'

Father says: 'Are you surprised if someone runs round all day and gets tired?' My Mother gives him an exasperated look. He says: 'Let him lie down and sleep, if he wants to and can,' then he starts walking round again.

I lie down. My Mother covers me up. She asks whether anything hurts—she presses a few places. I say impatiently: 'Nothing hurts.'

She says: 'Don't be cheeky.' She leaves her hand on my body under the coverlet. I don't mind—it feels quite pleasant. As time goes by I really do feel sleepy, what with the rain beating on the roof, the people walking round in slow circles, and her hand on my stomach. I think about what I would like to find in the empty houses in the night—it mustn't be too heavy as I will have to carry it, nor too big; I keep an open mind—just that the word 'marvellous' keeps going through my head. I'm sure I shall find something to make people stare and ask: Where in the world did you get *that*? Then I shall smile and keep my secret to myself, and they will all rack their brains and be envious. I feel I'll soon be asleep—there's always a humming in one's ears just before sleep. There's no chance of my oversleeping, I think, no matter how tired I may be: every night someone shouts 'Lights out!', loud enough to wake a bear. I am quite clever.

I sleep, then I'm awake again. It's almost time to go to bed. I am given my piece of bread and half an onion. I am a bit surprised that no one seems to notice what remarkable things are going on. Only my Mother insists that something's wrong with me; her hands keep fluttering over my forehead, and she reminds Father about my coughing. I am about to jump up and show her how well I am, but I remember just in time what a mistake that would be. I mustn't be well yet—I must go on coughing—otherwise they'll put me back between them for the night.

'There you see?' says my Mother.

She wants to fetch Professor Engländer, the famous doctor, from the next hut, but Father says: 'Go ahead, fetch him. He'll come and examine him, and if next time it's something really serious he won't come again.'

A voice calls: 'Lights out!' One more hour, I think in alarm. Itzek is lying there now, Julian's lying there now. I think, for each of them, one more hour. I'm afraid my parents may be able to feel how I'm trembling inside, but they are already at their kissing and whispering again. I never felt so wide awake in my life. Over and beyond the disturbance beside me I am aware of every single thing happening in the hut: the whispering in the next bed, the first snore, a groan issuing not from sleep but from misery, the second snore, the concert of snores, through a gap in the wall a light from the sky. I notice the rain has stopped—somewhere drops are still falling onto the ground, but no longer onto the roof. Two beds further along there's a very old woman who talks in her sleep. Sometimes it has woken me up. I am waiting for her to start again. Father says one can be a different person in one's sleep. She is silent. Instead someone is crying—that's not so bad—crying makes a person tired and soon drop off to sleep. Then I hear a snore that delights me because it is my Mother's. The sound is very soft and irregular, with little hesitations as if there were an obstacle in its path. None of the elves has put in an appearance yet. Perhaps the rain is keeping them away tonight. A good part of the hour has passed. I don't want to be the first at our meeting place. The hour will be over, I decide, when Father is asleep too. I sit up and dangle my legs over the side of the bed. If he asks me what's the matter it means he's not asleep. But he doesn't. Itzek is also sitting on his bed, that's a help. Julian's heart is also beating fast now. The crying has stopped, and for a long time there have been no more whisperings. So my hour must be up.

I stand beside the bed and nothing happens. Twice that morning I found my way to the door with my eyes shut—to make up for the lack of a rehearsal during the night—and I didn't bump into anything. All I did was step on the toes of an old man who was in my way, and he gave me a piece of his mind. I pick up my shoes. The hour is over. I take one step, then another. The floor creaks a little. During the day you don't hear that. The darkness is so black that it makes no difference whether your eyes are open or shut. My steps quicken, but suddenly everything stops. I almost fall over with shock because someone screams. It's that awful old woman. I don't budge till she is quiet again; what will happen if she wakes my parents, and then: 'Where's our child?' But they go on sleeping because the woman's screams are part of the night. My legs find the corner by themselves, then I see a grey shimmer from the door —light from the night. The last steps are recklessly fast because it suddenly occurs to me: what if the doors are locked at night! But the door opens with wonderful ease and closes quickly—at last, I'm outside in the camp! I sit down, put on my shoes, and could kick myself: I've forgotten my trousers. When I go to bed I always keep my shirt on, taking off only my trousers—that's my Mother's system here: the trousers are folded up as a pillow on the bed so no one will steal them. Now I have to climb over the wall in my shirt and underpants. Itzek and Julian will make fun of me.

I can't find the moon. Yesterday I asked Julian: 'What'll they do to us if they catch us?'

He replied: 'They won't catch us.' I found that very reassuring.

On the ground are puddles. In one of them I find the moon. Of course I stop at every corner and take no risks. I think: even if Father wakes up now, it won't do him any good.

Beyond the last corner I find Julian crouching by the wall. Of course he laughs and points at me. I sit down beside him on the ground. He is still enjoying the joke.

I ask: 'Isn't Itzek here yet?'

He says: 'Look round for yourself, stupid.'

The bottom strut is so low that I can hold it as I sit there; it wobbles a bit. 'Maybe he fell asleep,' I say. Julian says nothing—he seems very serious now that he's stopped laughing. Never before have I been so aware of his superiority. I ask: 'How long are we going to wait?'

He says: 'Shut up.' I imagine Itzek's horror when he wakes up in the morning and it's all over. But now there's no time for pity. I'm waiting for Julian's orders and begin to be afraid of the wall. It is much higher than during the day. It grows with every passing moment. When a crow caws overhead, Julian stands up; perhaps the bird's call was the signal he was waiting for.

He says: 'Your Itzek is a coward.'

Later, after we have returned with our booty, I shall be just as great a hero as Julian. It'll make no difference then who gives the orders now and who obeys. But Julian is silent for so long that I am afraid something may have gone wrong.

I ask: 'D'you want to postpone it?'

He says: 'Rubbish.' I admit there was also a bit of hope in my question, but now I know we're going to leave the camp tonight.

'What are we waiting for?'

He says: 'Nothing.' He pushes me aside because I am in his way. He tests the first strut, the second and the third. He can't reach the fourth from the ground. He steps onto the first strut and is now high enough to touch the fourth. Then jumps down again onto the ground. He says: 'You go first.'

I ask: 'Why me?'

He says: 'Because I say so,' and I feel how right he is.

Even so I ask: 'Can't we draw lots?'

'No,' he says impatiently, 'get on with it, or I'll go alone.'

That's the highest proof that Julian isn't scared like me; he gives me a little shove, to help me pull myself together. True, I can still think of a few questions I'd like to ask him; but if Julian means it and goes without me I'll look like a fool. I step up to the wall. He says: 'You must grab the third one and step onto the first.'

He pushes from below to make it look as if I couldn't have managed without his help. I stand on the bottom strut and no longer feel scared of the wall, only of the height. It is a consoling thought that I shall have conquered the wall when Julian still has to face it. It's like a ladder for giants. First take a big step, then grab hold of a higher strut—not much effort needed for that. On my right is the cool wall, on my left down below Julian stays farther and farther behind. He has turned his face up to the sky and is watching me.

He asks: 'How's it going?'

For the first time in my life I despise him, and from my height I say: 'Don't make so much noise.' I won't let him know how easy it is; it was only fear that made him send me first. Suddenly the top of the wall is level with my eyes.

I see a street. I see dark houses, the damp cobblestones on the square. Nothing moves. The Germans really are asleep.

Softly he calls: 'What can you see?'

I call back excitedly: 'Way down there is a cart drawn by horses. I think they're white.'

He calls out in surprise: 'You're lying!'

I say: 'Now it's turned a corner.' I lean my arms on the top of the wall. There is a bit of broken glass lying there. They are small pieces—you can't see each one. I grope along the wall with my hands. The largest pieces can be broken off, and I use it to scrape away the other splinters.

'What are you doing?' Julian asks from below.

I carefully brush off the glass with my sleeve and blow. Then I roll over onto the wall. The fear starts up again—most of all I'm afraid of the fear. I have to get my knees under my stomach, that's the hardest part. For a moment I put my knee on glass. Of course I mustn't scream. I find a better place for my knee. It must be bleeding now; and Julian, the idiot, calls out: 'What's keeping you?'

I have to turn myself round. I'm desperately afraid of losing my balance. If Julian says one more thing I'll spit on his head. Then, after turning round, I see him standing down there and for the first time realize how high up I am. Once again I lie down on my stomach. My legs are already outside. I can't worry about little pains. I let myself down as far as my arms will stretch. My feet find no support because there are no struts here. I hang there and can't pull myself up again.

I hear Julian calling: 'What's going on? Say something!'

I close my eyes and picture the wall from below, how small it seems when you walk round in the camp. So what can happen? I'll fall down and hurt myself a bit. I've fallen down thousands of times. I'll get up again and wipe my hands, while Julian will still have to face the climb. What happens if he doesn't come? I get cold shivers at the thought—I'm hanging here and Julian disappears and goes to bed. I can't very well go alone into the houses, after all it was Julian's idea from the beginning. I call: 'Julian, are you there?' Then I fly through the air: though nothing has been decided yet, the edge of the wall has detached itself from my hands. The ground is a long time coming. I fall slowly—the wall scraping along my stomach the whole steep way down—finally landing on my head too. I lie there comfortably on my back, keeping my eyes shut for a bit before calmly looking at the sky, which is exactly above me. Then I see Julian's face on the top of the wall. He's a good fellow, and he's got guts too.

He calls: 'Where are you?'

Now I must move. I have two pains to cope with, one on my right hip, the other in my head. I say: 'Here, Julian.' I feel giddy too. I must move to one side so he doesn't make matters worse by landing on my head. I think: But I've made it.

Julian has a different method. He sits on the wall. He slides forward; he seems to be hurrying; he supports himself left and right; his arms soon look like wings on him. No, he's not a coward. He flies to the ground, landing beside me on his back. He gets up much faster that I did. Since I am behind him I walk round him, but he turns so that I can't see his face and he moves off a few steps. I want to see him and grasp his shoulder, but he pushes me away because he's crying. Even so he's got guts.

My headache is sometimes a little one, sometimes a big one. My hip hurts at every step. I ask: 'Are your hands bleeding too?' As if this possibility had occurred to him for the first time, Julian looks at his hands, turns them towards the moon. They aren't bleeding. To comfort him I show him mine.

He says: 'What on earth did you do, you donkey?'
I say: 'The glass.'
He says: 'The whole idea is not to touch that.'

I am shivering—how many jackets does a thief need at night?
We are now people in a story, Julian walking ahead; he asks:
'Are you still there?' That means he can't hear me—I slink
along as stealthily as any expert. With each step I get more used to
my hip, whereas my headache gets worse. Everything is fine as long
as I don't turn my head. Somewhere a dog barks; it is a long way
away and has nothing to do with us.

I say: 'Why don't we go into this house?'

We go up to the next house, but the front door is locked. We
try every door, but it's the same with all of them. I cry a little, from
my headache and the cold too; Julian doesn't laugh. He tugs at my
sleeve and says: 'Come.' That makes my feel better. He says:
'D'you know what I think?' And when I shake my head and so cause
myself new pain, he says: 'I think there are people still living here.
That's why the houses are locked up. Only our street is empty.' I
stop outside a window and want to find out whether Julian is right. I
stand on tiptoe to see if there are people sleeping in the room. A
devil's face looks out at me—only the pane of glass is between us. I
run away, hip and all, so that Julian doesn't catch up with me until
the next street corner.

I say: 'There was a devil behind the window.'

Julian says: 'There are people living there, stupid.'

He finds our street. I hardly recognize it in the dark. We walk
past a fence where two loose boards seem familiar to me. I push one
of them with my finger and am right. I could show many a trick in
our street. I ask Julian why he doesn't simply take the next house;
yet I know he is afraid it might be locked up too. He says: 'I know
what I'm doing.'

Then I feel fine because my head feels better. We would have
been inside a house long ago if Julian felt as cold as I do. I think: I
hope he won't feel warm for too long. Some day or other I'll be the
leader, then I'll wear warm clothes. He asks: 'Are you still there?'
We go past my house—he can think only of his own; without him I
could walk in if I wanted to. I think of Father's torch. I must be

tired. We waste no words over the workshop of dead Muntek, the cobbler; in my day, anyway, he was alive and used to chase us. I have never felt so cold in my street—the wind blows round my bare legs—but Julian is the first to sneeze. He stands outside his house and can't get through the door. He rattles it a bit and kicks it a bit, but the door stays shut.

I say: 'Don't make such a racket!'

He answers: 'Shut up.'

Since it is a long way to my house, I go to the next one, and that's open. I call Julian; we're very close to our fortune. The house has three floors. We start at the top because Julian wants it that way. On the landing it's black, a door opens, a dark-grey hole. My heart pounds because I don't know whether Julian has opened the door or a stranger, until Julian says: 'What are you waiting for?' In the room there is a confusion of things: overturned chairs, a table, an open cupboard in which our hands find nothing.

I ask: 'What's that stink here?'

Julian says: 'You stink.'

I sit down on a broken bed. Julian goes to the window and opens it. It gets lighter. He leans far out and asks: 'D'you know where our camp is?'

I go over to him and say: 'No.'

He shuts the window again and says: 'I do.' That's Julian for you. On the way back to the door we stumble against a bucket, where the stink comes from.

All the rooms in the house are empty in the same way. In one there is an object that is much too heavy to take along. Julian says: 'That's a sewing machine.' In one we find a box half full of coal—what use is coal in the camp? In one the handle falls off the door. I pick it up and decide to take it along—it'll do for a start. Julian takes the handle away from me and replaces it. In the next house, in the very first room, Julian finds something. He examines it and soon calls out: 'Wow, they're binoculars!' I have never heard this word. He says: 'Come here and look through them.' I go over to him at the window, he holds his discovery up to my face, and sure enough you can see things in it that no one can see with ordinary eyes, although it's night. Julian shows how I have to turn the little wheel to make the pictures fuzzy or clear, but I can't see anything anyway because suddenly there are tears in my eyes. I give him back his binoculars. What rotten luck that he should be the one to find them.

In the next room Julian comes to me and says: 'We must go back.'

I say: 'I'm not going before I find something too.' He repeats that I must hurry, as if it were a question of skill whether I find something or not. He stays with me in each room, as long as I like. He opens every window and looks at everything with his damn binoculars.

I feel I would be content with less and less, but there is nothing there. Julian says: 'We must go. Or d'you want them to find out everything?' I say there is just one more room I want to go into, that's where the cloth ball is lying under the bed, then we'll run back to the camp. 'All right,' says Julian; since the binoculars he's a generous friend. While we walk along the street I have no answer to the question of what will happen if my house, of all the houses, should happen to be locked. Julian sees it long before I do, through his contraption, and says: 'The door's open.' There is no ball under the bed. I crawl into every corner. When we left the room it was here, no doubt about that, so someone came later and stole the ball. Now the whole thing hasn't been worth it.

Julian asks: 'What's wrong?' because I am sitting on the bed crying. He puts his hand on my shoulder, though he could easily be grinning. He's a pretty good friend. Now he should ask whether I want his binoculars; of course I wouldn't accept them, but it would help a lot. Then I remember Father's torch. It hasn't shown up in the camp so far; maybe it'll show up here, if the cloth-ball thief hasn't found it. I don't know where Father kept it hidden. I don't think it had any fixed place, sometimes it lay on the table, sometimes somewhere else.

I get up and ask Julian: 'If you had a torch as big as your fist, where would you hide it here?'

He looks round three times, then asks: 'Are you sure it's here?'

I say: 'It must be here.'

Julian puts down his binoculars on our table and begins to search; I like that but then again I don't like it. I hurriedly start searching; I must find the torch before he does. There are a few places I know that he doesn't—a hole in the floor, a little hollow under the windowsill, a loose board in the top of the wardrobe. My knowledge yields me nothing. I crawl on my stomach across the room, I climb on the chair: no torch. If Julian says once more that we have to leave, we'll have to leave. For the last time I crawl under the bed, and I hear him say: 'D'you mean this one?' He is quite calm. He has placed the torch on the table without waiting for any thanks.

I ask: 'Where did you find it?'

He says: 'In the drawer.' He says it like someone who can't understand that I almost went out of my mind over such a ridiculous object. He takes his important binoculars and goes to the door. Perhaps I would never have thought of the drawer: you don't need to crawl on your stomach to reach it; you don't have to climb on a chair; not even the ball thief had that much sense.

Back in the camp I'll make the light shine; just now Julian is impatient. I hurry after him to the stairs, yet I'm the one who knows every step of the way here. 'Thanks, Julian,' I say or think. Suddenly I feel sorry for Itzek. Julian forbids me to try out my torch in the street. I do as he says. I pay no attention to where we're going. I just follow him. I don't feel cold yet. I have to hold the torch in my hand because of course, having forgotten my trousers, I don't have pockets.

I ask: 'D'you remember the way?'

'You can go by yourself if you like,' says Julian, which means he knows the way. I've no idea why he is angry. I want to be nice to him.

I say: 'If you need the torch, you can borrow it any time.'

He says: 'I don't need your torch.' I believe he's just as keen as I am to be home again—that puts him in a bad mood; he dreads facing the wall again just as much as I do and having to climb it and jump down into the depths.

I say: 'If the Germans are all asleep, we don't need to climb. Why don't we simply walk through the gate?'

'Because it's locked, stupid,' says Julian.

It gets colder as we walk along. Of course Julian finds the camp, and since I've never doubted it I feel no relief. He even finds our spot. He whispers: 'Oh no, d'you know what's wrong?'

I whisper: 'What?'

'The iron struts,' he whispers back, 'there aren't any on this side.'

I'd like to have had a bright idea too and whisper: 'We have to go round the camp, somewhere there must be these things.'

'But there's glass all along the top of the wall, except at this place,' whispers Julian.

I look at my hands, which I had forgotten, and my knee. I whisper: 'If we find another place, we'll take a stone and first break up the glass.' I realize how good my idea is, for now Julian says nothing and looks round for a stone. He puts the stone in his trouser pocket and sets off as leader; if we should find struts on this side of the wall, it'll be me who has saved us.

While walking ahead Julian says: 'Stop playing with your stupid torch or I'll take it away from you.' He's always bossiest when he's right; I would be a better leader if I were the leader. We have to make a detour, a big detour away from the wall and past the camp entrance, where there's not a soul to be seen. That's how Julian wants it. He takes away my torch, though I've done nothing with it. For safety's sake, I don't resist; a leader must think of everything and needn't explain everything. We sneak across the street, which leads straight back to the camp gate. There's still no one there to see us. We get back to the wall. Julian returns my torch, which is what I expected. We walk and walk and find no struts.

I say: 'Julian, there won't be any.'

'I know that perfectly well,' he says, but keeps walking.

Then I ask: 'How much longer are we going to walk?' His answer is to stop, sit down, and lean his back against the wall. I sit down too and don't ask. I look at Julian and see something terrible: he is crying. Now for the first time we're stuck. He is crying because he's at his wits' end. His crying before, when he jumped down from the wall and fell, was nothing by comparison. We huddle together, most likely he feels just as cold as I do. He's probably a few months older.

I ask: 'Shall we go into an empty house and lie down?'

He answers: 'Are you crazy?' A few times my eyelids close. I think what a pity it is that it wasn't Julian who had the idea about the empty house. By now it's so light that my torch makes hardly more than a bright circle on the ground. I think of Father, wanting him to come and fetch us, first me, then Julian, or both together, one under each arm. I want him to lay me down on the bed and cover me up warmly: oh my, that would be good. He'd have to hold my Mother's hand. Both would have to stand beside the bed, looking down on me and smiling until I woke up.

Then something hurt. Before us stands a huge German. He has prodded me with his foot. He does it again, but not like someone meaning to kick. Out of his terrible eyes he utters a few words that are unintelligible; I'm too scared to try even to get up. Disaster won't really strike until I'm standing; I stay sitting down. But beside me Julian is on his feet, held up by his collar. The giant says in funny Polish: 'What are you doing here?' I look at my friend; the giant shakes me a little.

Julian points at the wall and says: 'We're from the camp.' That makes me admire him for a long time—the calm way he says it. The giant asks: 'And how did you get out?' Julian tells him the truth, meanwhile I look at the helmet and the rifle sticking up over the giant shoulder, the giant shoe on my stomach, pinning me down. I'm convinced we're soon going to be shot—we realized that from the beginning. The giant asks why the hell we didn't go back into our camp. Julian explains that too. He has never been as great a hero as now. The giant looks up to the top of the wall and seems to understand. He takes his foot away from my stomach—that's like an order to get up—and hardly am I on my feet when he grabs me by the collar. The torch is still lying on the ground. I have to get hold of it somehow before we leave.

The giant lets go of both of us and says: 'Come with me to the guardhouse.' But he just stands there without moving. So do we, of course—it's up to him to take the lead. 'Come along, get a move on now,' he says, giving us a shove. I turn towards the wall and pick up my torch—it's my last chance. The giant asks: 'What've you got there?' and grabs my hands, which are behind my back. He sees the torch, takes it, tries it out, and puts it away in his pocket as if everything here belonged to him. Every bad thing I have ever heard about the Germans is suddenly true. I hate him like poison. If it had been anyone else I would have tried to persuade him to give me back the torch, even if it had meant an argument, even with Father. With this huge German it was hopeless. I see Julian stuff his shirt well down into his trousers. Only the two of us know what he is hiding under his shirt. I hope for his sake that he can hang onto his binoculars—I don't want the giant to have them. The giant says: 'Get a move on now.' He gives us another shove. We walk along in front of him. I notice Julian moving his booty from his back to his stomach. If we're going to be shot, I think, his binoculars won't be much use to him anyway. The giant tells us to stop.

With his giant hands he turns us round to face him. He looks at us for a long time, like a person with something on his mind—I wish him the worst worries in the world.

He says: 'Do you know what'll happen to me if I don't take you to the guardhouse?' As if that concerned us: he's not only a thief, he's also an idiot. I think: Whatever happens to you, it can't be nearly bad enough.

Julian says: 'No, I don't.' I feel like answering that I don't care—it would be a good answer—but I see his great fists dangling. Oh how I'd love to be a giant! Suddenly he grabs us both by the neck and flings himself on the ground, bringing us down with him. He is still holding me by the neck as if it were made of wood. He says: 'Not a word.' I see a light at the far end of the wall, a motor-bike. Soon I can hear the sound of it; I seem to hear the giant's heart beating too; by now the pounding of his heart is louder than the sound of the motor-bike. He says: 'Not a word,' though he's the only one talking. He's a thief, a fool, a coward—I'm not scared of someone like that. I can't see Julian because the huge body is lying between us. A long way off the motor-bike turns a corner, but we have to stay where we are for a little while.

'Get up,' the giant then says. He lets go of us and brushes off his soldier's clothes. I look at my underpants and know I'll be in plenty of trouble with my mother, if I ever get out of this alive. The giant takes off his helmet and wipes his forehead; like all Germans he has fair hair. He takes his time, as if the cold existed only for me and not for him. His helmet is back on his head; now he takes hold of his rifle. This must be it: take you away and shoot you. They can do that.

Julian asks: 'Are you going to shoot us now?'

The giant says nothing, probably doesn't consider Julian's question worth answering. He looks up and down the street; no doubt he doesn't want anyone to see what he is about to do to us. He says to Julian: 'Don't you dare try and run away,' and wags his finger at him. Why has he taken hold of his rifle if not to shoot us? But he leans it against the wall. I suppose he doesn't know himself what he wants. The torch is a little bulge under his jacket. I should have simply left it lying beside the wall, then one day some lucky person would have found it. He points at me and says only: 'You there,' and I have to go up to him. He says: 'I'll lift you kids up onto the wall. But jump down quickly and run as fast as you can to your huts. Don't waste a second. Understand?' So that's what it's all about. I don't know whether I feel relieved—in a moment I'll have to jump again.

'We have a place,' says Julian, 'where there's no glass on top. It's not far from here.'

The giant says: 'There's no glass all along here,' and lifts me up with no effort at all. I have no time to think about it; it hurts me because he's holding me by my hips. He says: 'Stand on my shoulders.' I lean against the wall and do as he tells me; I still can't reach the top. He says: 'Now stand on my head.' He holds me by my ankles; I pay him back a bit for the torch: I make myself heavy and don't try to spare his head. The helmet is his salvation, without a helmet he'd have a surprise coming to him. He says: 'Hurry up.' I stand on one leg—there's not room on the helmet—now I can grab the top of the wall. He asks: 'Can you hold on?' I cautiously lift my foot from his head and he moves away from under me. I hang there, and will never get onto the wall; it's exactly how I hung there before, except that then I wanted to get down to the ground and not get to the top. I look down over my shoulder and see him pick up his rifle.

That's the ultimate shock. No one can imagine: to be hanging up there in the air just for him to shoot me, after all those nice speeches. There's nothing to hold me to the wall now; I let go. As the years pass, the fall gets longer and longer—no wall can be that high—then I am caught by the giant. It is as if I had never fallen. The giant puts his hand over my mouth before I can scream. He says: 'What d'you think you're doing?' He sets me on my feet, picks up his rifle from the ground, and props it against the wall again. Then he says: 'Once more, quick now.' Again he lifts me up, already I feel a bit more at home on his shoulders. This time I leave his head in peace. The sight of Julian standing down below makes me feel envious: I'm fighting a life-and-death struggle. I fall and I'll be shot or not shot, and he stands there looking on, calm as you please. And he's even allowed to keep his binoculars. I'll have to have a word with him about that later.

Once again I grab the top of the wall. The giant lets go of one ankle, the other remains in his hand. He says to Julian: 'Give me the rifle.' He presses the rifle butt against my behind and pushes me up. I can almost sit on it. With no effort I manage to get onto the wall. I lie on my stomach and can see how right he was—there's not even the tiniest scrap of glass in sight; the glass is a mystery. I can look into our camp where it is still as silent and empty as at night, though it's as light as day now. The giant calls from below: 'Get down there!'

I turn round on the wall, hang down on the other side and fall until I can fall no further. I lie there crying. I am back again and have brought nothing with me but sore places. Julian is no longer of interest to me; in future he'll have to find others for his ideas. I stand up. My parents feel closer. Father will be glad I'm still alive, my Mother will cry when she sees me, then she'll wash out my many wounds; I won't be able to tell them the truth. My hands are bleeding again, my knees are bleeding, my elbow looks as if it has been dipped in dirt and blood. One consolation is that they'll probably feel so sorry for me they'll stroke me. I start walking. Tomorrow I'll say to Julian: 'So all Germans sleep at night, do they?'

As I turn round, he jumps down from the wall by his own method. Though it's not a bad fall, he doesn't get up. Seeing him lying there on his stomach, I go back to him because he's my friend. He is crying, crying, and crying—I have never seen anyone cry like that before. I had already finished crying, now I start up again myself. I ask: 'Did he take away the binoculars?' It is a while before he pushes my hand away and gets up. I can see the binoculars under his shirt. He limps away, crying all the time. I run after him and at last feel superior. I ask: 'Are we going to meet tomorrow?' I see nothing wrong with this question, but what does Julian do? He hits me over the head. He looks at me as if he had more blows for me in his fists, then he limps on again. I stay where I am and can still hear him crying; I needn't be that sorry for him that I have to run after him again. I'm looking forward to the hut, where I won't have to feel cold any more.

Beyond the door it is dark. I close it so softly that I hear nothing; anyone who wasn't awake before will still be asleep. My parents are sitting on the bed, staring at me wide-eyed.

Someone whispers: 'Good God, what have they done to you?'

Right now nothing hurts any more, yet I feel as if the worst is still to come. My Mother holds both hands over her mouth. Father doesn't move. I stand between his knees. He puts one hand on my head and turns me once around. Then he holds me by both shoulders and asks: 'Where have you been?'

I say: 'I was outside and fell down.'

Father says: 'No one falls down like that.' My Mother has risen and is searching in our brown carry-all. Father shakes me so violently that my head, which for a long time had given me no trouble, begins hurting again.

I say: 'We met outside and had a fight and beat each other up. That's the truth.'

He asks: 'Who's "we"?'

I say: 'You don't know him.' Suddenly I can lie as never before. My Mother is holding a dripping towel. She takes me away from Father and leads me to the light by the window. Father follows us and looks on.

'Go and ask Professor Engländer whether he can come and look at him,' says my Mother.

Father asks: 'Can't we wait till after inspection?'

'No,' she retorts, 'or daren't you go outside?' Off he goes on tiptoe, and at last my Mother strokes me. She says: 'You must realize that he's upset.'

She lays me down on the bed and nurses my head on her lap. I think that later perhaps I'll tell her the truth, only her. She says: 'How tired you are, my little one.' It is bliss to lie in her lap, though her finger won't let me fall asleep. She speaks to someone, a few times I hear the word 'probably'. I open my eyes and she is smiling down at me as if I were something funny.

Father is holding a little dark bottle in his hand. 'Engländer gave me some iodine,' he says.

I ask: 'Will it hurt?'

My Mother says: 'Yes, but it can't be helped.' So I get up and back away because in my opinion enough things have hurt this past night.

Father says: 'Don't listen to her, it won't hurt. It just cleans out the wound.' That sounds a bit better. He says: 'I can prove it.' I watch very carefully—after all it's my pain—I look at his outstretched arm. He dribbles a few drops from the bottle onto his arm; they form a little black lake and slowly spread. Then he says: 'That's supposed to hurt? Do you think I would put the stuff on my own arm if it hurt?' I look into his eyes from very close up and can't see even the tiniest trace of pain. A further proof is that my Mother goes away; she was wrong and doesn't want to admit it, so she simply goes away. Father says: 'Come here now.' I hold out my elbow to him, he twists my arm a little so that the drops fall straight into the wound.

Translated from the German by Leila Vennewitz

GREGOR VON
REZZORI
MEMOIRS OF AN
ANTI-SEMITE

The big something falling from the floor above my grandmother's apartment cast a sudden shadow on the window before it bumped on the cobblestones, and my grandmother's gouty claw reached for the little bell beyond the flowery field of playing cards she had laid out on the table for her game of patience and shook it violently. Decades of strained impatience made her movement awkward, and the thin silver sound seemed to mock her intention to reach the deaf ears of old Marie. Nevertheless, as in a vaudeville gag, the door opened instantly, and old Marie appeared, trembling with age and the suppressed contradictions of nearly fifty years of service to a most complicated family.

'Yes, please?'

My grandmother majestically stretched her tortoise neck as if it still were encircled by half a dozen rows of pearls and turned her head towards the window. 'Something fell down from the upper floor. The Jews must have put their feather beds in the windows to air or something of that kind. Go and have a look.'

Old Marie pushed her head out of the window and then brought it back into the room. 'Please,' she said triumphantly. 'That's no feather bed. It is the young Raubitschek girl.'

I spent part of my youth in this apartment house, which was in a drowsy residential section of Vienna. When I met the 'old Raubitscheks' on the stairs, I greeted them with the same polite reserve they used in saluting my grandmother. Never a word was exchanged. They were educated people, though. Papa Raubitschek being a professor at the University of Vienna, famous artists came to their apartment, and every Wednesday evening the remote sounds of chamber-music reached my grandmother's apartment and would make her—she was very sensitive to noise—say contemptuously, 'They are playing Beethoven's "Allergique" again or something equally horrid.' Because so many Jews were successful in musical endeavours, my grandmother no longer considered it one of the fine arts.

Whether those chamber-music concerts got on the nerves not only of my grandmother but also of Minka Raubitschek I am unable to say. However, she was a high-spirited girl with a strong and stubborn will, and on the occasion I have just mentioned, during a quarrel with her mother, she jumped out of the window. 'Exaggerated' was my grandmother's comment. 'As those young Jewish intellectuals usually are.' Fortunately she didn't do herself much harm. She broke a hip and was slightly lame thereafter, that was all. In later years, when I had been accepted into the circle of her friends, we used to put a mountain climber's cord around her waist and let her down the steep stairs to the ladies' room of the Kärntnerbar. This was necessary not·only because of her lame hip but also because her sense of equilibrium was impaired by too many whiskeys. She used to thank us with bits of cultural-historical information. 'Do you realize where you are, you drunken swine? This place was designed by Adolf Loos, an architect as important as Frank Lloyd Wright. It is one of the early masterpieces of modern architecture—a room that would normally not be big enough for a dozen ignoramuses of your kind shelters half a hundred. If that isn't progress . . . .'

As the grandson of an architect who had done his share to make Vienna's monuments conform to the taste of the *fin de siècle*, I should have given particular consideration to such remarks of Minka Raubitschek. Her tastes were exquisite and her knowledge was profound. But at the time I was merely reminded of my grandmother. 'It is disgusting,' my grandmother would say, 'how very much like your father you have become. He is a perfect barbarian, with his monomaniacal passion for shooting. But when I think that I gave my daughters Renan to read in order to have them take up spiritualism . . . .'

The two neuralgic points in my grandmother's existence were the marriage of her eldest daughter, my mother, with my father and the 'exaggerated ideas' of my unmarried aunts. My grandmother never set foot in the back rooms of her apartment, which, after the death of my grandfather, were occupied by her two spinster daughters; for there, every Wednesday evening, accompanied by the remote sounds of the Raubitschek chamber-music, the meetings of the esoteric community of Mr Malik took place. Mr Malik was an engineer with supernatural powers that enabled him to massage the souls out of the bodies of ladies who had metaphysical talents so that the emptied vessel could be filled with some free soul of a dead person not yet reborn, who would then use the mouth of the medium to utter mystical nonsense, the theosophical interpretation of which was left to my aunts. The soul massaged out of the body remained attached to it by an astral navel cord, and when the free soul, who came like a guest into your body for the duration of the séance, had left, Mr Malik would massage your waiting soul along that very same astral navel cord back into your body, and you would be yourself again. In later years, when we were letting Minka down to the ladies' room of the Kärntnerbar, I had great success with what I had learned of Mr Malik's teachings. 'It's only her cursed *materia* that descends,' I would explain. 'Her soul stays with us and her whiskey.'

The presumably free, not yet reborn soul of Mr Malik will perhaps forgive me. I was only eighteen years old when I thus profaned his messages, and all during my childhood nobody had done much to make me take him very seriously. 'I am sure that man is not an engineer at all but just a cheap crook,' my grandmother used to say. 'Probably a Jew who has changed his name.'

The suspicion that somebody could have changed his name already made him a Jew—provided, of course, he was not an Englishman, like charming Mr Wood, who one beautiful day became Lord Halifax. But that was quite another thing. It was typically Jewish to change your name, for Jews quite understandably did not want to be taken for what they were. Since their names usually made it quite clear what they were, they had to change them, for camouflage. Had we been Jews, we should certainly have done the same, because it must be painful to be a Jew. Even wellbred people would make you feel it—either by their reserve or by an exaggerated politeness and coy friendliness. But fortunately we were not Jews, so, though we could see their point, we considered it a piece of insolence when they changed their names and pretended to be like us. Part of the certain esteem my grandmother had for the Raubitscheks came from the fact that they had not changed their name. Jews who changed their names, like Mr Malik, were crooks and swindlers. Their camouflage was but a falsehood to which they were driven by their disgusting greed for profit and their repulsive social climbing. This was particularly the case with the so-called Polish Jews—the prototype of the greedy, pushing little Jew one met so often in the Bukovina. There were crowds of them; you could not take a step without running into swarms. The elder ones and very old ones, particularly the very poor, were humbly what they were—submissive men in black caftans and large-brimmed hats, with curls at their temples, and in their eyes a sort of melting look which the sadness of many thousands of years seemed to have bestowed. Their eyes were like dark ponds. Some of them were even beautiful in their melancholy. They had spun-silver prophets' heads, with which the butcher's face of Mr Malik would have compared very unfavourably, and when they looked at you, humbly stepping aside to let you pass, it was like a sigh for not only themselves but all the burden of human existence which they knew so well. But the young ones, and especially the ones who were better off, or even rich, showed an embarrassing self-confidence. They wore elegant clothes and drove dandified roadsters, and their girls smelled of scent and sparkled with jewelry. Some of them even had dogs and walked them on leashes, just as my aunts did. When they spoke to one another, it was in a pushing, impatient way, even when they had just met. They asked direct personal questions and looked around for someone more worth knowing. They were not humble at all.

My father likewise hated Jews, all of them, even the old and humble ones. It was an ancient, traditional, and deep-rooted hatred, which he did not need to explain; any motivation, no matter how absurd, would justify it. Of course, nobody seriously believed that the Jews wanted to rule the world merely because their prophets had promised it to them (even though they were supposedly getting richer and more powerful, especially in America). But, of course, other stories were considered humbug: for instance an evil conspiracy, such as was described in the *Protocols of the Elders of Zion*, or their stealing communion wafers or committing ritual murders of innocent children (despite the still unexplained disappearance of little Esther Solymossian). Those were fairy tales that you told to a chamber-maid when she said she couldn't stand it here anymore and would much rather go and work for a Jewish family, where she would be better treated and better paid. Then, of course, you casually reminded her that Jews *had*, after all, crucified our Saviour. But our kind of people, the educated kind, did not require such heavy arguments to look upon Jews as second-class people. We just didn't like them, or at least liked them less than

111

other fellow human beings. This was as natural as liking cats less than dogs or bed-bugs less than bees; and we amused ourselves by offering the most absurd justifications.

For instance, it was well known that it's bad luck to run into a Jew when you go hunting. Now, my father did little else but hunting; and since there were so many Jews in the Bukovina that it was impossible to go hunting without promptly running into several of them, he had this annoyance almost every day. It made him suffer, like an ingrown toe-nail. There were violent scenes between him and my mother because she attracted crowds of Jews to our house. She used to give our cast-off clothing to rag-picking ped-dlers—Jews, needless to say, so-called *handalés*. You couldn't sell them the clothes—my father was the first to realize this. But it was better to throw the stuff away than to support the Jews in their dirty business, thus possibly helping them in their despicable social climbing. For the Jews dealt in second-hand clothes in order to emigrate to America. They arrived there as Yossel Tuttmann or Moishe Wassershtrom and soon earned enough dollars to change their names. Wassershtrom became Wondraschek, of course, and eventually von Draschek, and finally they'd come back to Europe as Barons von Dracheneck and buy themselves a hunting ground in the Tirol or Styria. And this was a personal affront to my father, for he could not afford a hunting ground in Styria, and thus he believed that all his privileges had been usurped by the Jews. More than anything, he felt it was their fault that he, as an Old Austrian, was forced to remain in the Bukovina and become a Rumanian, which made him too a kind of second-class human being.

He felt exiled in the Bukovina—or rather, as a pioneer, betrayed and deserted. He counted himself among the colonial officials of the former realm of the Austro-Hungarian Dual Monar-chy; and it was the task of such officials to protect Europe against the wild hordes who kept breaking in from the East. 'Civilization fertilizer' was his bitterly mocking term for the function he ascribed to himself and his kind: they were supposed to settle in the borderland, form a bulwark of Western civilization, and show a bold front to Eastern chaos. He had come to the Bukovina as a young man, after growing up in Graz during the most glorious era of the Dual Monarchy; and everything that had become sad and dreary and hide-bound after the collapse of 1918 was, he felt, represented in the land where he had been cast away.

The Bukovina is probably one of the most beautiful areas in the world. But for my father—aside from one tip of the forest Carpathians where he hunted—it was a landscape without character. He even went so far as to deny that I had any character, because I passionately loved the Bukovina. 'No wonder,' he said with undisguised scorn. 'You were simply born into corruption—I mean, the corruption of character. If these borderlands didn't constantly pose the danger of corroding character, then they wouldn't have needed our kind of people as civilization fertilizer.'

In my boyhood, I found it very difficult to reach any precise notion of what 'character' really was. For my father—he repeated it often enough—Styria had a distinct character. Naturally, I had to assume that this was connected to its 'mountainous character', which was always brought up in Austrian books on local history and geography. *A propos*, instead of 'character' or the lack thereof, they occasionally talked about 'backbone'. 'The boy simply has no backbone,' I had once been forced to hear when refusing to own up to some prank. Styria had character because of its mountain backbone. Now, the Bukovina did have a mountainous backbone, too, although not quite such a spectacular one as the Hohe Tauern. But rocky peaks did loom here and there from the green cones of the forest Carpathians, and the poetic gentleness of the flowery slopes was all too deceptive in obscuring the wildness of the deep forests in which they were embedded. If the word 'character' signified what I sensed about it, then these tremendous, wind-swept black forests had at least as much character as the glacier-crowned massifs of Styria.

Even my father had to admit that hunting in the Bukovina was better, more adventurous, more primeval than in Styria. Nevertheless, he dreamed of a hunting ground in Styria and shrugged his shoulders when he was sharply reminded that owners of hunting grounds in Styria dreamed of having a hunting ground in the Carpathians. When I finally asked him what character was, he replied without hesitating: 'Troth, more than anything else.'

Now I thought I understood him. 'Troth' was a much clearer fetish than the throat-scratching concept of 'character'. Since earliest childhood I had been taught to idolize this notion of loyalty, or troth. It was obvious my father could not love the Bukovina, because he had become a Rumanian citizen after its defection from the Dual Monarchy. He had been compelled to commit an act of disloyalty, like the engineer Malik, who had changed his name. Only in my father's case, the conflict was tragic: through loyalty to the hunt, he had been forced to be disloyal to his flag. And what that meant was urgently brought home to me.

In those years, the first great war was still close by. Traces and evidence of it survived throughout the countryside: shot-up farms, barbed-wire entanglements, ditches and dugouts in the heart of the woods, the wasteland of villages over which the Russian offensives had rolled. When I viewed such things, I was seized with a strange excitement, a mixture of fear and yearning, which—projected out of myself into the world comprising my experiences back then—I found mirrored in certain evening moods. In the oppressively hopeless dove-blue of the twilights, as in the dramatics of blood-red and sulphur-yellow sunsets, I experienced the shock that the war had brought to my parents' lives. Under such skies, the flag of our allegiance had sunk in the tumult of battle and amid the croaking of ravens over the field of warriors. It was the golden flag with the black, two-headed eagle of the Holy Roman Empire which had been carried on by Imperial Austria. And anyone who had not died in the battle around that flag had betrayed his troth and was now living on without character.

With the mind of a child, always open to thrilling sublimity, I kept reviving the catastrophe of that destruction and that unwilling disloyalty over and over again. This alone explained the oddly empty grief of the people in my immediate surroundings, their resigned and only ironically reflective stance: their deadness, which allowed them to continue existing in an everyday rut that was barely aglow with the melancholy of golden memories, kept them going even though they seemed not to care about the present. My father and mother in the Bukovina were as old and as much a part of a previous era as my grandmother and my crotchety maiden aunts in Vienna. Their dogs had grey heads and trembled when they walked, like Marie. They lived only when they talked about bygone days. The golden glow of their memories came solely from that sunken golden flag.

This sunkenness even explained the melancholy of the landscape in which I grew up. Beautifully canopied by the silky blue of a usually serene sky, the woodland was afflicted with melancholy, the melancholy of eastern vastnesses, creeping in everywhere: into the dove-blue of twilight hours as into the summer heat brooding over the fruit-bearing earth, into the submission of the peasants and the Jews to God's will, into the gentle flutes of shepherds from the meadowed slopes of the Carpathians. These flutes died out when the wintry winds began whistling from the steppes and high deserts of Asia, which suddenly shifted close to us. The Jews and peasants then pulled up their shoulders and curled into themselves even more humbly; the earth turned to stone beneath the frost; and the twilight hours were no longer ambiguous stages of the universe, leading to mute and colourful celestial dramas: they now were a deeper freezing and darkening over a greyish-white, skeletal world. This was a landscape of catastrophe: the proper setting for a destruction growing from a mythically ancient dichotomy. For not only *one* empire had gone under with the sinking of that golden flag. Not only we—or, as we said, 'our people'—had carried it, but also our adversaries, the Imperial Russians. Not only our emperor had gone down with the flag, but their emperor too.

The myth at the source of this tragedy had been drummed into me like a litany. It was the myth of the Holy Roman Empire of the Caesars, which had split apart. The black eagle in the golden field of the sunken flag had two crowned heads rising from his breast —shielded with coats of arms—because the empire had two capitals and two heads: Rome, and Byzantium, the Constantinople of the Emperor Constantine. A breach of troth was at the beginning of this myth: the defection of a part from a unified whole. Two empires arose from one and soon were bloodily fighting one another. For each considered itself the true descendant of the original one great Imperium. Each symbolized this claim in the same flag. Under this flag, Eastern Rome and Western Rome unpeacefully divided the world, until one of the Asian storms that had menaced Western civilization since time immemorial broke loose once again, and Byzantium decayed and ultimately fell into the hands of the pagans.

Western Rome too had gone through dark and disorderly times, which were historically conjured away, as it were, under the term 'Dark Ages' and inadequately bedizened with monarchical figures like Alaric and Odoacer. We leaped across centuries in order to come up all the more sensationally with the figure of light: Charlemagne, whom the Germans call Karl the Great, the reviver of the idea of Holy Empire and the founder of the Roman Empire of the German Nation. I cannot evoke my boyhood without his image. A bronze replica of a mounted statue of him stood on my father's desk, and I often gazed at that replica in deep meditation. The thought that after more than a millennium, his slippers and gloves still belonged among the Imperial treasures filled me with awe.

Nevertheless, I was puzzled by one enigma: how could Charlemagne, who was a Frank, after all, and thus, strictly speaking, a Frenchman (and, as a French governess furiously assured me, still viewed as a Frenchman by the French)—how could he be the new founder of an Empire of the German Nation? Needless to say, my father had explanations at hand which, while not dispelling my qualms, did divert me from them. In a higher sense, he maintained, one could think of Karl the Great as a German emperor because his descendance was thoroughly German. Germans, with the glorious Stauffers in the lead, had worn his crown and given the Holy Roman Empire an eternally German stamp. Besides, my father added, not quite logically, in medieval times (which had now lightened from the 'Dark Ages' to the 'High Middle Ages', the epoch of cathedrals and many-towered cities, of knights and ladies, of minstrels, inspired master stone-cutters, and altar-piece painters)—in those times, such distinctions had been meaningless. People didn't have national sentiments in the modern sense. You just followed a flag, that was all. Either you were born lowly and were a serf belonging to a lord—you followed him blindly wherever he went, and you never thought beyond your own parish—or else you were born into knighthood and served some count or prince as a true liegeman, which might expand your horizon by a few provinces; but in the end it was all the same. It made no difference whatsoever which of the many nations of this imperium these lords belonged to with their little flags and their liegemen and serfs; it made no difference what language they spoke or what costume they wore. For they were all vassals and subjects of the Emperor and the Empire.

This was comprehensible because it was graphic. The world seemed well ordered to me. The empire was the epitome of order. From the emperor at the top down through the great vassals and their liegemen with their subliegemen and serfs, it was all as hieratically articulated as a pyramid. This could be enacted. This could be represented in the parades of my tin soldiers. This could also be grasped abstractly. Its mechanism was simple. One person protected the other, the higher one always the lower one; and one served the other, the lower one always the one higher above him. And thus up and down the ladder, like the hierarchy of angels under the Almighty's Heavenly Throne. And that was why the Empire was Holy, said my father. It was God's state on earth. Not just purely and simply a political construction, a state constitution that offered uniform protection, uniform leadership and administration to a gigantic territory that was inhabited by many nations and threatened by many dangers. It was more than that: it was an idea and ideal; an ordered image of the world, of human society striving to make God's will come true. The divine right of the Emperor was not as it would be today, an arbitrary usurping by power-drunk demagogues mounted on a pedestal made up of interwoven interests—financial, mercantile, and political. Oh no! It was the very symbol of what God wanted the state to be. And this state was held together not by material interests alone but by the ethical principle of troth, loyalty, allegiance, the allegiance of vassals, the unconditional obedience that the liegemen had sworn to their lord and his flag, just as we, the immediate liegemen of the Habsburgs, had sworn allegiance to the Austrian imperial house and to the flag of the Empire with the two-headed eagle in the golden field.

Usually at this point my mother got up and left the room. Whereupon my father felt obliged to help me, as a small boy, to understand things better. He explained to me that in spite of the fact that we were of Italian descent and had become subjects of Rumania, we were still Austrians, and that living in the Bukovina meant a sort of unfaithfulness forced on us by unlucky circumstances—one of which was that shooting in the Bukovina was much better than in Styria. Still, as Austrians, we should have stuck to our flag. Unfortunately that flag didn't exist anymore; the imperial flag of Austria had been replaced by the vulgar flag of the new republic, with which, fortunately, we had nothing to do. The old imperial flag was the flag of the emperors of the House of Habsburg, who for six hundred years had been the emperors of the Holy Roman Empire, founded by Charlemagne. For six hundred years, the emperors of the House of Habsburg had worn his crown and defended the world of Christendom against another storm from Asia: the Turks. Under the house of Habsburg most of the nations of southeastern Europe had united in that noble task. That's how we, as Italians, had become Austrians, though we had neither come to Austria in the time of Charlemagne nor come in order, as true defenders of Christendom, to fight the Turks, but arrived only in the middle of the eighteenth century as bureaucrats from Sicily. But never mind. Nobody asked you where you were born. They asked only how you were born, and whether you were brave and just and faithful to your liege lord's flag. If you had been brave and just and faithful to your liege lord's flag, you got a coat of arms that obliged you to be even more brave and just and faithful to your flag.

But in the end it was agreed that I should be brought up in Austria, and this I resented very much, because I loved the Bukovina. It seems to be the lot of every good childhood to be lonesome, and I was lonesome in both places. In Vienna I was lonesome as a little boy who came from a now remote country of the Balkans and lived with old people and fools. At home, in the Bukovina, I was lonesome as the little snob with a foreign education who tried to avoid contact with others of his age. As a matter of fact, this was not at all my intention. It was the logical consequence of the isolation into which the monomania of my father and the nostalgia of my mother had manoeuvered us.

My mother too felt the Bukovina as a sort of exile, but simply as a woman who, with an unloved husband, lives far from those she loves. As my father's monomaniacal passion for shooting estranged him more and more from family life, my mother's various unfulfilled desires found an outlet in a no less monomaniacal love for me, her child. She watched over every step I took and every breath I drew. Between her terror that I would get pneumonia from running too fast and the suspicion that a contact with the gardener's children could give me lice, or that through the friendliness of a Rumanian officer who had put me in the saddle of his horse I would get syphilis, I did not develop into a very social youngster. In winter-time, on the big public skating rink, I found myself lonely in a corner, cutting my circles and loops into the ice, an enormous woollen shawl wrapped six times around my neck, while all around a whirl of hilarious liveliness filled the sparkling winter day.

The majority of the young skaters were Jews. Among them were some extremely pretty girls, with whom, one by one, I clandestinely fell in love, suffering not only from the overpro-tectiveness of my mother but from guilt. My mother came to fetch me every day and, in spite of my violent protests, had me wrapped in blankets and furs in order to protect my frail health after the exhausting exercise. My departure became a public amusement so humiliating that I did not dare to look the Jewish girls in the eye even when my mother had not yet turned up. At the same time I felt guilty because my tender feelings were a betrayal of everything that in the geography of my inner world formed the moral massifs, the mountainous backbone, so to speak—the Carpathians, without which that inner landscape would have had no character. Of course, there were some people who, with a dirty smirk, would say, 'A Jewess is no Jew'. But those were swine. For our kind it was impossible to fall in love with a Jewish girl. It meant being unfaithful to our flag. Love makes you long for intimacy, it leads to the most direct of all human relationships, and it was unthinkable to get into a human relationship with Jews. Jews were human beings, too; that could not be denied. But we did not have intimate relationships with other people, either, just because they were human beings. My father would not have anything to do with Rumanians, because they considered him part of a minority more or less equal with the Jews; nor with Poles, because they usually hated Austrians; nor would he have anything to do with other former Austrians who had stayed on in the Bukovina for mere personal interests, and not for a noble purpose like his, and who therefore had been unfaithful to their flag. That did not mean that we wouldn't regard them as human beings and behave like educated people when we came in contact with them. We answered every greeting more or less politely, with the same mixture of joviality and distance with which my grand-mother in Vienna greeted the Raubitscheks, and, when it was inevitable, even shook hands with them, and, should the occasion have demanded it, we would presumably have done the same with the Jews of the Bukovina, the Polish Jews, unless they pretended they could come shooting with us. But that did not mean that we wished to enjoy a closer relationship either with them or with the Jews in general. As a matter of fact, it was not really true that we hated Jews. It was more a *façon de parler*. Hatred, too, is a direct human relationship. If there had been a real hatred for the Jews, it would have been just as much as loving them. No, Jews were simply people of another star—the star of David and Zion. It might be a shining star, but for us, unfortunately, it shone under the horizon. Therefore, falling in love with a Jewish girl could not be considered a pardonable perversion, like, for instance, that of a sodomite. It was *the* incomprehensible, a sudden gap in one's mind, worse than treason and breach of troth. I had good reason to be ashamed.

I would soon have some more, and better, reasons. Thanks to a few lessons from a skating teacher at the Wiener Eislaufverein, my circles and loops had very much improved. I was even capable of doing a few jumps. Home again in the Bukovina, I performed them in my corner of the skating rink. This aroused the curiosity of a group of sturdy youngsters—Jews, of course—who had formed a sort of wild hockey team. One day I found myself encircled by them. I felt a trifle uncomfortable, for they were tough and I did not know what they wanted. So I pretended not to notice their nearness and continued to perform a tidy eight with a Dutch jump at the conclusion of each circle. This went on for a while, till finally the biggest of them said, 'Not bad, what you're doing. How about playing on our team?'

'No, thank you very much,' I said.

'Why not? Because we're Jews?'

I did not answer and they came nearer.

'Well, what are you?' another of them asked. 'A Rumanian? A Pole?'

'Neither the one nor the other.'

'Well, then, what? A German?'

'No,' I said. I felt an Austrian; that is: I was no German.

'But you speak German. So what the hell are you? A Jew, maybe?'

Why I did not answer I did not know at that moment. It was not cowardice, for it was obvious they meant me no harm. I did not like them very much; they were not my kind, and they were Jews. But I did not dislike them, either, and that made it worse. They had asked me to join their team, and here I stood and lacked the courage to say simply, 'I would have liked to play with you, but I can't, because you are Jews and I am not, and I don't need to say any more. However, I thank you for having asked me.' I did not fear hurting their feelings. What I feared was that open words of that kind could have meant the direct contact of which I was afraid. A direct human relationship could have resulted—esteem or hatred, either one, would have meant the same. I didn't answer.

'Well, speak, baby,' one of them said and came so near that our noses nearly touched. 'Are you a Jew or aren't you?'

I still kept silent, and finally the first one said, 'Oh, leave him alone. He's only a stuck-up pissing *goy*.' He threw the puck into the field, and they leapt after it, he with them, and there I stood alone again in my corner, with my beautifully tidy eights, and the huge shawl around my neck.

I believe that must have happened in the winter of 1927. I was thirteen or fourteen years old. In order to have the vagaries of my adolescence corrected, my benevolent and crazy parents, after a slight effort to have me tamed by a couple of relatives, put me in a Styrian boarding school renowned for its severe methods of education. To it I owe—along with the ever since vainly fought habit of smoking cigarettes and a profound knowledge of the pornographic folklore of the German and English languages—the insight that all public education's task is to vulgarize the genius of young people in such a way that only natures of extraordinarily strong neurotic tendencies are enabled to escape banality. The holidays I spent, usually, in the Bukovina, grateful for the utter loneliness that received me there, luckily freed for a few short summer weeks from the company of school-mates in whose minds and muscles manhood fermented and from teachers deformed by their profession into baroque monstrosities. I passed my time hunting with my father in the Carpathian forests and walking the streets of Czernowitz and Sadagura, just watching and listening to what was going on. I don't know how I ever managed to pass my final examinations, for my mid-year reports were catastrophic. My father, when he got the good news, sent me a cable with the single word *'Ahi!'*—an exclamation of Bukovinan Jews expressing unusual astonishment at the unexpected. Later, he explained that, in point of fact, the exclamation was a survival from the days of chivalry. Yiddish, he said, was mainly Middle High German, with Hebrew and Polish elements. For example, take the Yiddish expression *'nebbish'*, which was nothing but the 'squire' (*neb-ich*: 'near I') who runs with the knight, carrying his shield. *'Ahi!'* was what the knights shouted when, at a tournament, they put their lances under their armpits and ran against one another.

This explanation was given to me not without a trace of embarrassment, for it was rather uncomfortable to think that the language of our models for a noble attitude of life should be faithfully preserved only by the Jews. Therefore my father did not fail to add that a certain decline of forms, as well as of habits and even of costumes, of the upper classes to the lower ones is the rule. The caftan of the rabbis, for instance, and their fur-lined caps and boots were actually the costume of Polish noblemen in medieval times, and a Jewish wedding preserved many a custom that originated in the court ceremonies of the dukes of Burgundy. It is about the only cultural-historical lesson put into my mind between my fourteenth and my seventeenth year that remains there today.

The diploma of a *Gymnasium* is a poor substitute for the rites of initiation with which primitive societies make a young male understand that he has become a man; yet in my youth nobody hesitated to take it as such. When I went back to Vienna, in order to follow in the footsteps of my late grandpapa and study architecture, I was merely a boy of seventeen, but I enjoyed all the liberties of a grown man, with none of the responsibilities. I could go to bed when and with whom I pleased, drink liquor to my heart's content and the revolt of my intestines, and spend my money and time as economically or wastefully as I felt like. My parents were not rich; my father's passion for hunting was expensive and soon devoured what the war had left of a former certain opulence. Yet, in the Bukovina, my monthly allowance would have sufficed to keep a Jewish family of seven from urgent need. Anyhow, I was not forced to begin my studies under the mental pressure of lack of time. But all this did not alter my solitude, which by now had become not only a habit but a deliberate, proud attitude. I did not have a single friend, and I did not long for one. With girls I was extremely clumsy and shy. Besides, my mother, fearing that I would abuse my new status and fall into debauchery, had arranged that I again live with my grandmother. Though my mother knew very well that the old lady was too much of a recluse to keep an eye on a young man, she counted on my aunts, whose theosophical preoccupations and love for dogs were evidence of a high morality that would perhaps keep me from immediately getting lost in a swamp of vices.

It was at this time I learned that we had done Mr Malik an injustice by calling him a Jew. On the contrary, he was a man of high moral standards. A very important free and yet not reborn soul who had followed his invitation and slipped into the emptied vessel of the body of his sister, Miss Weingruber, a highly gifted medium, revealed to the esoteric community that great things were in preparation. The universe was a big system of perpetual perfection. Everything in it had but the sole wish to dematerialize more and more and finally become pure spirit and unite with God. *Materia* was the contrary of God.

My aunts were full of joy and expectation telling me about all this. By the good behaviour of those who lived for the spirit, they said, our world had slowly potentialized and dematerialized and was now on the verge of potentializing into a nearly butterfly-like world. For there were very high-class souls—people like Buddha, Plato, and Jesus Christ—who deliberately took on the burden of *materia* in order to teach the others what was good or evil. Each of them was announced by some soul of a high category materialized for this very purpose. And as Jesus Christ had been announced by John the Baptist, Mr Malik had come to announce the arrival of another dematerializer. His name was Adolf Hitler, and one could already see what enthusiasm he had created in Germany by spiritualizing the Germans and cleansing Germany of the low, materialistic Jews. Mr Malik was no Jew, in spite of the fact that he had changed his name (as had Mr Hitler, whose real name was Schicklgruber—and he certainly was no Jew, either); he had done this for a different reason, for Malik was the name given to him in the outer world

—the name of his spirit. The name given to his material burden, which he had voluntarily undertaken to carry, was Weingruber. He and his sister were actually one high-category soul divided in two and inhabiting two bodies.

The potentialization of the world could already be felt in my grandmother's home by the fact that it, too, had to a certain extent been cleansed of Jews. No longer were the séances of the esoteric community accompanied by the chamber-music of the Raubitscheks, for on the same day both Professor Raubitschek and his wife died of Spanish flu—a typical Jewish extravagance, as my grandmother said, because there was no epidemic, as in 1918, when many people died of it; therefore there was no cause to do it out of season, so to speak. Anyhow, they both died and left their daughter alone, and—alas!—what had been gained by their disappearance was largely spoiled by the scandalous behaviour of Minka Raubitschek. Not only did she have an official lover, whose roadster often stood parked in front of the house all night, but other gentlemen were seen going into the Raubitschek apartment and coming out the morning after. Instead of chamber-music on Wednesday evenings, one could hear the noises of carousing nearly every night.

I rather liked Minka. She was friendly when we met on the staircase. Her voice was full and warm, and her smile beautiful. She looked Spanish, with her shining black hair and large black eyes. Her skin was lovely, and she used a lipstick of a most provokingly vivid red. She dressed well, and even her slight limping had a certain charm; she did not try to hide it but limped ahead courageously and decidedly. On Sunday mornings, I was invited by my grandmother to breakfast in her room. From the window I could follow the spectacle of Minka's being called for by her official lover, a tall, fair, athletic chap, for their weekend outing. He was obviously an ice-hockey player. Sometimes he got into his roadster wearing his hockey uniform, vividly striped in red and white and yellow. Minka carried his sticks, knee pads, and shoulder pads. It all looked very smart and gay, and made me feel my isolation.

The courses in architecture at the Technische Hochschule bored me to tears. Instead of giving me a taste for harmony, the instructors tortured me with the theory of statics of rigid bodies, equations, the use of vectors, and so on, and I have always been a hopeless mathematician. Very soon I began to cut classes, and finally I did not go there for months at a time. I was too ignorant to enjoy either a concert or the theatre. With the exception, perhaps, of a few operettas starring Fritzi Massary, I saw nothing of the good theatre in Vienna of that time. My grandmother still kept a seat at the opera and never went there herself, so I drowsed through *Rheingold* and *La Traviata*, wondering why people sometimes sighed with delight and sometimes expressed their disapproval. But I walked a lot. I crisscrossed Vienna from one end to the other, sometimes walking as far as from Döbling to Hietzing, and then taking the tramway back. I walked, preferably at night, through the inner city, watching the swarms of whores on the Kärntnerstrasse. During the day, it was the most elegant of all Viennese streets, and at night it turned into something like the Canebière in Marseilles. Or I would stand and marvel at the beauty of the empty Josefsplatz and Fischer von Erlach's National-Bibliothek, wondering why my grandfather had never achieved this perfection. Nobody cared that I came home at four o'clock in the morning, and old Marie had long since given up trying to wake me, knowing that I usually slept till noon.

But of course I was too proud to admit my solitude to anybody. I spent most of my money on clothes, and when I set out for a stroll in the afternoon I would be most elegantly dressed, like some young dandy who is just about to get into his car and drive out to the golf course at Lainz or to the five-o'clock tea dance at Hübner's Park Hotel in Hietzing. In the evening, I never left the house except in a very smart dinner jacket or sometimes, when I felt like it, even in tails, with a silk hat on my well-brushed head. After a couple of hours of lonesome walking through empty streets and sombre parks, along the tracks of railways or the banks of the Danube Canal, I would sit down for a coffee and a brandy in the lounge of the Hotel Imperial, slipping off my patent-leather pumps under the table to ease my sore feet. One would have thought I was a young man with an exquisite social life.

Once, well after midnight, I came home to my grandmother's house in tails and silk hat and found Minka at the door, fumbling in her handbag for the key she had either forgotten or lost. She was amused at the misfortune of having no key, and at my arriving just in time to open the door. She was a little drunk. Her eyes sparkled, and her teeth shone moist between those provoking red lips. But, of course, I behaved like a well-bred young man. I unlocked the door and held it open for her with the particular politeness of a certain reserve, and she smiled at me and said I looked splendid. Where had I been, so elegantly clad? At a dance, I said. Where and with whom? With people she would certainly not know. What was their name? she asked. Oh, Rumanians, I said stiffly. It was typically Jewish, I thought, to be so insistent and to ask such personal questions, and I did not like it. The Rumanians were passing through Vienna, I said, on their way to Paris.

She knew frightfully amusing Rumanians in Paris, she said. Had I been there lately? Not lately, I said, following her up the stairs. The steps were flat and easy to mount, but she had a little difficulty with her lame hip and the one drink too many she might have had, so I offered her my arm, and she leaned against it freely. My elbow registered that she was not so bony as the fashion of the early 1930s demanded. It was delightful, and a little embarrassing, so when we reached my grandmother's floor, I stood still, and she let go of my arm and smiled again. 'Thank you,' she said. 'You are charming.'

'Would you like me to accompany you to your floor?' I asked, and then bit my lip at my own clumsiness.

She laughed. 'Does it show that I'm drunk? I never realize it myself unless I have to get up these stairs on all fours. Come on, then, my young dandy, give me your arm again. . . . I once broke that silly left hip of mine,' she said, leaning trustfully against the length of my body. 'Because I was in love—imagine! If I had gone on that way, I wouldn't have a sound bone in my body. How are you making out with the girls?'

'Well . . . ,' I said, and smiled shyly, as if I were too modest to tell her the full truth.

She laughed. I said nothing more. I wasn't quite sure she hadn't seen through me and just been teasing me. 'Would you like to come inside for a nightcap?' she asked when we arrived at her door.

'Thank you very much.'

'Thank you, yes, or thank you, no?' She looked straight into my eyes.

'Yes.' I said, and felt that I was blushing.

She handed me a key and said, 'Fortunately, I haven't lost this one.'

Again I unlocked the door and held it open, and she went in, dropping her fur coat on the floor. I picked it up and put it on a chair. 'What nice manners you have,' she said. 'It must be lovely to have you around. How old are you?'

It seemed too silly to say 'I'm going to be eighteen next May,' so I lied. 'Twenty-three.'

'Just my cup of tea. There is a phonograph in the corner. Put on a record if you want some music. What will you drink? Whiskey, or a brandy?'

'A whiskey with soda, please.' The flat did not look at all as I had imagined it would. She must have redecorated it since the death of the old Raubitscheks. With the exception of a huge library with black carved-wood bookcases that could have belonged to the chamber-music-loving Professor Raubitschek, there was no trace of the particular Jewish-middle-class stuffiness I had had glimpses of through open windows at home in the Bukovina. There were flowers all over the place—her lovers seemed to be quite generous, I thought. Through an open door I could see into her bed-room, gay and feminine, the huge bed covered with a soft, flowery comforter. While she fixed the drinks, I had a look at the records. There were masses of them, piled up carelessly around the phonograph. I put one on with the label 'Star Dust', hoping it was Mozart and not as violent as Beethoven's 'Allergique'. With the first sweet sounds, she came towards me with the drinks. 'Here's yours,' she said, putting a glass in my hand. 'Let's see how you dance.' I did not know what to do with my glass, but finally took it in my left hand and put my other arm around her, and we danced a few steps. I could not feel that she limped. 'All right,' she said, and moved away from me. 'A little stiff, but there is hope. I can't dance long, because of my hip, but I love it.'

I took a gulp of my whiskey. She dropped down on the couch, leaned back, and shut her eyes. Suddenly she yawned, her beautiful mouth wide open. She yawned with a melodious cry that sounded like a happy weeping and that faded away in a sigh of utter relaxation, at the end of which she opened her eyes and said, 'You are sweet. Now go downstairs to your grandma and sleep well.' She got up with an unexpected swiftness and went to her bedroom, already unbuttoning her dress at the back.

I stood still in bewilderment, not knowing what to think of all this, not even knowing whether I had imagined something else would happen or what—just simply not knowing how to put my glass down and say 'Good night' and 'See you soon'. She turned and looked at me, still fumbling with buttons at her back. 'If you don't want to go,' she said, 'you can listen to a few more records, if you like. But don't mind if I fall asleep, I'm dog-tired.'

I felt humiliated to the core. The situation was totally out of my control, and I wished I'd never accepted her invitation to come in for a nightcap. But, on the other hand, she was so kind, and sweet, and pretty. Her mouth had excited me.

She had turned round fully and stood watching me. Then she came towards me, smiling, and before I could say anything she took my head in both hands and kissed me softly and affectionately. Then she smiled again, close to me, under my eyes, and said, 'What's all this? Do you want to stay with me?' I didn't answer. Still looking into my face, she said softly. 'Then come!'

She very soon found out the full truth about my worldliness, and it seemed to touch her. She was all sweet understanding, treating me with a tenderness and intimacy I had never known before or even been able to imagine. If it had been possible for me to think such a monstrous thought, I should have called it gay and tender love-making with a sister.

I put 'Star Dust' on the phonograph again, and we lay in the dark and listened till it came to an end. She laughed and said, 'Won't your grandma be upset when she finds out that you've been with me in the middle of the night?'

'She doesn't necessarily need to know.'

'Well, certainly not. But she will find out sooner or later. I want to have you around, you are so cosy.'

I said, 'May I put on that record once more?'

'You do like it, don't you? Well, it's yours. You can take it with you and play it till you can't stand it anymore.'

'Thank you.'

'I wish I had a little more money, so I could buy you things you ·

like. I have always longed for a little brother to spoil. What is your name?'

'Arnulf.'

'What?' she cried, with an outburst of her delightful laughter. 'It can't be true. Arnulf? Who ever thought of such a dreadful name?'

'My father,' I said, smiling against my will. 'It comes from his mother's family; they're Bavarians. I think he thought it would oblige me to behave like a good knight.' I sighed. Yet I was very much amused myself.

'But you can't possibly expect me to call you Arnulf,' she said.

'Well, I have a few more Christian names. I have about half a dozen. Other people I know have up to fifteen.'

'Don't tell me. I expect your other names are even worse. No, I shall call you Brommy—that fits you very well.'

'Why, and how?'

'Oh, I don't know. It simply fits you.'

'Did you have a pet dog with that name?'

'No. I don't know where I got it from—there was an admiral, I think.'

'What have I to do with an admiral?'

'Lots. You are very much like a young cadet who will become an admiral someday. And you don't want me to call you Wilhelm von Tegetthoff.'

I laughed. The totally illogical jump was typically Jewish. It sounded like one of the surrealistic jokes that were told in the Bukovina about the merry rabbis of the Hasidim and their shrewdly twisted logic. I could not help feeling very much at home with Minka.

'Now, come,' she said. 'Be a good boy and let's get some sleep.'

She did not send me away. She simply put her arms around me and curled close to me, and instantly fell into a deep and innocent sleep, smelling of well-groomed feminine hair and skin, good perfume, and a little whiskey. I lay for a while with open eyes, listening to the fading sounds of 'Star Dust' which was now mine, and thinking how funny it was that at the very moment you got mixed up with Jews you changed your name. Soon I, too, fell asleep, my arms around her.

I have often wondered since whether I had an affair with Minka. Whatever it was, it did not interfere in the slightest with her amorous life, and though it altered my life completely, there seemed not the faintest tie that would have given me the impression that I couldn't do whatever I pleased. From that first morning —when I woke in her arms and watched her face, so fresh and well rested, and she opened her dark eyes and, with joyful laughter, said, 'Now, who are *you*? Surely not the boy from downstairs?'—we were together day and night. 'I am getting so accustomed to having him in my bed,' she would explain to her friends—among whom some were even a little more than friends. 'Like a child with its teddy bear. He doesn't kick or snore. He's just sweet and appetizing.' And, turning to the nearest female in the circle, 'If you really want a good night's sleep, I'll lend him to you.'

Of course, there were also moments when she said to me, 'Listen, my dear Brommy, there is a certain gentleman who is arriving from Paris, so would you do me a great favour and go skiing with Bobby? He's treating, so you needn't spend your pocket money on that. And please don't show up around here before next Friday.'

Bobby was her official lover—the fair, athletic chap who skied and played ice hockey and swam and rode horseback. We had become great friends. 'You know, my boy,' he would explain to me, 'if it were any other girl, you'd become jealous. But not with Minka. First, it would be pointless. Second, she wouldn't let you. She makes it quite clear to you that it's not you who possess her, it's she who possesses you. Now, since she is not jealous of you, what right have you to be jealous of her? It's as simple as that.'

There was no use trying to explain to him, or anybody else, that our relationship was, in fact, relatively—and even in great proportion—innocent. When Minka and I went to bed together, it was mainly to curl up in one another's arms and fall asleep. It gave her comfort to have someone near. I have sometimes thought that it may have been an atavism or, let us say, a tradition that she had inherited, like the passion for hunting and shooting among our kind. After all, many of her ancestors must have slept six in one bed, like most of the poor Jews in Galicia and in the Bukovina. But certainly such an explanation would not have helped my grandmother or aunts to understand my affection for Minka; in their eyes it would have made things even worse. In fact, it was all rather scandalous, and I was afraid my father would hear about it—particularly as neither my grandmother nor my aunts gave the slightest sign of knowing what was going on. That they knew perfectly well I could detect from old Marie's trembling resentment whenever I went up to Minka's flat or came down from it, and the resentment increased when the hours I spent downstairs in my room became short intervals between the sojourns upstairs at Minka's. I could only pray to God that the hatred of my mother's relatives for my father would not allow them to give him the satisfaction of saying that it was not surprising I got involved with Jews while staying in their house. He had always warned my mother against her own family, and he would no doubt say that it was her fault for letting me go to Vienna, instead of—as he had wished—sending me to Graz, the capital of Styria, where there were fewer Jews.

There is an old saying that when you change your life you also change your ideas. This is not necessarily so. You can very well change your life and in the meantime send your ideas, so to speak, on a holiday. My life had changed entirely, and though I kept right on disliking Jews, I lived among them—for most of Minka's friends were Jews—from then on. One of them, a monstrously fat and ugly yet highly amusing journalist from Prague, who regularly came to Vienna as a theatre critic, gave me the password. Once, after a brief encounter with a well-known actor who was not a Jew and who had treated him with special friendliness, he turned towards me and said, 'My mother used to say, "More than of an anti-Semite, my boy, beware of people who just love Jews".' Right she was, I thought, laughing heartily. For disliking Jews was not something you could change. It was an inborn reaction that did not hinder you from even liking them in a certain way. I liked Minka tremendously, and if she hadn't been a Jewess, I would have fallen madly in love with her and, in spite of my eighteen years (and to her utter amusement, I presume), probably have asked her to marry me. But even when she woke up in my arms and I in hers, after an innocent night's sleep, there was a taboo that controlled my feelings and made everything even more delightful. I felt so free and unburdened with her. As she said, she liked having me around. She could not take me seriously as a lover. I was her toy, and everything was light and nice and uncomplicated. She could summon me and send me away whenever she wanted. I asked no questions, and she could tell me everything. We would both laugh at our particular adventures and misfortunes, share our joys, our money, our problems. Her girlfriends were sweet and of a charming libertinage. I can't remember a time in my life since when I have had such pleasures. She took me to museums, to concerts, to the theatre, to dinner parties, and to the *Heurigen*—the tasting of the new wine in the vineyards of the nearby village of Grinzing. That little kingdom of hers, which became my universe, was composed of all that was best in Vienna in the early 1930s, the most intellectual and most amusing. Her friends came to her home as birds fly in and out of the foliage of a tree. Among them was Karl Kraus, who at that time was considered merely a satirist but whose life stands as an example of moral uprightness and courage which should be put before anyone who writes, in no matter what language. Thanks to Minka, I had, at the age of eighteen, the privilege of listening to his conversation and watching his face, lit up by the pale fire of his fanatic love for the miracle of the German language and by his holy hatred for those who used it badly. There was also a young man, not a Jew, who was a gifted musician. 'Come on, Herbert,' Minka would say, 'play something on the piano.' Many years later, I remembered that his name was von Karajan.

What gave me the right to stand my ground among those people was a rather strange talent Minka had discovered in me. Not for nothing had I passed a great part of my childhood and adolescence among Polish Jews. While walking through the streets of Czernowitz and Sadagura and Lvov, I had kept my ears open, and I spoke better Yiddish and knew more of the customs and behaviour of the so-called Polish Jews than most of the refined Jews of Vienna or even Prague. I was an expert in all shades of Jewish slang and the way Jews spoke when they wanted to speak select German. And when somebody told a Jewish story, which at that time, and especially among Jewish intellectuals, was cultivated as an art, and told it badly, Minka would impatiently interrupt him, saying, 'Come on, don't bore us. Tell your story in a low voice to

Brommy, and he'll tell it to us much better than you do.' If for some reason she chose not to interrupt the imperfect story-teller, she and I would exchange a short, vague, yet significant look, very much in the way that my eyes would meet those of my mother or father, my grandmother or my aunts, when somebody who was not of our kind committed some lapse of manners or language. If, on the other hand, some master told a Jewish story to perfection, then Minka would pull my sleeve and say, 'Pay attention, Brommy!'

Brommy . . . . It was a name of quite another form of existence, which ran parallel to my existence as son, grandson, and nephew — very much as Guru Malik within the esoteric community of my aunts led a life parallel to that of brave engineer Weingruber, who lived his petit bourgeois life as an employee of the Styria Motor Company. Once, when someone called me on the telephone, one of my aunts answered, and afterwards she asked me with an expression of amazement, 'What do your . . . friends call you? "Brommy"? But you have such nice other Christian names. What a regrettable lack of taste.'

Furious, without knowing why, I said, 'You mind your own business!'

'Now, really!' she exclaimed. 'Have we come to the point where boys of your age speak to adults in such a way? Don't forget, you're only eighteen, after all.'

I certainly did not forget it. It weighed on me that I had lied to Minka about my age. One day I could bear it no longer. We had been talking about some of her troubles, and she said, 'It's astonishing how understanding you are for your age, my boy.'

'Minka,' I said, 'there's something I have to confess. I lied to you.'

'What about?' she said and smiled. 'Oh, I see. You want to tell me that in fact there *is* a drop of Jewish blood in you.'

'No,' I said. 'I am sorry there isn't. But I'm not twenty-three. I am only eighteen.'

'What? But you're not serious?'

From then on, she treated me as a sort of wonder child. 'Would you believe it? He's only eighteen!' They probably all thought I was Jewish, and were proud of my precocity.

Well, it did not go on forever, alas. Very soon I was nineteen, and at twenty I had to do my military service in Rumania, and my gay time in Vienna was over. But it was soon replaced by another fascinating experience. I now became aware that I knew almost nothing about the country I belonged to, the Rumanian people, or their language. In order to fill that gap, a young Rumanian student was hired to teach me Rumanian and something of Rumanian literature and history, and I not only formed friendships with my tutor and some other young Rumanians which have lasted till today but also learned the historical past of the three Rumanian principalities—Moldova (to which the Bukovina had once belonged), Muntenia, and Oltenia—and their struggle to unite against their Turkish oppressors and Phanariot rulers and become a nation and the kingdom of Rumania. By tracing some rather remote lineage of my pedigree until it found root in Rumania, I was able to justify my newly discovered love for that country and my claim to belong there not merely as part of a former Austrian minority but by inheritance. Then I exchanged my first name, Arnulf, for the third of my Christian names, Gregor, which also happened to be the Christian name of some half-Greek, half-Russian ancestor originating in Bessarabia and beautifully outfitted with a Turkish wife. My father watched with intense disapproval my Rumanian friendships and my attempts to tie myself genealogically to Rumania, but by that time I had—thanks to Minka Raubitschek—acquired a certain independence of mind, and when my father said that he loathed the Bukovina and if it hadn't been for the Carpathians would long since have left it, I said boldly that, according to my taste, it was better to have a free outlook over a lovely rolling country with a vast horizon than to be always running your nose against some stone wall, as in Styria. Whereupon my father turned his back, and did not speak to me for a couple of weeks.

I came back to Vienna in the summer of 1937 as Gregor, sporting an enormous Phanariot moustache. I hurried upstairs to embrace Minka and break the news that I was in love. It was not a very happy love story, though, for the lady in question was married, and, to make matters worse, I liked her husband very much. Minka, as usual, was full of understanding, comfort, and good advice. We passed a few gay days together, but no night. I had outgrown my teddy-bear stage and, besides, would have considered it treason to my love to sleep soundly in another woman's bed instead of lying alone, sighing for her. I was going to meet her shortly in Salzburg, where she wanted to attend the festival. Minka took me to the station. Looking up at me while I looked down at her from the open window of my compartment in the train, she saw my excited happiness. Her eyes shone tenderly, with a strange, more profound tenderness than ever. 'If you were wise,' she said, 'you would now get off this train and never see that girl again.'

'What do you mean?'

'Everything you have had with her so far is beautiful—all promise and expectation. Now come the troubles.'

'Oh, don't talk rot. We are going to be very happy.'

'I do hope so,' she said. 'I am very, very fond of you, you know.'

The train started up, and I sat back in my seat in a state of bewilderment. It could not be that Minka was in love with me, could it? No, that was impossible. Yet the thought flattered my vanity, and, rather the prouder for it, I looked forward to meeting my adored one.

Minka was right. Things became frightfully complicated, and Salzburg in the summer of 1937 was just awful. It was overrun with Jews. The worst of them had come from Germany as refugees and, in spite of their luggage-laden Mercedes cars, behaved as if they were the victims of a cruel persecution and therefore had the right to hang around in hundreds at the Café Mozart, criticize everything, and get whatever they wanted faster and cheaper—if not for nothing—than anybody else. They spoke with that particular Berlin snottiness that so got on the nerves of anyone brought up in Austria, and my sharp ears could all too easily detect the background of Jewish slang. My Turkish blood revolted. I could have slaughtered them all. I fled to Styria, for a visit to my old boarding school, and then followed my ladylove back to Rumania.

When I came back to Vienna again, it was February 1938, and what I found was chaos. Minka had come to fetch me at the station. She merely said, 'Poor boy, I am afraid that your aunts' guru is right and the Weingrubers and Schicklgrubers and Schweingrubers will soon potentialize the world.' Most of her friends—Bobby among them—had already gone to Switzerland, she said, or England or France, or were preparing to leave Austria even at the price of their material existence.

'Oh, don't exaggerate,' I said. 'You Jews are always making a fuss about something. What in the world is going on, anyway?'

'Poldi will explain it to you. We're having dinner with him. You just listen to what he has to say.'

Poldi was the fat journalist from Prague, who, as a theatre critic, went regularly not only to Vienna but also to Berlin. He had lost a lot of weight and was not half so amusing as he used to be. What irritated me most of all was the self-complacent way he treated me—and I could not rise to the occasion, because he resolutely kept aiming at my cultural gaps. 'I understand that we have sworn off allegiance to the ancestor of the Carolingians,' he greeted me, 'even though the moustache is downright Merovingian.' And when I shook my head uncomprehendingly, he went on, 'I mean, we are no longer calling ourselves Arnulf, now, but Gregor. Good, very good. Gregory the Great, as we all know, was a protector of the Jews.'

I dryly answered that this was certainly not the reason I had been given this name, and he threw in, 'Very well, let's stay with the Carolingians. We are then not far from Bishop Agobard, and we can look forward to a new *De insolentia Judaeorum* or, even worse, a new *De Judaicis superstitionibus* with a few blood libels. Today, you see, there are two schools of thought—two camps, I must involuntarily say: one outside and one inside the concentration camps. And uncomfortable as the latter may be, it is, still and all, the only one for decent people.'

'And I would rather end up there myself than let Brommy get in,' said Minka. 'But just tell him seriously how things look politically. He's straight out of the Middle Ages, you know. That's where his father lives, in the Carpathians.'

Now I realized that Poldi's irony was put on in order to conceal an enormous fear. Most of the things he told us, in a whisper, looking around to make sure he wasn't overheard, did not make much sense to me. In the landscape of my mind, politics had not figured prominently. As a subject of Rumania—that is, of His

Majesty King Carol II—I knew, and was expected to know, that he was the sovereign of a constitutional monarchy, and that in Bucharest there was a parliament where deputies represented the party of the peasants and the party of the liberals and whatnot, and that they were a bunch of crooks who did nothing but steal the money of the state. There were also some Jews, who were Communists, and therefore, rightly, were treated as such—that is, as Russian spies and *agents provocateurs*. But fortunately there were also some young Rumanians who, under their leader, a certain Mr Cuza—which was a good and noble name, though only adopted by that gentleman—beat up those Jews from time to time, thus keeping them in a hell of a fright, and preventing them from spreading more Communist propaganda and provocation. I knew, too, that in Austria there were many socialists, called Reds, who were beaten up by or beat up the Heimwehr, which was a national guard defending the ethical values—such as the cleanliness of mind guaranteed by the fresh mountain air, and the love for shooting goats and plucking edelweiss—of Styria, Tirol, Carinthia, and other of the old Austrian lands. With the help of the Heimwehr, Chancellor Dollfuss had cannonaded the Reds, only to be shot down later by a Nazi. Nazis, in Austria, were rowdies who dynamited telephone booths, but that was not necessarily true of German Nazis, who, after all, had done very well. They had built up a state of order and justice and genuine social welfare, in spite of the fact that Adolf Hitler was a frightful proletarian, as my father said, and looked exactly like a Bohemian footman my grandmother had once employed, against his advice. The footman turned out to be a thief and stole my father's cuff-links and some other items, including a very nice hunting knife. Only people like my mother's family could be wrong about somebody with such a face, my father said.

The Reds were bad because they were proletarians and wanted to do away with people of our kind, as had happened in Russia. Jews had a fatal inclination for Reds; therefore they ought to be kept in a hell of a fright, so they would keep quiet. Nazis were also proletarians, but they had some very sound ideas, like the theory of breeding and some exemplary laws about hunting only in season, which gave the game the chance to regenerate and even improve in number as well as in size. And on the whole they were against Jews

137

and Reds, so it was quite obvious that we had to stick with them. I really did not think there was much more to the subject, and I got rather bored with Poldi's Cassandra-like whispering, so I proposed that we go to the Kärntnerbar for a whiskey. If, as Poldi said, the Germans wanted to conquer Austria, so much the better. The German-speaking peoples would be united again, as they had been in the Holy Roman Empire of Charlemagne. And if the Jews were frightened, it served them right. It would keep them from becoming Russian spies and propagandists of Communism and also make them behave a little more decently at the Salzburg Festival. As for the reaction of the English and French and so on, they should mind their own business. I did not see any reason to start a war just because the German-speaking peoples did what the Czechs and Poles and Rumanians had been encouraged to do by the very same French and English. Of course, I did not say any of this to Poldi and Minka, because they were friends and it would have hurt their feelings. So we went to the Kärntnerbar.

When Minka went to the Kärntnerbar, it was the crest of the wave. We let her down to the ladies' room by a rope and pulled her up again, and Poldi became his old self and was highly amusing. At three o'clock in the morning, we found ourselves in the beer cellar of the Paulanerbräu, sitting between a stone-drunk chap—who shouted in a loud voice that he was a former cavalry officer with a golden decoration for bravery and the official title of the Hero of Zaleszczyki—and a shy little tart I knew fairly well from midnight strolls on the Kärntnerstrasse. We had hardly had a spoonful of our goulash soup and a sip of beer when a huge, rather shabby-looking young man roared in our faces, *'Juden raus!'* 'Jews out!'

The former cavalry officer got up in stiff dignity and said that he felt offended by having been called a Jew, and would the gentleman instantly follow him to the men's room in the basement in order to fix the place and conditions of the duel. Poldi pushed him back on his stool. The rowdy then, surprisingly, sat down on the other side of the little tart and stared with a dull expression at the wooden table. Suddenly he lifted his head and looked at me. 'Don't you remember me, you swine?' he roared. 'Arnulf! I'm Oskar. Oskar Koloman.'

I could scarcely believe my eyes. He was one of the boys at the boarding school in Styria, a good deal older than I but in the same class. 'Where the hell have you come from?' I asked.

He rose to his full height and volume. 'You really want to know?' He nearly fell over the table in the attempt to grasp my shoulder. 'Come with me to the men's room in the basement. I'll *tell* you where I've come from.'

'I think you'd better go,' Minka said, in a low voice. 'It'll give Poldi and me a chance to disappear.'

I followed my schoolmate past a row of gentlemen standing against a tarred wall, showing us their backs, till he found a gap where we could stand next to one another. He had that very day been released from Steinhausen, the Austrian concentration camp for Nazis under the regime of Chancellor Schuschnigg. As one of a group of Nazi students, he had blown up a telephone booth in Graz and had been caught doing it. He had spent three years in the camp. 'For a cigarette butt no bigger than this,' he howled into my face, showing as well as he could with his thick fingers how small, 'for such a tiny little butt, they made me clean the latrines for a week!' Then, hammering his fists against the tarred wall. 'They have forsaken us! They have betrayed us—our brethren of the Reich! They left us in the mire while they became great and mighty. Now they will come and take over here, too!' He leaned his forehead against the wall and wept.

So that was Austria. Hadn't my father been right to keep out of it? Again I fled to the clean mountains of Styria to ski for a couple of weeks. I had nothing to do anyway but wait for the lady I still loved. We had made an appointment to meet in Vienna on the eleventh of March. I was there a day earlier, and felt as if I had wandered into a mad-house. A sort of regimented revolution was going on under the watchful eyes of fat Viennese policemen in long bottle-green coats. On one side of the Kärntnerstrasse, people with swastikas in their button-holes promenaded, shouted *'Heil!'* and sneered at the people on the other side. The people on the other side, young workers—many Jews among them—shook their fists at the Nazis and shouted *'Rotfront!'* I could not get hold of Minka, who was helping relatives in Mödling prepare their departure, somebody in the Café Rebhuhn told me. So I went home to my grandmother's flat, where I found that my beloved had already arrived in Vienna and would be waiting for me next evening at ten o'clock in an apartment house on the Opernring. I did not go out all the next day but spent the day in great uneasiness waiting for the telephone to ring. The cable with that precise information could only mean that something had gone wrong. But no call came. When I left the house at a quarter to ten, the streets were strangely dark and empty. I walked the short distance from the Florianigasse to the Rathaus, and through the Rathaus arcade—one of my grandfather's dubious architectural masterpieces. Coming out, I found myself in the middle of an uncanny procession. In blocks that in their disciplined compactness seemed made of cast iron, people marched by thousands, men only, in total silence. The morbid, rhythmic stamping of their feet hung like a gigantic swinging cord in the silence that had fallen on Vienna. This cord seemed to originate somewhere in the outskirts. I could detect it through the length of the Alserstrasse, then winding round towards the Rathaus and leading down the Ringstrasse. Parades of all kinds were not rare in Vienna. They were nearly always led by a detachment of street-car conductors and were in protest against something or other —unemployment, or the rise in the price of milk, or the pollution of the city water, brought in from the clean mountains of Styria by aqueducts. But this was different. It had an uncomfortably decisive character. I tried to break through between the blocks, but I did not succeed. Two or three times I asked a bystander what was going on, and got no answer. Impatient, fearing I would be late for the appointment with my beloved, I squeezed myself into the last row of a marching block and marched with them.

'What the hell are we marching for?' I asked the man beside me.

'*Anschluss,*' he barked.

Well, that literally meant 'connection', and that was exactly what I was looking for. If I could march with them down to the Opernring and get out of the parade there, I'd be in time for my appointment. But they wouldn't let me. I was pushed out. I had come far enough to see the full height of the tower of the Rathaus, towards which the marchers turned their heads, starry-eyed. The tower was surmounted by the statue of a knight in armour, a statue I had loved as a child, so I turned my head, too, and saw a huge flag hanging down from the tower's peak, attached to my knight's armoured feet—a red flag with a white circle, in which there was a black swastika. 'So that's it. It's come, finally,' I said to myself. 'Austria has united with the German Reich.'

It was not unexpected. For weeks people had spoken of little else. Yet how did all these people know that it would happen this very night? And how, for heaven's sake, did they know their place in the serried ranks? They must have been drilled for months—but where? In cellars? Austrian Nazis had been underground up to this moment, an underground everybody knew about and spoke about quite openly and—with the exception of Jews and Reds, of course—with a certain sympathy. And now here it was. The whole male population of Vienna seemed to be marching in that silent parade. I felt a sudden resentment at being left out. After all, I was an Austrian myself; I had been born under the flag of the double-headed eagle as well as they, and though I was a subject of Rumania, it seemed unjust to deny me a place in one of their marching blocks as if I were a Red, or even a Jew. Politically, too, I wasn't much different from them. Anyway, the event in itself was something I welcomed, even if I didn't much care for the *Pieffkes* (as we Austrians called Germans). These people probably didn't care for them either. Oskar Koloman had already expressed his disillusion. In any case, the unity of the Reich was restored. The dream of a century had come true. Such a political reversal would change many things, perhaps even the decision of my beloved to get a divorce from her husband, whom, unfortunately, I liked so much. There was a promise of hope in the atmosphere. In spite of that uncanny silence all over Vienna, something was happening, some-thing important, and not merely a protest against the diminishing size of *Wiener Kipfeln*—the beloved Viennese croissants—and the pollution of the city water. Again and again I inserted myself into the marching blocks, trying to keep step so it wouldn't be too obvious that I did not belong, and was pushed out of the ranks each time. At last, I came to the Opernring and hurried up the staircase of a certain house, and there she was. We both burst into hysterical laughter. 'Can you imagine!' we said. 'What an effort to celebrate our union!'

It wasn't a union, though; it was the opposite. With great emotion, and not without tears, she had to tell me that in spite of all her love for me she couldn't divorce the man whom we both liked so much. She had been married to him for too many years. It was the old story of an engagement more or less arranged by their parents; then, suddenly, she had felt that she could not marry him, and was about to tell him so when he went on a trip, and while she was waiting for him to come back so she could tell him how she really felt, he wrote her such charming, loving letters that—well, she finally married him. And he had been sweet to her and decent, and everything I knew so well, too, and—well, that was that. I had to accept it.

Next morning, we stood at the windows and looked down at the Opernring, now empty, where all the night through there had been ecstasy—a sudden ecstasy that had its source in the silent marching blocks, and that drew people out of their houses and made them run towards the marchers, shouting, roaring, embracing one another, swinging flags with swastikas, throwing their arms to heaven, jumping and dancing in delirium. It was an icy-cold yet gloriously sunny day, quite unusual for the middle of March. It was so cold that you would not allow your dog to stay outdoors for longer than five minutes. There was nobody as far as you could see except two or three of the old hags, wrapped, onionlike, in layers of frocks and coats, who sold flowers in the New Market. They were running across the Ring and throwing their roses and carnations in the air, yelling 'Heil!' What did they have to do with it, anyway? Over the radio we had learned that Austria was about to unite with the German Reich, and the Germans were expected to come here triumphantly, as our brethren, in a huge parade, under a rain of flowers. And that the great unifier and renewer of the German-speaking peoples, Adolf Hitler, was also about to arrive in Austria any moment and would come down the Danube, the old stream of the Nibelungen, to Vienna, the former capital of the Holy Roman Empire.

She stood at one window, I at another. I turned my head towards her and saw her face, pale and suffering. I knew it was not only because we had to part but also for that clear, icy-cold emptiness outside. Out of a sudden intuition, without even thinking about how cruel it was, I said, 'I know how you feel about what happened out there last night.' She swung her head round and looked coldly at me. 'You feel,' I said, 'precisely the way you did on the day of your marriage.' She covered her face with both her hands. 'I can't help feeling the same,' I said. 'We are at a wedding day of sad promise.'

I could have gone back to Rumania or somewhere else. But I felt that, at last, I should do something properly. I had wasted so much time, never finishing—if you could say I had ever seriously begun—my studies. Also, there was promise in the air, even if the appearance in Vienna of the great Führer of the now Greater Germany had turned out to be sort of a flop. His voice blared through the loudspeakers, over the heads of some million ecstatic listeners who were crammed together in a compact mass that covered the Heldenplatz. But the voice was choked by emotion (or by the rhythmic uproar of some million voices' *'Sieg Heil! Sieg Heil! Sieg Heil!'*) and could only stutter, 'I—I—I—I—I am just so happy!' In spite of all that, as I say, there seemed to be born a new reality, clearer, more transparent, more energetic, more dynamic. It felt as if the fresh mountain air of Styria were blowing through Vienna. Then several divisions of the German Army came down the Danube, in marching blocks that were even more solid, more resolute, more dangerous, in their silence and grey metallic hats, than the ones on the night of *Anschluss*. After that, German civilians swarmed in and took everything into their administering hands. They filled that mountain air with their snotty Berlin slang and, to our utmost surprise, cynically mocked the great Führer and the Nazi Party, so that the Austrians had to take over the task of enthusiastic confirmation that everything was wonderful, really great, marvellous—particularly my aunts, who had now interrupted their *Anschluss* with the world beyond and entirely devoted themselves to the Nazi Women's Union. Mr Malik, I learned, not only had become the leader of his department at the Styria Motor Company (which very soon united with a German company and disappeared) but also was a *Sturmbannführer* of the SS—a very mighty position, so I had better make friends with him and stop saying that his real name was Schweingruber. Old Marie, for whose senile eyes the victorious symbol 'SS' read '44', insisted that he would be made a colonel of the 44th Regiment of the Imperial Infantry, which, as a young girl, she had very much admired. My grandmother shut herself in her rooms and received nobody. Coming back from Mass, she had been laughed at and shouted at in the open street, and nearly man-handled, by a handful of young rowdies who were forcing a group of Jews to wash slogans for the Schuschnigg regime off the wall of a house. Among those Jews, my grandmother recognized a physician who had once cured one of my aunts of a painful otitis media, and she interfered, attacking the young rowdies with her umbrella and shouting that this was going too far. Only the interference of Sturmbannführer Guru Malik saved her from serious trouble.

As for Minka, she was in despair. Of course, I had seen her immediately after the first big events. We were together a few days later when *Anschluss* was officially declared, in an impressive ceremony that we followed on the radio. And there was a rather embarrassing moment when, for the first time, we heard the 'Deutschland, Deutschland über Alles' and she burst into tears. 'Listen, old girl,' I said to her, 'it's not all that bad. It's just the first letting out of an old hatred that will soon calm down. Don't be afraid. It appears they really want to build discipline and order.'

She turned to me and shouted, 'Don't you realize, you imbecile, that it's the "Gott Erhalte", our old Imperial Austrian anthem, composed by our Haydn, that they've embezzled for their dirty anthem of Greater Germany? Why, it's a breach of . . . troth!'

Troth. She must have used it quite unconsciously, without a second thought as to the word's immeasurable profundity. This made me rather pensive for a couple of days. She was right: an incredible breach of troth was taking place all around us, but which troth was actually being broken? One already sensed that the faith, the pure enthusiasm with which this transformation had been yearned for and then greeted, was being betrayed. Troth itself was betrayed, I thought. For instance, the troth to the old empire. This Reich had no more to do with my dream of the Holy Roman Empire than with the glorious dream of the Habsburg Dual Monarchy. But I was soon tired of brooding about it. After all, I was a Rumanian, and even if I had been an Austrian, how could I have prevented what all the other Austrians obviously welcomed? I felt frightfully sorry for Minka and all our friends, but it was not my fault that they happened to be Jews, and in the event that they got into serious trouble I could use my connections with the SS to help them out again.

These connections were by no means limited to Sturmbann-führer Malik. I had run into my old schoolmate Oskar Koloman again, and this time he looked prim and tidy, in a splendid black uniform, with the insignia of an even higher rank than that of *Sturmbannführer*. '*Heil*, Arnulf,' he greeted me. 'How is it you're in civilian clothes? Don't you want to join us?'

'I am Rumanian, you know.'

'That means nothing. You were born an Austrian. Sooner or later, all German-speaking people will come home to the Reich. I can easily arrange for you to change your nationality.'

'I'll think it over,' I said. 'Thank you anyhow.'

'You were a fairly good skater, and not bad at horseback riding, as I recall. We need sporting types, you know. We have some excellent horses at the Mounted SS. Come and ride them, if you want. What are you doing otherwise?'

'Well, I'm trying to get on with architecture. But it bores me stiff.'

'You see! Studying bored me, too. That's why I amused myself blowing up a telephone booth. It cost me three years, all right, but look what I've become now. Not bad, hey? You can have the same if you want. But tell me'— he looked at me mistrustfully—'don't you have contact with Jews? I remember that dark girl you were with when we met again for the first time.'

'Oh, she's a Turk,' I said, and laughed.

'A Turk. I understand.' He laughed, too. 'However, a Jewess is no Jew, and a Turkish girl even less. I do understand, you old swine. Now, don't be a fool, and come riding one of these days?'

I did. They had excellent horses. I rode one that had belonged to the Rothschilds, and was very good indeed. The cavalrymen were fantastic yokels. They clicked their heels and threw up their arms and shouted '*Heil Hitler!*' every time they saw me. Sometimes I had the impression they did not take it seriously themselves, because they tried so hard to *do* it seriously. On the whole, they seemed quite harmless, happy with their uniforms and their obsolete importance. Oskar, in order to avoid silly questions about my riding there without being a member of the SS (also, perhaps, in order to give himself an air of clandestine importance), had told them that I was a Rumanian engaged in some special intelligence work, and I did nothing to destroy this legend, so I was treated as if I were the bearer of top secrets that would soon enable Adolf Hitler to unite the Carpathians with the Styrian Alps. I knew I could certainly count on Oskar, because, in a drunken moment, he had confessed to me that his group of Austrian Nazis had been deceived by the men of the Reich. He and his friends had not at all wanted *Anschluss* but a separate Nazi Austria under their own leader, Dr Rintelen. The next day, he came to me and implored me never to mention what he had told me. I grasped his arm and said, 'Well, Oskar, after all, we have always been friends. Let's not fuss about how reliable we are.' He then grasped my arm and said, 'Arnulf, I always knew you were a fine fellow, though you sometimes'— and here he laughed heartily —'have a trifle too much to do with the Turks. However, I would very much like to meet that Turkish girl of yours. She has something that appeals to my particular taste. If you don't mind.'

Of course, Minka knew about all this, and laughed when I told her that she had only to smile at Oskar and he'd immediately make her an honorary Aryan. 'Aryans,' she said. 'I can't stand the sight of them any longer. The sooner I get my affidavit the better. I want to get out of here. It breaks my heart, but I simply have to.' She was waiting for her affidavit for England, as most of our friends were. It was not easy to get an affidavit. The English would take only people who wanted to be employed as servants, so very soon some clever man opened a butlers' school on the Praterstrasse, where Jewish bankers and intellectuals were taught how to wait on the British. I once went there with Minka, and we laughed our heads off. Old stockbrokers were waddling around with aprons about their hips, balancing trays and opening bottles of champagne. My talent for imitating Jews made me invent a sketch in which a Scottish laird, reading in the newspapers about the said destiny of the Viennese Jews, decides to dismiss all his wonderful Highland servants and replace them with Dr Pisko-Bettelheim, Jacques Pallinker, Yehudo Nagoschiner, and such. Minka's house had become a sort of centre for the few Jews left in Vienna and some Aryans unfaithful to their new flag, like myself. My sketch was a great success.

During that summer and autumn of 1938, most of the Jews I knew went away. Some of them were arrested and locked up for a while, and came home with some rather gruesome stories about what was going on in the prisons of the Rossauerlände. Some disappeared, and we did not know whether they had been put in jail or had just fled at the last moment. All this was pretty awful, I had to admit. But one knew, after all, how people were—some being horrid, others really very nice—and those who got arrested were not always entirely innocent. A Jewish lawyer, telling about his cruel treatment at the hands of the SS, said proudly, 'But I was not arrested for just being a Jew, I am a criminal.' However, I was becoming bored with the Nazi attitude of promise, hope, and expectation, as nothing really happened, and the whole thing was nothing but a great mess with some sordid highlights. Vienna had become a dreary place. Even Oskar complained; he didn't enjoy the *Heurigen* anymore, God knows why. Then he said, 'Do you remember our school library? Well, there was a book called *The City Without Jews*. Actually, I never read it. Have you? Anyway, I sometimes have the feeling that Vienna is just that. There's nobody left to hate.'

There was a young boy of great musical talent around Minka in those days—not Herbert von Karajan but a little Jew by the name of Walter, whom I had come to like very much. He was intelligent and funny and extremely well read. Minka protected him, as, in happier times, she had protected me, and he showed me a touching affection and confidence that I could not resist. Since he had relatives in America, he got an affidavit rather quickly, and we decided to give him a farewell party. We chose an out-of-the-way place—a small wine-grower's cottage behind the Kobenzl—with the poetic name, in the Viennese dialect, of Häusl am Roan [Cottage at the Edge of the Vineyard]. We were a party of sixteen, and there were some pretty girls. Someone still had a car, and it took two trips to get us all out there, and we were gay as in the old days. Walter played the nice old Viennese *Heurigenlieder* on the piano. I performed the butler Yehudo Nagoschiner, serving the wine and the fried chicken. Below us, beyond the hills that smelled of mown hay, lay the sparkling lights of Vienna. Suddenly this idyllic happiness was interrupted by a voice that roared, 'I've finally caught you in the very act, you scoundrel!' I felt the marrow of my bones freeze. In the door stood Oskar, with a group of sturdy men in civilian clothes behind him. My poor Jewish friends stood or sat motionless as he came towards me, followed by his silent men. Then he threw his arms up and said, 'But don't let me interrupt your good time. I'm a schoolmate of Arnulf's, and I wanted to show a few friends from the Reich what a true Viennese *Heurigen* looks like.'

It was true. He had not come to arrest me or anything of the kind. When I asked him how he knew where I was, he said with a smile, 'Old boy, there are very few things we don't know.'

'Come on, don't give me that. Who told you, really?'

'Your grandmother.'

'My *grandmother*?'

'Well, that old witch with the trembling voice who answers the telephone at your house.'

Old Marie, then. I was a fool. For months I had told her where I could be reached when I went out, hoping that a call might come through from Bucharest to tell me that things had changed again and that my beloved was getting a divorce. I was more than a fool; I was blind to what was going on around me. I felt this very strongly when Oskar poked his elbow into my side and said, in a loud voice, with a glance towards his companions, 'Now, how about introducing me to your beautiful *Turkish* girl friend?'

'She is my wife,' I said. 'We are celebrating our wedding.'

The Germans were very pleased to hear this, and clicked their heels and congratulated us, shaking our hands so hard they almost pulled our arms out of their sockets. One of them sat down next to Minka in order to tell her about a cousin who lived in Istanbul. Oskar clapped my shoulder and said with a wink, 'Don't look so frightened. Tell that little Jew there at the piano to play some *Heurigenlieder*.'

The Germans soon got very drunk. The one with the cousin in Istanbul flirted with Minka, in competition with Oskar. The others danced with the pretty girls, and finally one of them performed a most courageous jump over a small stone wall in the garden, misjudged the distance to the ground, fell, and broke his leg. The

Germans made a stretcher for him, so they could carry him to the nearest hospital, and then, in a great hurry, they shook our hands, clicked their heels, threw their arms up, shouting *'Heil Hitler!'* and 'Long live Kemal Pasha Atatürk!' and disappeared as spookily as they had come, with Oskar waving and calling good-bye.

'You bastard,' Minka said to me. She went out into the vineyard and sat down on a stone. I followed her.

'I'm sorry, Minka. I know I am a mindless ass.'

'Never mind. After all, it was funny. Did you see darling little Walter playing the piano as if the devils were standing over him?' She laughed her enchanting laugh. 'But still . . . .' She sank back with a deep sigh.

It was dawn. Out of a mist in the valley Vienna rose, the peaks of its towers first, then the Riesenrad, the Ferris wheel, in the Prater, the monuments, the roofs, the streets. I sat beside Minka, looking down at all this. Suddenly I heard a strange sound coming out of Minka's throat, and thought she was going to cry, but she was laughing instead. 'Do you know what happened to Friedel Süssmann?' she asked. 'I told you that in order to get her affidavit she got married at the British Consulate to an English sailor she had never seen before? Well, when she got to England, she was met by some gentlemen in black. They had come to break the news to her that her husband had fallen from the mast and broken his neck. She now has a widow's pension—one pound a month.'

'Listen, Minka,' I said. 'After all, I am a Rumanian. My hands are not tied. I need not tell you what it would mean to my parents, and you know that I love somebody else, but if it would help you—I mean, just in order to get you a passport that would enable you to get out of here, and, of course, with an immediate divorce afterwards—if you want to, we could bloody well go and get married. You won't get a pension, though, if I break my neck.'

She drew herself up slowly till she was looking into my face. Then she took it in both her hands, as she had done when I first came to her flat, and kissed me. 'You know, my darling Brommy,' she said, 'that you are the dearest person on earth to me. I could never have felt closer to a brother, if I'd had one. You are a bastard, it's true, but I am more fond of you than of anybody else. Just kiss me, once—and kiss me tenderly.' Her mouth was as beautiful as

149

ever, and I could even feel more than the tenderness I would have felt for a sister. In that moment, it appeared to me that if she had not been a Jew, I could have loved her even in the same way, or perhaps more than, I loved the one I had lost. Still, I felt a twinge of bad conscience, as if I were being a traitor to my flag.

'All right,' she said. 'That's that. And now don't be afraid that I'll say yes to your kind offer. I couldn't possibly marry you. Apart from the fact that it would hurt your parents and that you love somebody else—we would certainly get an immediate divorce, but that is not the point—I would not want to marry you, if you understand what I mean. Because of certain goyish qualities of your soul. But still, you are the dearest to me. Come, let's see how the party is getting on.'

A few days later, she got her affidavit, and within a fortnight she had sold her things, even Professor Raubitschek's carved-wood bookcases, and gone to London.

There I saw her once more, in the year 1947. God knows how she had found out where I was living—near Hamburg at that time. Anyway, I got a letter from her saying that she was all right, and married to a man—not a Jew, by the way—who had left Austria in 1938 and who was as sweet and decent as could be, a professor of philology and a great admirer of Karl Kraus. They were about to emigrate to America, and she would very much like to see me once more. She enclosed in the letter a ticket to London and all the papers necessary to get me, as a former Rumanian, a visa for Great Britain. I accepted all this more than gratefully. I was as penniless, as starved, as miserable as any displaced person could be in the rubble of Germany in early 1947. As she had known how—and where—to trace me, she must also have known that my father had fired his last shot into his temple when the Russians took the Bukovina in 1940, and that, two years later, my grandmother had died in Vienna. I had not had a chance to build up a life or settle in a place for all those years.

There was only one difficulty: I had no valid passport. But Minka had even thought of that. A friend who was with the British Military Government arranged to get me a travel document. It defined me as an 'individual of doubtful nationality' but brought me to England, all right. Her husband fetched me at Victoria Station, took a closer look at me, and said, 'Let us go to have lunch first. She doesn't know that you are arriving today. I have not told her, in order not to excite her too much.'

'Why?' I asked. 'Is there anything wrong with her?'

'That trouble with her hip seems to have affected her spine. She is in great pain, and you will have to be very patient with her.'

They lived in a nice house in Cadogan Square. Minka's husband showed me in, fixed me a drink, and then called up the stairwell, 'Oh, Minka, would you mind coming down? There is a friend of yours.' She came down the stairs, a middle-aged woman with grey hair, bent and torn by the atrocious pains of cancer of the bone. 'Who is it?' she asked sharply. Then she saw me. 'Brommy!' she said, and covered her face with her hands, her poor, tortured body shaken by her sobbing.

On the evening before their departure for America, all of our old friends who had managed to emigrate to Britain came to their house to bid them good-bye. Even though they had been told I would be there, they marvelled at seeing me, as if I were a creature from another star. They could not stop asking about Vienna during the war, and how it had looked when I last saw it. They remembered things I had long since forgotten. Had Oskar survived? Oh, he had been hanged in Poland? Poor chap. And Guru Malik, the spiritualist I had told so many funny stories about? No! Had he really been dematerialized by a bomb? Great success, that one. Every one of the guests had brought me a gift, things I badly needed at that time—mostly second-hand clothes. And when, at the end of the evening, I had kissed Minka good-bye—forever, and we both knew—and had shaken hands with everybody, I went back to my hotel carrying two large suitcases full of old clothes that I hoped to sell in Hamburg like a *bandalé*, to make enough money to follow Minka to America.

She died there a few months later.

SOUR SWEET

A NOVEL

Timothy Mo

'Adopting the severe approach of a French 19th-century
realist novelist, Timothy Mo has drawn an amazing picture
of a family of Chinese living in London in the 1960s... an
excellent book.'

Claire Tomalin, *Sunday Times*

'The characters and atmosphere are enthralling, and Mo
has a deliciously gingery sense of humour.'

John Mellors, *Listener*

£7.95

Nominated for the 1982

Booker
McConnell
Prize

✿ **ANDRE DEUTSCH**

EICHMANN
INTERROGATED

Commentator: More than once in his public speeches, Hitler announced his intention of exterminating the Jews. On October 8 1942, addressing the 'old warriors' of the National Socialist Party at the Munich Löwenbräukeller, he said, 'People have laughed at my prophecies. Countless numbers of those who laughed are no longer laughing today. And those who are still laughing may not be laughing for long.' The chimneys of the crematoriums in the death camps were already smoking day and night. That speech was broadcast by every radio station in Germany and was printed word for word in the newspapers. Yet most Germans regarded those words as rhetorical threats designed to frighten Hitler's enemies. Reichsführer-SS Heinrich Himmler spoke much more concretely of the 'extermination of the Jewish people'. On October 4 1943, addressing the highest- ranking leaders of the SS in Posen, he said: 'Most of you probably know what it is to see a hundred corpses lying together in one place, or to see five hundred or a thousand. To have gone through that and yet, aside from exceptions due to human weakness, to have preserved our decency—this is what has made us hard.'

Since neither the Führer nor the Reichsführer wanted to bloody their hands, they needed tools; in other words, an apparatus of commanders and followers, organizers and thugs, murderers and white-washers. Most of these were provided by the SS, the élite of the National Socialists; they were the most disciplined and the most unscrupulous. One of this breed was Adolf Eichmann, head of the Bureau for Jewish Affairs at the Reich Security Headquarters. In the Third Reich, Adolf Eichmann was as little known by the general public as ten thousand other high-level bureaucrats. But at the end of the war, his name came to be identified, all over the world, with genocide and murder.

The man chosen to interrogate him was Police Captain Avner Less, a one time Berliner, who was familiar with conditions in Germany before 1933 and could speak to Eichmann in his mother tongue. To throw the accused off balance, Less resorted in his questioning to the criminal investigator's old trick of jumping from one set of crimes to another and back again. This makes the

3,564 pages of the transcript difficult reading. Jochen von Lang and Claus Sibyll have consequently collated the dispersed parts of the different complexes, so, to the best of their ability, presenting the record in logical and chronological order.

Less: I believe we should begin with your curriculum vitae.

Eichmann: I was born on March 19 1906, at Solingen in the Rhineland. My father was a book-keeper at the Solingen Light and Power Company. In 1913 he was transferred to the Light and Power Company in Linz on the Danube, and in 1914 he moved his family to Austria, that is, to Linz on the Danube in Upper Austria, where I attended elementary school up to the fourth grade, and then *Realschule* (scientific secondary school) at the Kaiser Franz Staatsoberrealschule. Later it was renamed Bundesrealschule.* I must have finished elementary school in 1916 or 1917. I was at secondary school during the revolution. I can still remember that there was rioting during classes. I then went on to a vocational school [the School for Electrical, Mechanical and Structural Engineering]. Still in Linz.

My father took an early retirement about then and went into business for himself. First in Salzburg, where he founded the Untersberg Mining Company, in which he held fifty-one per cent of the stock. Next he decided to acquire an interest in a mill-construction enterprise in the Inn region of Upper Austria, a decision he later often regretted as this was just at the time of the economic crisis. He not only failed to make money, but also lost his savings and my second mother's as well. My father had also bought interest in a machine shop in Salzburg that made locomobiles. The original owner later hanged himself after spending the money that my father had invested in the business. Then one day my father shut down the Untersberg Mining Company, although for years after he continued paying prospecting fees to the mining authority.

---

*At one time, Eichmann would indoubtedly have pointed out that Adolf Hitler had gone to that same school a few years earlier.

Less: In which of your father's firms did you work?

Eichmann: When I—well, you see, my father had taken me out of school and put me in the Untersberg Mining Company, because, I may as well admit that I hadn't been the most conscientious of students. I then had to work in the mine both below and above ground. I was there about three months and was then sent to Austrian Electrotech as a volunteer: it was called a volunteer period instead of an apprenticeship, and I stayed with Austrian Electrotech for two and a half years. My father wanted me to become a salesman. Radio was just coming in and it attracted my interest because of its novelty. But after two and a half years my father said I wasn't getting anywhere and decided I should become a travelling salesman for the Vacuum Oil Company in Upper Austria. It seems that my parents had just seen an advertisement in the daily paper, and my mother, who usually took the initiative in these matters, had got in touch with a cousin of hers, the president of the Austrian Automobile Club. He lived in Vienna and was a close friend of the head of the Vacuum Oil Company for Austria. A Herr Weiss.

In 1928 I was twenty-two. I went to Vienna, reported to the main office of Vacuum Oil and was taken to a Herr Popper, who told me I was too young but I had been hired at the request of Herr Weiss, the president. I reported back to the Linz office and spent the next few days learning about Sphinx gasoline, kerosene, and the various grades of Gargoyl-Mobiloil. After a week or two of preparatory work I was then assigned a district of Upper Austria as my exclusive territory.

Less: Were you living with your parents at the time? With your father and stepmother?

Eichmann: Yes, but I came home only on Saturdays and Sundays, or occasionally during the week when my route was changed. That year most of my work consisted of setting up petrol pumps in my territory and arranging for kerosene deliveries in most of the Mühlviertel where electrification wasn't completely available.

I was especially interested in the kerosene deliveries as they took me into territory that hadn't been touched by the high speed of modern life. The Mühlviertel was a dreamy little district, where the people still lived as they had fifty or even a hundred years before. And then there was its natural beauty. Mixed forests, partly deciduous, partly evergreen. Plus the romantic feel of the place. It's amazingly rich in old castles, or what might be more accurately described as the ruins of many generations of nobility; some are very old, genuine ruins that I made a point of visiting on all my trips. I stayed there until 1933, and was then transferred to Salzburg. That transfer went against my temperament. At first I was happy, because it was winter and the high mountains were covered with snow. But then spring came, and the tourists crowded into Kitzbühel, Hofgastein, Dorf Gastein, and Bad Gastein, and all that bustle repelled me. I didn't enjoy my work any more, and lost interest in selling and calling on customers. After the Whitsun holidays of 1933, Director Blum said that they had to cut down on personnel and that, as I was the only unmarried salesman, I was to be given my notice.

Less: And what did you do after returning to Linz?

Eichmann: I stayed with my parents and tried to figure out what to do next. I thought of starting a business of my own, selling lubricants—as agent for some unknown brand, not for any member of a cartel. I knew many prospective customers, especially in Upper Austria—but while I was making preparations, I ran into some sort of difficulties—I don't remember what, something financial or maybe something was wrong with the idea. I remember only that I was on my way to Eferding to see my first customer and suddenly decided to turn back. I said: 'After all, I'm a German citizen; why not go to Germany and try my luck with Vacuum Oil?'

Less: What prompted that decision?

Eichmann: I was a relatively young man and used to being led, in business and everything else. Maybe I just lost my nerve, I really

157

don't remember. In any event, I broke off my trip and told my parents I was going to Germany. Germany was a big country, I said, and there was sure to be work there, probably even in the oil business. At that time there was a lot of unemployment in Austria.

Less: All that was in 1933?

Eichmann: Yes, Herr Hauptmann.* To make this part of my story perfectly clear, I have to switch from my business matters to those of the 'political sphere'.

Commentator: It should be pointed out that in 1933 unemployment in Austria was scarcely worse than in Germany. True, Hitler kept trumpeting his promise that the six million German unemployed would be back at work within four years, but in the context of the world crisis, his promise was hardly credible. As the following sentences show, it was something very different that brought Eichmann to Germany.

Eichmann: Quite apart from economic considerations, I had other reasons for wanting to get away. Even in my school days, we had political groups, all perfectly harmless, of course: nationalists, socialists, monarchists. The kind of thing youngsters go in for, without thinking about it very seriously. For instance, you'd join the monarchists or the nationalists just because a good friend was already a member of one of these groups. At that time, I had an old friend in Linz, Friedrich von Schmidt, whose father was Field Marshal Lieutenant von Schmidt, although I never met him because he died before I met his son. The family was enormously proud of the father, who had risen from private to field marshal lieutenant in the days of the Emperor Franz Joseph. It was a distinguished family. My friend's mother had been a countess and although their world had collapsed in 1919, they still lived with

---

*'Herr Hauptmann', meaning 'captain', is the formal term Eichmann uses whenever he addresses Israeli Police Captain Avner Less directly.

the old ideas, keeping up the old forms as if nothing had changed. My friend Friedrich von Schmidt had connections with First World War veteran organizations, as he was associated with many military men, and one day he persuaded me to join the Young Veterans' Association. Its slogan was 'Public Need Before Public Greed'. It was the only organization that dared to march through the streets, and evidently had the support of the government. Most of the members held monarchist opinions. Some were Christian-oriented, and only a vanishing minority were nationalists. National Socialism was still unheard of.

As a group we sometimes took the tram to Klein-München, a suburb of Linz where a marksman's organization had a rifle range. A rifle was put into my hands for the first time and I was taught marksmanship. I remember that well. Those early days in the Veterans' Association must have been in 1928 or 1929. Around 1931, friction developed between nationalists and monarchists, and by that time the SA [Nazi storm troopers] had begun marching through the streets. The SS tried to recruit members of the Veterans' Association in Linz, because we were tolerated by the government and allowed to practise marksmanship. One day the National Socialist German Workers' Party or the National Socialists—as its members called themselves— staged a mass meeting in the Märzenkeller, a big Bavarian-style beer hall. Gauleiter Bollek made a speech, and someone named Ernst Kaltenbrunner approached me. His father was a lawyer in Linz who had had business connections with my father for twenty years. Ernst Kaltenbrunner put it to me straight: 'You're going to join us!' That's how it was done in those days, all very free and easy, no fuss. I said: 'All right.' So I joined the SS.

In Salzburg I attended to my regular work at Vacuum Oil, and returned to Linz every Friday where I did my SS duty. Every Friday, I went to the 'Brown House', which the Party had bought, and slept on a straw mattress and did night guard duty. Since I was one of the few who had work I was always welcome as I regularly treated the boys to beer or cider and cigarettes at the restaurant next door. That was when the uniform with the beret came in, and I had one of those uniforms made, just before we went to Frielassing.* In Frielassing, we attended the SS auxiliary police unit where SS members from Salzburg, and Linz went every Sunday to be whipped into shape. In the evening we'd be driven back to Salzburg, and the next morning I returned to my work. I happened to be in Pinzgau when I heard that the Party had been suppressed in Austria.

Commentator: In May 1933, three important German Party officials—the Lawyer Dr Hans Frank, later Governor-General of Poland; Dr Hans Kerrl, the future Church Minister; and Dr Roland Freisler, the future president of the notorious People's Court—tried to organize National Socialist demonstrations in Austria. As soon as they landed at the Vienna airport, however, Engelbert Dollfuss, the Christian Socialist Chancellor of Austria, sent them back to the Reich. On June 19 1933, as a result of the ensuing diplomatic incident between Berlin and Vienna, the National Socialist German Workers Party and all its subsidiaries were prohibited in Austria.

Eichmann: My uniform was at the tailor's, bought and paid for, but I never called for it, because the Party was suppressed. Moreover, as I told you, I had been fired from my job. I was on the way to Eferding when I said to myself: 'There's no point to this. I'm going to Germany.' So one fine morning I set out from Linz with my parents' blessing, a German passport, and a letter from the German consul stating that I belonged to one of the most respected families of the Linz German colony.

Commentator: Eichmann left Austria in 1933. But it is perhaps not surprising that Eichmann, a failure in school and business, did not pursue his possible career with Vacuum Oil in Germany with much enthusiasm. On arriving, he was invited to join the German army, and Eichmann accepted the invitation in the same casual

---

*Frielassing was near Salzburg, just over the German border. Parades of uniformed National Socialists were then forbidden in Austria.

fashion with which he had previously decided to join the National Socialist Party in Austria: 'All right with me, I thought, why not become a soldier?' The decision, as Eichmann's statement shows, was not particularly well-informed.

Less: Have you read Hitler's *Mein Kampf*?

Eichmann: Never all of it and never carefully.

Less: Were you in agreement with his doctrine?

Eichmann: When I was still in Austria, on January 30 1933, I heard Hitler's seizure of power on the radio in some village in the Tyrol, where I happened to be on Vacuum Oil business. I have to admit that I was enthusiastic at the time. In this seizure of power I saw, with my youthful—relatively youthful—eyes and impulses, I saw, I saw a nationalism that appealed to me. Hitler fulminated against Versailles, work and bread were promised, and the promise was kept later on. But this would take us too far, Herr Hauptmann. At the time I was happy about the whole development, because I thought to myself: now things will change.

Less: In other words, you supported Hitler's doctrine at the time.

Eichmann: Yes, at the time I supported it.

Less: Had you read the Party Program?

Eichmann: The twelve points? Yes, I must have read them, but today I couldn't tell you what they were.

Less: How did you feel about the point denying Jews the right to be German citizens?

Eichmann: When I joined . . . when I joined the National Socialist Party . . . I didn't give these details . . . these details . . . a thought. And these details were never discussed among, among so-called comrades.

Less: Have you read Rosenberg's *Myth of the Twentieth Century*?

Eichmann: No, I have not read it. To tell the truth, I never read any books about National Socialism either before or after. Before going into the Secret Service I didn't read at all—much to the dismay of my father, who often pointed out to me that he had an excellent library in the house, with all the classics, which he had built up over the course of his life, evidently to no purpose. When I was with the Secret Service, it wasn't those books that I read but others. I read specifically Jewish books; I read books about Freemasonry. I doubt if I read any other book in all that time. Novels, for instance. In my entire life, I've never read crime thrillers or love stories. I still don't.

Less: Those books you read about the Jews—were they critical?

Eichmann: I only read books written by Jews. No others were of any use to me in my—in my study. My mind was not clouded by any previous knowledge.

Less: Did you know that Hitler accused the Jews of causing the defeat of Germany in the First World War?

Eichmann: At that time I belonged to a category of people who formed no opinions of their own.

Less: Did you read *The Protocols of the Wise Elders of Zion*?*

Eichmann: No, I did not, but I heard about it. When I asked about it, it was described as rubbish. I accepted that opinion.

Less: Were you a loyal, unconditionally obedient SS man?

The Protocols is the alleged resolution of a non-existent Jewish conspiracy to subject the entire world to Jewish domination. This notorious forgery figured prominently in the propaganda by Streicher and his school.

Eichmann: Yes. I can say I was. I had taken the oath, and I obeyed orders. In the first years I had no conflicts, no inner conflicts of any kind. I sat at my desk and did my work. My unconditional, my absolute allegiance underwent a change when I . . . when the . . . the . . . the so-called solution of the Jewish question became more violent—I mean, that is—when the gassing and shooting started. I made no secret of the fact and I said—yes, I believe I said . . . to my superior, Gruppenführer Müller . . . I said, that is, I said, this isn't what I imagined; it probably isn't what any of us imagined, because it's not a political solution. We were still talking about a political solution . . . up until then that was the approved line. But this wasn't a political solution. And then I . . . .

Less: Did you unconditionally support the National Socialist philosophy?

Eichmann: Yes and no. In those years, the first years, I didn't give the National Socialist philosophy and such things a thought. In those first years what mattered to me, as I've already said, was work and bread for seven million people, an Autobahn, and the fight against Versailles—in those matters my attitude was unconditional. And later on in my military service—to all intents and purposes it was military service, and at first I liked it until the time came when I wanted to get out and go into private industry, but found myself behind a desk instead. And in this desk work, Herr Hauptmann, in the first place you weren't asked to consider— and in the second place you didn't waste your time thinking about—unconditional allegiances, unconditional loyalty, because you threw yourself completely into your —into your—work.

Less: In other words you were a convinced National Socialist, a loyal SS man, true to the oath you had taken. How then do you explain your contention that you have never hated the Jews and were never an anti-Semite?

Eichmann: That is true, Herr Hauptmann. I would certainly have had conflicts sooner, in Dachau for instance, if instead of being in

163

the Austrian SS, I had found myself behind the barbed wire, serving as a concentration camp guard. But since for many years I had no contact with such things, I didn't worry my head about them. Because I didn't have to deal with them.

Less: But you must have had anti-Jewish opinions, because they were required. A large part of the program had to do with the Jews.

Eichmann: But not in the early period, Herr Hauptmann. In the early period the Jewish problem wasn't the main thing. What interested us in Austria was work and bread, freedom and an end to servitude.

Less: But wasn't hatred of the Jews a leitmotiv running through Hitler's *Mein Kampf*?

Eichmann: That is possible. I've told you I never read it carefully; I never read it through; I didn't need to. Yes, sir, of course there was hatred of the Jews in it. But in those days there were many Party members with Jewish relatives by blood or marriage. I myself knew an SS Scharführer who was a Jew.

Commentator: Eichmann was initially trained as a soldier, but found the life so tedious that when he heard of openings in the Security Service of the Reichführer, he applied immediately for a position and was accepted. His new employment required him to research into a number of opposition groups—especially Jewish organizations—and, within a short period, Eichmann was seen as an expert on Jewish affairs. After *Anschluss*—the incorporation of Austria into Germany in January 1938—Eichmann was sent to Vienna as head of the newly established Centre for the Emigration of Austrian Jews. The human assembly line that Eichmann set up—effectively expelling Austrian Jews but appropriating their wealth and property before allowing them to leave—was terrifying in its efficiency: by July 1938, four months after Eichmann's arrival in Vienna, 45,000 Jews had emigrated; within a year and a half, 150,000 Jews had left or what was roughly sixty per cent of the original Jewish population. In September 1939 war broke out, and one month later Eichmann was called back to Berlin, where he was appointed head of Bureau IV B 4 of the Secret Service of the Reichführer. Each of the Head Offices of the SS was divided into sections and subsections; subsection IV was organized to combat 'opponents hostile to the State'. IV B 4, Eichmann's department, was simply entitled 'Jews'. In his new position, Eichmann addressed a number of ways of dealing with the Jewish problem, including the establishment of a Jewish ghetto in the Nisko region of Poland and the Madagasgar plan: the scheme to settle four million European Jews in an area of 227,678 square miles of a poor land that already supported an indigenous population of 4,370,000.

Between 1937 and 1941 Eichmann was promoted four times. Within fourteen months he advanced from Untersturmführer to Hauptsturmführer (second lieutenant), and in another year and a half he was made Obersturmbannführer (lieutenant captain). That was October 1941, shortly after the Madgasgar plan had been abandoned and after Eichmann had been assigned his role in the Final Solution.

Eichmann: As I had nothing interesting to do after the Madagascar plan fell through, I asked to be transferred to some city as police president. The answer: a soldier can't decide where he chooses to fight. Later I tried several times to be sent to the front, always with the same negative result.

Toward the end of 1940 the ghettoization measures in the Government General went into an intensive, or you might say final, phase. The same also occurred in Warthegau [from the Warta river in southwestern Poland], an action which did not concern Bureau IV B 4.

Commentator: Both Gauleiter Greiser in Posen [Poznan], formerly Polish territory in West Prussia, and Governor General Frank with Headquarters in Cracow for West Poland, had been empowered by Hitler to concentrate the Jews in their territories in ghettos, and to have those unfit for work killed. For this they did not need Eichmann. Nevertheless, his Bureau was not inactive.

Eichmann: At this time, Gruppenführer Müller, my immediate superior, sent me on frequent trips to Poland with instructions to inspect one thing or another and report to him. He himself never left Berlin, but he insisted on being thoroughly informed. So I inspected the ghetto of Litzmannstadt—now it's called Lodz again—and the Warsaw ghetto too.

Less: You might tell me what the functions of your department were at this time.

Eichmann: Yes, Herr Hauptmann.. Yes, Herr Hauptmann. Bureau IV B 4 had undergone a number of slight changes. When I took over, it was simply called Jewish Affairs. I can't say for sure whether over the years, before it acquired the official title Weltanschauliche Gegnerbekëmpfung [Defence against Ideological Enemies], it ever bore the title Final Solution of the Jewish Question. Originally the words 'final solution' had nothing to do with physical extermination, of which I shall have more to say. I already had the words 'final solution of the Jewish question' in mind when I took up the Madagascar project.

Less: Was it already called Final Solution of the Jewish Question at that time?

Eichmann: I am certain, Herr Hauptmann, that the term 'final solution' was usual even before that. It was one of the terms employed by Heydrich and Himmler. When I took over the Bureau, it handled withdrawal of nationality and citizenship and the confiscation of property. That was a complicated business. The State Police never saw the property, only the orders.

Less: Now tell me about the deportation of Jews from Western and Eastern Europe.

Eichmann: As far as I can remember, Jews were deported from

Holland, Belgium, France, Greece, Slovakia, and Romania. Whether any were deported from Croatia, I don't know. From—what's the name of that country up there?— Denmark, I believe. From Hungary. I don't know if I've forgotten some country.

Less: Italy?

Eichmann: Italy proper, no, but possibly from places in the Côte d'Azur region that were somehow connected with border disputes. Of course I haven't the faintest idea how many were evacuated from these countries, how many shipments were sent out.

Less: Very well. You have touched on the final solution of the Jewish question. Would you now like to speak about that or about the war with Russia first?

Eichmann: The final solution depends . . . it's mixed up with . . . something that happened after the start of the German-Russian war. At that time Reich Marshal Goering issued a document conferring a special title on the head of the Security Police and Secret Service. I'm trying to remember the wording. Was it 'Deputy charged with the Final Solution', or was it 'For the Solution of the Jewish Question'? The war with the Soviet Union began in June 1941, I think. And I believe it was two months later, or maybe three, that Heydrich sent for me. I reported. He said to me: 'The Führer, well, emigration is . . . .' He began with a little speech. And then: 'The Führer has ordered physical extermination.' These were his words. And as though wanting to test their effect on me, he left a long pause, which was not at all his way. I can still remember that. In the first moment, I didn't grasp the implications, because he chose his words so carefully. But then I understood. I didn't say anything, what could I say? Because I'd never thought of a . . . of such a thing, of that sort of violent solution. And then he said to me: 'Eichmann, go and see Globocnigg in Lublin.' Gruppenführer Globocnigg, the former Gauleiter of Vienna, was then head of the SS and police in the

Lublin district of the Government General. Anyway, Heydrich said: 'Go and see Globocnigg, the Führer has already given him instructions. Take a look and see how he's getting on with his program. I believe he's using Russian anti-tank trenches for exterminating the Jews.' As ordered, I went to Lublin, located the headquarters of SS and Police Commander Globocnigg, and reported to him. I told him Heydrich had sent me, because the Führer had ordered the physical extermination of the Jews.

Globocnigg, sent for Höfle, a member of his staff. We went from Lublin to, I don't remember what the place was called, I get them mixed up; I couldn't say if it was Treblinka or some other place. There were patches of woods and the road passed through a Polish highway. On the right side of the road there was an ordinary house, where the men who worked there lived. A captain of the regular police welcomed us. A few workmen were still there. The captain had taken off his jacket and rolled up his sleeves—which surprised me—somehow he seemed to have joined in the work. They were building little wooden shacks, two, maybe three of them, which looked like two or three-room cottages. Höfle told the police captain to explain the installation to me. And then he started in. He had a, well, let's say, a vulgar, uncultivated voice. Maybe he drank. He spoke some dialect from the southwestern corner of Germany, and he told me how he had made everything air-tight. It seems they were going to hook up a Russian submarine engine and pipe the exhaust into the houses and the Jews inside would be poisoned.

I was horrified. My nerves aren't strong enough . . . I can't listen to such things . . . such things, without their affecting me. Even today, if I see someone with a deep cut, I have to look away. I could never have been a doctor. I still remember how I visualized the scene and began to tremble, as if I'd been through something, some terrible experience. The kind of thing that happens sometimes and afterwards you start to shake. Then I went to Berlin and reported to the head of the Security Police.

Less: What year was this?

Eichmann: After the war broke out between Germany and Russia. That would make it the autumn of 1941. Then I was sent on to Culm in Warthegau. I received orders from Müller, my immediate superior, to go to Litzmannstadt and report back to him on what was going on there. He didn't put it the same way as . . . as Heydrich . . . not as crassly. 'An action against the Jews is under way there, Eichmann. Go take a look. And then report to me.' I went to State Police Headquarters in Litzmannstadt —now it's Lodz again—and there I was told. It was a special team, put in by the Reichsführer [Himmler]. And they told me exactly where this Culm is situated. I saw the following: a room, perhaps, if I remember right, about five times as big as this one here. There were Jews in it. They had to undress, and then a sealed truck pulled up and drove up a kind of ramp. The doors were opened, and the naked Jews had to get in. Then the doors were closed and the truck drove off.

Less: How many people did this truck hold?

Eichmann: I don't know exactly. The whole time it was there, I didn't look inside. I couldn't. Couldn't! What I saw and heard was enough. The screaming and . . . I was much too shaken. I told Müller that in my report. I drove after the truck . . . and there I saw the most horrible sight I had seen in all my life. It drove up to a fairly long trench. The doors were opened and corpses were thrown out. The limbs were as supple as if they'd been alive. Just thrown in. I can still see a civilian with pliers pulling out teeth. And then I left. I got into my car and drove off. I didn't say another word. I sat there for hours without saying a word to my driver. I'd had enough. I was through. The only other thing I remember is that a doctor in a white smock wanted me to look through a peep-hole and watch the people inside the truck. I refused. I couldn't; I couldn't say another word; I had to get out of there. In Berlin, I reported to Gruppenführer Müller. I told him the same as I've told you now. Terrible, an inferno. I can't. It's . . . I can't do it . . . I told him.

Less: What did Müller say?

Eichmann: Müller never said anything. Never! Not about these things and not about other things. He was always very terse and unemotional; he only said what was strictly necessary. He'd say yes or he'd say no. And when he didn't say yes or no, he usually said: 'Eichmann, my friend . . . .' That wasn't yes and it wasn't no.

Less: Did you report on this in writing?

Eichmann: No, I couldn't do that. I was expressly forbidden to; by Heydrich, I believe. Müller especially wanted to know how long it takes; I wasn't able to tell him that, I couldn't hear. I should have gone out there a second time, but naturally I didn't volunteer, and nothing was said to me.

Less: Did you also see Jews being gassed with a submarine engine by Globocnigg's outfit?

Eichmann: No, I did not see that, but I'll come back to it. I was sent there another time. Let me think a moment, Herr Hauptmann. I was sent there after the following places: the two I've mentioned, and then Auschwitz, Auschwitz, and then I was sent to Treblinka. And then to . . . what's the name of that double battle near Minsk? . . . near Minsk. Anyway, to Minsk, Auschwitz, Treblinka, Minsk. . . . That's all, I believe. Oh yes, and Lemberg Lemberg. That's it. Those are the six places.

Less: Where these just information-gathering missions? Or did you have some special assignment?

Eichmann: No assignment, no assignment. I had no orders to give or anything else. No instructions about who to gas, or whether anyone was to be gassed, whether the gassing could or should be stopped or started or intensified: I never had anything to do with all that, Herr Hauptmann. If the newspapers said I did, it's a lie; I'm telling you the whole truth.

Less: What was the function of your Bureau within the framework of the extermination program?

Eichmann: Evacuation.

Less: Herr Eichmann, you wished to speak of your visits to the extermination camps.

Eichmann: Yes. That's right. Müller said to me: 'In Minsk the Jews are being shot. I'd like a report on that.' So I went to Minsk. I had nothing at all to do there; I didn't know anybody. I went to the command post—what was it called again . . . Commander Security Police or could it have been Action Team Security Police?—and asked for the commanding officer. I still remember, he wasn't there. I spoke to someone else and told him I had orders to see what was going on. I spent the night in that town, and next day I went to the place, but I got there too late. The work for that morning was already done, almost done—and I was very glad of that. When I got there, I was just in time to see some young riflemen, I believe they were riflemen, with the death's-head collar patch, shooting into a pit . . . maybe four or five times as big as this room. Maybe bigger, say six or seven times. I . . . I . . . my orientation in this case is unreliable, because I saw this thing without thinking; I didn't think anything at all. I just saw it, and that's all. They fired into the pit. I can still see a woman with her arms behind her back, and then her knees crumpled, and I cleared out . . . .

Less: The pit was full of corpses?

Eichmann: It was full. It was full. I went to my car; I got in and drove away. I drove to Lemberg. I had no orders to go to Lemberg, I remember now. Somehow I went to Lemberg and found the man in charge of the Gestapo command post and I said to him: 'It's horrible what they're doing there. They're training young men to be sadists.' I told Müller the exact same thing. I told Günther, too. I told everybody. I told them all. And I said to that SS officer in Lemberg: How can they stand there firing at a woman and children? 'How is it possible? . . . It's just not . . . Those men will either go mad or they'll turn into sadists . . . our own men.' He said to me: 'They're doing the same thing right here, shooting. Want to see?' 'No,' I said. 'I don't want to see anything.' 'We're driving past there, anyway,' he said. There had been a pit there—it was already filled in—and blood was gushing out of it . . . how shall I say? . . . like a geyser. I've never seen anything like it. I'd had enough of that mission. I went back to Berlin and reported what I'd seen to Gruppenführer Müller. I said to him: 'This is no solution to the Jewish question. And besides, we're training our men to be sadists. We shouldn't be surprised if they all turn out to be criminals, all criminals.' I still remember Müller looking at me with an expression that said: Eichmann, you're right, that's no solution. But there was nothing he could do about it. Müller definitely couldn't do a thing. Not a thing. Not a thing. Who gave the order for those actions? The orders, the orders. Obviously the orders were given by the head of the Security Police and the Secret Service: namely, Heydrich. But he must also have had his instructions from the Reichsführer SS, namely, Himmler; on his own hook he can't . . . he could never have done such things on his own hook. And Himmler must have had express orders from Hitler. If he hadn't had orders from Hitler, he'd have been thrown out before he knew what hit him.

Less: Didn't Himmler give written orders about this final solution of the Jewish question?

Eichmann: Writt . . . for extermination, physical extermination?

Less: For physical extermination.

Eichmann: I never saw a written order, Herr Hauptmann. All I know is that Heydrich said to me: 'The Führer has ordered the physical extermination of the Jews.' He said that as clearly and surely as I'm repeating it now. And those were the first, the first results . . . small-scale results . . . that I'm telling you about now. I implored the Gruppenführer: 'Please, don't send me there. Send someone else. Someone with stronger nerves. They never let me go to the front. I was never a soldier. There are plenty of other men who can bear to see such things, who won't keel over; I can't stand it; I can't sleep at night; I have nightmares. I can't stand it, Gruppenführer.' But it didn't get me anywhere.

Less: Were Jews from the Reich, Austria, and the Protectorate of Bohemia and Moravia sent to Riga and Minsk in the autumn of 1941?

Eichmann: In 1941, Herr Hauptmann, that is possible. I don't know. I only know that there were trains going to Minsk and Riga.

Less: Did you receive periodic reports about the 'action groups', so-called occurrence reports, and hence communications about the liquidation of the Jews in Russia?

Eichmann: Yes. About the liquidation of the Jews along with other activities of the 'action groups'. Here I must add something that, chronologically speaking, should have been mentioned before. Shortly before the start of the German–Russian war, a conference was held in Berlin, attended by all the top men from Reich Security Headquarters. There for the first time I heard the code name for the war preparations against the Soviet Union. Someone read a paper, prepared long before, that mentioned the 'action groups' in the East. As the German troops advanced, 'action groups' followed right behind and took over police power. The leader of one of these action groups was Ohlendorf, who testified at the war criminal trial in Nuremberg that his group shot 84,000—or maybe it was 94,000—Jews.

Less: Was it stated what the function of these 'action groups' was to be?

Eichmann: No. I thought it was something to do with the offensive, and I was upset about it at the time, because I thought I'd been passed over. My advancement had been relatively rapid and I said to myself: 'Now I'm an Obersturmbannführer, but if they send me to the front I'll be promoted to Standartenführer in no time.' As it happened, I stayed an Obersturmbannführer until May 8 1945. I couldn't be promoted any more.

Less: You were also in Auschwitz?

Eichmann: I kept getting orders to visit Auschwitz. Müller told me they were expanding the plant, and he wanted me to take a look and report back to him. Herr Hauptmann, those fellows were very cruel. Describing those things as gruesomely as possible to a man accustomed to desk work, putting it to him as abruptly as possible. Naturally, they laughed their heads off when my nerves broke down and I couldn't keep up my military dignity—that's what they called it—as they did. Höss told me Himmler had been there, and taken a good look at everything. He told me the Reichsführer himself had gone all weak in the knees. He meant that, meant that, in a disparaging sense, because Höss himself was thoroughly hardened. That was the day when Himmler, after seeing that—undoubtedly to screw up his own courage and hide his weakness from his concentration-camp men—told Höss that those were battles the coming generation wouldn't have to fight. When I visited the installation, Höss sent for an all-terrain car. We drove to a certain place—I don't know my way around Auschwitz. I never got any further than the command post at the main entrance. Had no desire to. As we were driving, I saw some big buildings. Almost like factories. Enormous chimneys. Höss said to me: 'Working to capacity! Ten thousand!' A job was under way. They were separating the able-bodied from the ones who were supposedly unfit for work. I didn't watch the gassing. I couldn't. I'd have probably keeled over. And I thought: Whew, I've got it over with again. But then he drives me to a big trench. It was very big—I can't say exactly how big—maybe a hundred metres long, maybe a hundred and fifty or a hundred and eighty. And there was an enormous grating, an iron grating. And corpses were burning on it. Then I got sick to my stomach. Sick to my stomach.

Less: But you were in Treblinka again?

Eichmann: I'd like to say something about this last, about this last point of this terrible, terrible business. I mean Treblinka. I was given orders. I went to see Globocnigg in Treblinka. That was the second time. The installations were now in operation, and I had to report to Müller. I expected to see a wooden house on the right side of the road and a few more wooden houses on the left; that's what I remembered. Instead, again with the same Höfle as my guide, I came to a railroad station with a sign saying Treblinka, looking exactly like a German railroad station —anywhere in Germany—a replica, with notice-boards, etc. There I hung back as far as I could. I didn't push closer to see it all. I saw a footbridge enclosed in barbed wire and over that footbridge a file of naked Jews was being driven into a house, a big . . . no, not a house, a big, one-room structure, to be gassed. I was told they were gassed with . . . what's it called? . . . potassium cyan . . .

Less: Cyanide.

Eichmann: Potassium cyanide . . . or cyanic acid. In acid form it's called cyanic acid. I didn't look to see what happened. I reported to Müller and as usual he listened in silence, without a word of comment. Just his facial expression said: 'There's nothing I can do about it.' I am convinced, Herr Hauptmann, I know it sounds odd coming from me, but I'm convinced that if it had been up to Müller it wouldn't have happened.

Commentator: Cyanic, or prussic, acid, is a colourless liquid which boils and becomes a gas at room temperature. When breathed, sixty milligrams of it are fatal. It was used in the gas chambers in the form of Zyklon B, a commercial product designed for the extermination of vermin. The National Socialists' first experiments with poison gas as a means of mass murder date from the so-called euthanasia campaign, when mental patients were done away with on the alleged grounds that they were a useless burden to the national community. This action was directed by the Office of the Führer and was broken off when it became known and aroused protests, despite the claim that it was a mercy to put the incurably ill out of their misery. In the conquered eastern territories the murder teams were given a new and far larger field of activity. One of the most notorious figures was Police Captain Christian Wirth, whom Eichmann met on his first visit to Treblinka. He was killed by partisans towards the end of the war.

Less: What do you know about Zyklon B gas?

Eichmann: I don't know anything but what I heard there, that it's contained in beer . . . I mean, I've heard today for the first time that it's called Zyklon. Then I was told that it came in tablets that looked like beer mats, cardboard mats. But whether it was Zyklon B or prussic acid, I have no idea.

Less: I am now going to quote from the German edition of the proceedings of the trial of the leading war criminals before the International Military Court in Nuremberg. From the sworn testimony of Rudolf Höss, the camp commandant at Auschwitz from 1940 to 1943. He said: 'Eichmann was repeatedly in Auschwitz and knew exactly what was being done.'

Eichmann: Herr Hauptmann, I knew no more than what I have said. I knew the killing was done with those round cardboard things. Höss told me that. He even showed me one. Then I saw the outside of that big building. Neither in Auschwitz nor anywhere else did I observe the extermination process. It was only in Minsk that I got there while the shooting was going on. Everywhere else I refused, because the burning, the burning of the corpses was as much as I could stand. I wasn't up to it.

Less: When Rudolf Höss was under arrest in Poland, he made autobiographical notes. Here I have his book: *Commandant of Auschwitz*. I'm going to read a passage: 'Eichmann told me about the killing by exhaust fumes in trucks, as had been practised in the East up until then. That, however, would not have been possible for the mass shipments that were to be expected. Killing by spraying with carbon monoxide in a bathroom, as had been done with the mentally ill in some places in the Reich, would have required too many buildings. Moreover, it was questionable whether sufficient gas could be procured for mass shipments.

Eichmann undertook to find out about a gas that was easily obtainable and required no special installations, and report to me about it.' Have you a comment to make?

Eichmann: Yes, Herr Hauptmann! The overwhelming majority of these assertions are pure invention. It is obvious to me that Höss was interested only in one thing: clearing his own department. I never in any way—and to this I will take any oath, Herr Hauptmann—discussed this matter with Höss. On the contrary, when Müller sent me to Auschwitz for the first time, it was Höss who showed me those cardboard mats.

Less: I will now read you parts of the statement made under oath by your one time subordinate Dieter Wisliceny on January 3 1946 at the Nuremberg war crimes trial: 'Until the spring of 1943 I was in Bratislava, at the German embassy. In the spring of 1942, roughly seventeen thousand Jews had been sent from Slovakia to Poland as labourers. At the time, Eichmann gave the Slovakian government the assurance that these Jews would be given decent, humane treatment in the Polish ghettos. As a result of this assurance, approximately thirty-five thousand more Jews were shipped from Slovakia to Poland. Premier Tuka repeatedly sent for me and expressed the wish that a Slovakian delegation be permitted to visit the territories where the Slovakian Jews were located. Eichmann told me that he could not under any circumstances authorize such a visit. When I asked him why, he replied after various evasions, that a large part of those Jews were no longer alive. I asked him who had given him such an order. He said the order came from Himmler.' So much for Wisliceny. And now your comment.

Eichmann: Obviously, Herr Hauptmann, Wisliceny was trying—as he had every right—to distance himself as much as possible from the whole business. I can only repeat that I had no power whatsoever over what went on in the Government General.

Less: I shall quote again from Wisliceny's testimony: 'Eichmann then said he could show me this order from Himmler in writing, if

177

it would put my conscience at rest. He went to his safe, took out a thin file, and showed me a letter from Himmler to the head of the Security Police and Secret Service. The gist of this letter was that the Führer had ordered the final solution of the Jewish problem. The head of the Security Police and the Secret Service and the Inspector of Concentration Camps were entrusted with implementation of this final solution. Pending the final solution, all able-bodied concentration-camp inmates of female or male sex should be employed on labour projects.' Have you any comment?

Eichmann: Yes, Herr Hauptmann. As I hear it now, it's possible . . . I won't deny it, there may have been an order from Himmler. As I hear it now, it's possible; I don't . . . don't deny it . . . though I never saw this paper with my own eyes.

Less: Wisliceny was asked about the date of that order. His answer: 'The order was of April 1942, and was signed by Himmler in person. Eichmann told me that he personally had been charged with carrying out this order at Reich Security Headquarters. I said to Eichmann: "God grant that our enemies never get an opportunity to do the same to the German people." To that Eichmann replied that I shouldn't get sentimental, that it was the Führer's orders and had to be carried out.' Have you any comment?

Eichmann: Yes, Herr Hauptmann. According to this statement, I had a special mandate, mand . . . er, er . . . to direct, to take central command of the whole business, the evacuation and killing of the Jews. That is not true. That is not true at all. Wisliceny made it up. I never had any special mandate and had—I cannot insist too much—nothing to do with the killing. With the evacuation, yes—I can't wriggle out of that, I have to admit it. But once a shipment was delivered to the designated station as per the decisions of the scheduling conference, my powers ended.

Less: So you were responsible for the shipments, but if the shipments hadn't got there, the killing wouldn't have been possible. With regard to the killing of the Jews, you say . . . .

Eichmann: I'm not . . . it's not . . . it's not possible. The Security Police had no authority, Reich Security Headquarters had no authority.

Less: But isn't it strange that both Höss, the camp commander at Auschwitz, and Wisliceny, your co-worker, who advised the government in Bratislava on Jewish questions, should make almost identical statements? I don't believe they had a chance to compare notes.

Eichmann: No, neither do I. But isn't it just as strange that even Pohl, head of the SS Administration—who after all held rank of general—should also try to wriggle out of the whole business like a born coward? It's beyond me how, when the going gets rough, a man of his rank can shamelessly try to clear himself at the expense of men of lower rank. I've read in the papers that General Pohl blames everything on Reich Security Headquarters. At the height of their power, these generals have courage to spare, but when facing a court, they lose their nerve and try to shift everything . . . everything to somebody else's shoulders. I'm not calling anyone else to account for the evacuations. I was responsible. I'm ready to take my punishment. I'm not short on courage. Of course, it's a . . . sad kind of courage I need now. But in those days I had the resolve to say, 'Yes sir, will do!' and today I have the resolve to say: 'All right. I'm ready. Here's my head . . . ready to go where it belongs.'

Less: In the English edition of Rudolf Höss book—*Commandant of Auschwitz*—there are some things about you that are missing in the German edition. I've translated them for you: 'I became acquainted with Eichmann after I received orders for exterminating the Jews from the Reichsführer SS. He came to see me in Auschwitz to discuss the details of the extermination process with me. Eichmann was a lively, active man in his thirties, always bursting with energy. He was always hatching new plans and always in search of innovations and improvements. He could never rest. He was obsessed with the Jewish question and the order that had been given for its solution. He regularly had to give the Reichsführer SS direct, oral reports about the preparation and implementation of the various actions. Eichmann was convinced that if he succeeded in destroying the biological foundation of Jewry in the East, Jewry as a whole would never recover from this blow.' Do you wish to say something?

Eichmann: Basically, I reject all that as untrue, totally untrue. I'm covered with guilt, Herr Hauptmann, I know that. But I had nothing to do with killing Jews. I've never killed a Jew. And I've never ordered anyone to kill a Jew.

Less: You have said that in Reich territory it was the Gauleiters who pressed to have the Jews in their Gaus evacuated as quickly as possible. I'm going to read from the minutes of a meeting: 'Gauleiters or Kreisleiters are to be informed of the evacuations, because several Gauleiters complained that they have received no notice of such crucial measures.'

Eichmann: Naturally, with so many actions under way, the local evacuation authorities didn't always observe the guidelines. But the Bureau never took it on itself to say: 'Look here. There are still . . . two thousand or five thousand Jews here . . . in, say . . . Rhineland-Westphalia, and we want to get them out of there, immediately.' That wasn't the province of Bureau IV B 4. It never did anything like that, because we were already getting so many orders that were were glad if we could just get half the transportation to fill them, let alone arranging the routing and scheduling with the Transportation Ministry. We, the Bureau I mean, really had no need to make extra work for ourselves. We already had it up to here.

Less: You keep saying that this, that, and the other thing weren't in your department. There are hundreds and thousands of details which you took an interest in but which were not in your department. If they were not in your department, why do we find time and again in all these documents, that you did take a hand in them?

Eichmann: Well, Herr Hauptmann, all those things were insepar-
ably connected with evacuation.

Less: That's just it. One might say for instance: no evacuation, no
gas chambers.

Eichmann: Yes . . . you could put it that way . . . though I had
nothing to do with that sector.

Less: You say you had nothing to do with the killing?

Eichmann: That's right.

Less: But you delivered the people to be killed!

Eichmann: Yes, Herr Hauptmann, that is true, insofar as I received
orders to evacuate them. But not all the people I evacuated were
killed. I had no knowledge whatever of who was killed and who
was not. Otherwise, 2.4 million Jews, according to one count,
would not have been found alive after the war.

Less: It's no thanks to you that any Jews were found alive after the
war. If the war had gone on longer, those two million would in all
likelihood have been killed. Your plan called for total extermination of the Jews.

Eichmann: Not my plan. I had nothing to do with that plan, Herr
Hauptmann.

Less: You certainly had the plan in your possession, because . . . .

Eichmann: I am obviously guilty of complicity. That is plain. I've
said so before. To that extent, Herr Hauptmann, I cannot deny
my responsibility, and any attempt to do so would be absurd.
Because from a juridical point of view I am guilty of complicity.

Less: We're not talking about the juridical point of view. We're
talking about cold facts.

Eichmann: Yes, but I mean, on the strength of these cold facts I am guilty of complicity . . . from the standpoint of jurisprudence. That's obvious. I realize that, and I'm not trying . . . I can't try . . . to sidestep . . . to talk myself out of it.

Less: Very well, but in all your statements you keep hiding behind 'it wasn't in my department', 'it wasn't in my province', 'the regulation' . . . .

Eichmann: Yes, Herr Hauptmann, I have to do that, because as head of Bureau IV B 4 I was really not answerable for everything, but only for my rather narrowly circumscribed department. And this narrowly circumscribed sphere is easily definable, because we were a central office.

Less: In the course of time I shall show you documents that make many things clearer.

Was it the duty of Höss, the Auschwitz camp commander, to record the number of Jews sent to Auschwitz?

Eichmann: I don't know that, Herr Hauptmann. I am not informed about his official duties, and if I had asked him I don't believe he would have given me truthful answers. Those Auschwitz people always kept you at a distance—Höss too, at first—because they didn't want anyone to see their cards, and I was from a different outfit. They had the death's head on their collar patch, and I didn't have anything.

Less: How many Jews were gassed and killed at Auschwitz?

Eichmann: I've read, Herr Hauptmann, and Höss is supposed to have said 'that he killed four million Jews. Up to now, I've thought that figure exaggerated. But if we're going to talk about figures, one million, four million, or a hundred amounts to the same thing in principle. In the last fifteen years, I've done some figuring myself. At the end of the war I spoke to my officers of five million. I saw that figure as a kind of cloud in my mind's eye. In that brief—hmm, how shall I put it?—apocalyptic speech, or whatever you may choose to call it, I wasn't looking for exact figures.

I don't remember whether the Jewish *Yearbook* published then gave the figure of ten million Jews for Europe, or whether that figure covered the German-occupied Russian territories. In any case, I tried to work out a basis to figure on. I've read somewhere that a few months after the war the Allies reckoned that 2.4 million Jews were still in existence. I said to myself: 'Let's say that 1.2 million Jews emigrated from Austria, Germany, and the USSR. Then comes natural diminution. I'm no statistician. I just figured that out for myself. So on that basis I said to myself: 'Yes, one way or another about six million Jews must have been killed.' Whether I was right or not, I don't know, Herr Hauptmann.

Less: You did know, though, how many Jews were shipped to the camps over the years?

Eichmann: To the camps, yes, I can't deny that.

Less: You also knew that the camps were synonymous with final solution. That is, extermination. Consequently, you had every reason to believe that the Jews you shipped had been exterminated. Even when you said labour service, you probably knew that no one could survive such treatment for long. Whether a forced labourer dropped dead at his work or was clubbed, or whether he starved to death or was gassed—in any case he was dead.

Eichman: All the same, Herr Hauptmann—I believe—as I said before, that 2.4 million Jews were counted by the Allies after the end of the war. And hundreds and hundreds of thousands came out of the concentration camps. And some had been in labour service. Anyway, those things weren't my province; I had nothing to do with the concentration camps. Once the guidelines for shipment were sent out, the Bureau's responsibility stopped. If I wanted to go a step further, I might say—though there's room for argument—that at the very latest my responsibility ceased when the military police took over the shipments at the evacuation stations.

Less: I shall now read you a passage from Höss's *Memoirs*: 'Eichmann came to see me in Auschwitz and acquainted me with the plans for action in the various countries. First Upper Silesia and the adjoining parts of the Government General were to be drawn upon. Then, proceeding geographically, the Jews from Germany and Czechoslovakia, then those from the West —France, Belgium, and Holland. We went on to discuss the extermination process. It transpired that only gas could be considered, because to eliminate the masses that were to be expected by shooting was absolutely impossible and also too hard on the SS men involved, having to shoot women and children.'

Eichmann: I will not shoulder the blame for things I didn't do, Herr Hauptmann. All this was made up by Höss; it has nothing whatever to do with me.

Less: Other people made similar statements, not just Höss, and there is no reason to suppose that their stories were made to order. They had no means of getting together and saying: 'Now let's all of us save our skins by testifying against Eichmann.' Everyone of those who testified knew what was in store for him.

Eichmann: Herr Hauptmann, I myself have read a good deal about it, and I've always wondered: why is it always me? The only explanation I can think of is that I was always at the focal point, at the centre of everything connected with Jewish affairs. Höss knew that, so he lumped everything together in his statement, said he got his instructions from Eichmann rather than Administration and Supply Headquarters.

Less: Höss made that statement at a time when he had no reason to conceal or embellish anything. His situation was a foregone conclusion.

Eichmann: My situation is pretty much the same. There's so much against me that my rejection of Höss's monstrous lies can't have much effect on my punishment.

Less: I would like to quote one more short passage and hear your answer to it. He writes in his book: 'As I once heard from Eichmann, the jewelry and foreign exchange were sold in Switzerland; in fact, they swamped the whole Swiss jewel market. Ordinary watches were brought from the Sachsenhausen concentration camp by the thousands.'

Eichmann: I had no more to do with the property of the killed Jews, Herr Hauptmann, than with the rest of it. A department of the Administration and Supply Headquarters took care of the, the— how shall I say?—the realization of valuables and all that. After the war, a member of Adolf Hitler's Body Regiment, living in Brazil, told me these watches came from Administration and Supply. He said it made the troops sick to be given watches for special achievements.

Less: You keep trying to make it look as if you were nothing more than a transportation officer.

Eichmann: That was true, Herr Hauptmann, as a rule.

Less: The documents thus far produced show that your duties went much further. Whether or not you were acting under orders is irrelevant in my opinion. The fact is that along with the technical problem of transportation, as you call it, you had other occupations that certainly had nothing to do with transportation. Did you concern yourself with the personal fate of individual Jews and make decisions affecting them?

Eichmann: Except for the Jewish functionaries, with whom I worked for years, I did not decide a single personal fate; and as for the functionaries, I never decided their fate; I never had any of them evacuated, let alone killed . . . or anything of the kind.

Less: Now let me show you a letter of December 2 1942 from your

185

Bureau to the Foreign Office. '*Re*: The Jew and former French prisoner of war Roger Massé, born in 1884. The above-mentioned Jew was deported to the East—Auschwitz—on June 5 1942. For reasons of principle, I cannot agree to having him shipped back. Per proc. Eichmann.'

Eichmann: That's a normal routine communication, drafted by a clerk.

Less: But it shows that you personally . . . .

Eichmann: Herr Hauptmann, it's a form letter. A routine communication. It's not a decision on my part.

Less: But it says 'I': 'for reasons of principle I cannot agree . . . .'

Eichmann: Yes, yes, of course. That's a bureaucratic . . . always the same old story . . . obviously. I was the Bureau head. It had to have my name on it. This letter had no effect on the fate of the man concerned.

Less: Of course not, because he wasn't sent back. Quite right. This next document concerns the owners of the Kapitol Cinema in Heidelberg. A letter of February 2 1943, from you to the Foreign Office in Berlin. Is this your signature?

Eichmann: My signature? Yes, it is.

Less: It concerns the Jewish family of Jakob Hirsch, alias Eugen Romani, Hungarian national. From here on I quote: 'From the above, it follows that the motion-picture industry is almost completely Jew-contaminated. In the here prevailing view, this Eugen Romani is obviously a Jew, who appears to have managed, on the strength of his connections with influential Hungarian circles, to get himself transformed into an Aryan in return for bribes. It therefore seems pointless to ask him or his children for proof of their alleged Aryan descent. I therefore intend to give instructions not to renew the residence permit of Eugen Romani, his wife, and his son Rudolf, which expires on February 12 1943, and to expel said persons from the Reich. Rudi Romani, because of his incredible conduct, is to be sent to a concentration camp. Before I have this measure executed, however, I should like to be informed as soon as possible whether there is any diplomatic objection. Per proc. Eichmann.' It seems to me that you decided that family's fate. Right?

Eichmann: Right. Though the text as such was not drafted by me, but by one of the clerks. I signed for the head of the Security Police and the Secret Service.

Less: Here I have a letter of March 23 1943 from you to the Foreign Office. Is this your signature?

Eichmann: Yes, it's my signature.

Less: I'm going to read you this document. '*Re*: the Jew Israel Hirschberg, residing at 34 Sodenerstrasse, Berlin-Wilmersdorf. According to his own statement, the Jew Hirschberg, of German citizenship, is employed by the Thai ambassador in Berlin as a language teacher and instructs both the ambassador and members of his family. Apart from the fact that suitable persons of German blood must be available for this activity, I am of the opinion that in employing the Jew Hirschberg, the Thai ambassador's sole purpose is to shield him from difficulties. I should therefore be grateful if your office could persuade the Thai ambassador to dispense with the further employment of the Jew Hirschberg, and request notification of the results. Per proc. Eichmann.' Was your purpose in protesting about Hirschberg's further employment to have him sent to a death camp?

Eichmann: Herr Hauptmann, that was written in 1943 . . . .

Less: When you were involved in the final solution of the Jewish question . . . .If the man was dismissed by the Thai ambassador, only one fate awaited him: deportation on the next or one of the next shipments. You have claimed that you never took a hand in the fate of individual Jews. But these documents speak for themselves. They show that you had full powers.

Eichmann: That is true, Herr Hauptmann. But on the other hand, these were not personal decisions. They were not personal decisions. If I had not been sitting there, someone else would have had to make exactly the same decisions on the basis of the instructions, regulations, and orders of the higher ups. I wasn't expected to make any decisions at all. At the most, I wrote letters per proc. for somebody else, for the Head of the Security Police and Secret Service. Not for Bureau IV B 4, because that was me.

Less: The next document has to do with the evacuation of the Romanian Jews. It's a telegram from Rintelen, the German ambassador in Bucharest, to the Foreign Office.

Eichmann: In it he says that the Chief of the Security Police and Secret Service has announced that the political and technical preparations for the solution of the Jewish question in Romania have been completed and shipments can soon begin. It is planned to transfer the Jews from Romania, in a series of shipments beginning September 10 1942, to the Lublin district, where the able-bodied will be assigned to labour service and the rest subjected to special treatment. It has been arranged that these Jews will lose their citizenship on crossing the Romanian border. On instructions from the Reich Security Headquarters the adviser for Jewish questions in Bucharest, has requested and obtained a personal letter from Mihail Antonescu, the deputy premier. I request authorization to carry out deportation measures. Rintelen.'

Less: What does it mean that the rest will be subjected to special treatment?

Eichmann: They will be killed. That's the technical term.

Less: Am I to infer that in this case and others the Jews declared unfit for labour were automatically given special treatment?

Eichmann: That's the way it was, by order of the Reichsführer SS and Chief of the German police.

Less: Was this order drafted by you?

Eichmann: Yes. Yes, it was. It must have been signed by . . . by a superior. Kaltenbrunner or Müller.

Less: And what is the point of 'It has been arranged that these Jews will lose their citizenship on crossing the Romanian border.'

Eichmann: Some bureau must have insisted on that.

Less: Wasn't it *your* Bureau? Once these people were stateless, it was all right to seize them and send them to the camps. Then no one could say: You've sent Romanian citizens to the death camps. They were stateless.

Eichmann: The Foreign Office must have imposed that condition. In such matters, the Foreign Office always took precedence. We were always extremely careful in such matters.

Less: Because Herr Ribbentrop of the Foreign Office might otherwise have felt slighted?

Eichmann: No, no. If the Foreign Office said no, the Security Police couldn't make a move in foreign countries. The various departments defended every inch of their competency tooth and nail. Otherwise, there'd have been no need for all this stupid paper work. The bureaucracy, the—what shall I call it?—red-tape specialists stuck to the regulations with an obstinacy, a punctilio . . . that's why you've got tons of these documents.

Less: The Germans have always been famous for their thoroughness. And that includes thoroughness in killing. On that score, one more letter from your Bureau. Dated July 26 1942, the very same day, to the Foreign Office. *Re:* Solution of the Jewish question.'

Eichmann: This is a letter from my Bureau, stating that it is planned to send Jews from Romania to the East by special trains as of September 10 1942.

Less: What sort of instructions did your Bureau give your agents in connection with these shipments?

Eichmann: They had to do with provisions for the trip, things like that. And then always and invariably the same identical sentence: 'Avoidable cruelties are to be avoided.'

Less: Cruelty to be avoided. Doesn't that sound rather ironical when you consider that these people were being sent to a death camp to be killed?

Commentator: Under interrogation, Eichmann admits that he took part in the extermination of Jews in Hitler Germany, but insists that he never killed anyone or gave orders to kill anyone. On the contrary, he alleges, he tried for many years to help Jews save themselves by emigrating. It was only when the Second World War sealed the German frontiers and made deportation to a reservation in Africa or Siberia impossible, so Eichmann tells us, that Hitler thought up the Final Solution.

In his last and worst campaign, Eichmann no longer operated from his desk in Berlin. He now commanded the anti-Jewish action from headquarters in Budapest. Hungarian agencies and gendarmes did the dirty work of rounding up the Jews and loading them into trains. He and his men supervised the operation and intervened only in case of bottlenecks and delays. In the late autumn of 1944 when the railway lines between Budapest and the Reich were severely bombed, Eichmann tried to send tens of thousands of his prisoners to Austria on foot. The roads were littered with the dead and dying. Eichmann's activity continued unchecked until the second half of November 1944 when the mass marches to the Austrian border were prohibited by Himmler. Though Eichmann was now no longer needed in Hungary, he did not return to Berlin. Nor was he ordered to. If he is to be believed, there was nothing he desired more than to die a hero's death at the front. Still, it was easier to make heroic statements than to die. Moreover Eichmann, like many others who possessed the secrets of the Third Reich, was strictly forbidden to go too near the front, for fear that he might be captured and questioned. And so, from the end of December he sat idle in his Budapest office, waiting for the end or for a change in the fortunes of war.

Less: Again, let me read you a few lines from the notes of Auschwitz Camp Commandant Höss. 'On the occasion of a visit in the summer of 1942, the Reichsführer SS inspected the whole extermination process from the unloading of the trains to the removal from Bunker 2. A short time after the Reichsführer's visit, Standartenführer Blobel came from Eichmann's Bureau, bringing the Reichsführer's order that all mass graves should be emptied and the corpses burned. The ashes were also to be disposed of to make sure they wouldn't serve later on as an indication of the number of people burned. In Culmhof, Blobel had already experimented with different methods of incineration. He had orders from Eichmann to show me these installations.'

Eichmann: I don't know what Höss has against me to keep bringing up these things. It sounds as if there'd been hostility between us, but there wasn't. Blobel wasn't under me.

Less: And what does your subordinate Wisliceny say here in his confession?

Eichmann: It's not true what he says: 'Furthermore there was a special team, formally under Eichmann's command, for eliminating the traces of the executions, Team 1005, set up by Standartenführer Blobel.' SS Standartenführer Blobel had previously commanded an action team in the East. He came to my Bureau—as Müller said—for economic housing purposes. He and his men had permission to spend the night in the rooms belonging to my Bureau when they were in Berlin. Blobel's job was to find mass graves all over the East, have them opened and burned and the traces destroyed. For that purpose he moved westward and did his work as the front came closer. For a long time there was tension between me and Blobel. He was a crude man with a rough voice and he drank a lot. When he was drunk, he'd order my men around and behave like he was at home in my office. He had no right to do that. I gave him a piece of my mind. Naturally he fought back, because he was a Standartenführer and I was an Obersturmbannführer, one rank below him. Why I challenged him to a duel with pistols I don't know. Müller stepped in and stopped the whole business. Later, when I was in Argentina, I heard the Americans had hanged him in Landsberg because he had belonged to one of the 'action teams'.

Commentator: Team 1005 consisted of a half dozen SS officers, who merely supervised operations. The actual dirty work was done by concentration-camp inmates under the guard of auxiliary policemen, who had been recruited from POW camps in the East. When the work was done, the auxiliary policemen had to murder the camp inmates and then an SS team murdered the auxiliary policemen.

Less: Didn't Blobel's work suggest to you that Germany was losing the war?

Eichmann: In 1941 I made statements for which Müller reprimanded me in the presence of other Bureau heads. I often remarked to my men that if things went on as they were we would lose the war instead of winning it. Even before that I had conversations with Wisliceny, in which I said: 'I don't believe in the Thousand Year Reich. I believe that when Hitler dies the Reich will disintegrate. Because Alexander the Great's empire disintegrated. You just have to take a look at history. Whenever a large empire has been founded anywhere, it has usually disintegrated and been divided up at the death of the founder. Quarrels, struggles, general disintegration.' During the war years I also once remarked to Günther that I had no faith in a victory. He still did. I must say, though, that when I heard about the rockets for the first time and then when I kept hearing about miracle weapons, I actually did believe we could win the war. I was always one of the people who believed in miracle weapons. We had all set our hopes on the German miracle weapons, and when faith in them began to crumble, when our hopes dwindled and then vanished at about that time, many men got together and tried to work out a security formula that would put them in a halfway bearable position in case the war was lost. That accounts for their changed attitude toward me later on. It accounts for the relative uniformity of their respective statements, especially as the propaganda directed against me in the newspapers and so on, was no secret to those men. Some of them larded their testimony with the crudest lies and slanders with respect to my person—all this, of course, after 1945. Propaganda, you see, transformed me into a person I never was.

Less: Aren't you, too, distancing yourself from those events?

Eichmann: You see, Herr Hauptmann, the officers who planted the bomb in Hitler's headquarters on July 20 1944—well, in my eyes, in everybody's eyes up to May 1945—were not guilty of high treason. They were common traitors, oath-breakers, and scoundrels. Today I divide them between men who committed high treason, breaking their oath out of idealistic motives, and men who are common traitors—because it is not permissible in wartime . . . regardless who the chief . . . regardless who the chief . . . the chief of state is . . . . In many things—questions of philosophy or similar matters of interest to no one but me, let's say ultimate things—I had an entirely different point of view up until May 8 1945 from what I have today. Then we had an entirely different . . . call it psychological attitude toward all these things, because in time of war the life and death of the nation was at stake. At that time we thought of nothing else. Whether that was the product of propaganda or sense of duty or something else is of secondary importance. That was the situation. I wasn't the only one; there were millions; otherwise, the German nation wouldn't have held out for so many years against so many armies and so many powers. I'm not trying to put heroic ideas on record—I'm far from all that today, fifteen years later—but our attitude then was very different from what it is today.

Less: But why do you think differently today?

Eichmann: It was only after 1945 that I saw I wasn't the only one who had revised his way of thinking. Some chucked the whole business overboard from one day to the next. It seemed to me that such people had no better . . . er . . . no better moral values than the ones who made a show of loyalty during the war but actually thought differently. But there were also people who thought the matter over and who struggled . . . yes, struggled, that's the word . . . with themselves. I too had an inner struggle. I shifted to a different stage only gradually and it took me a long long time to arrive at my present attitude. Herr Hauptmann, to be perfectly frank, it took me a very long time. To tell the truth, it took a rocket landing on the moon. From then on, a radical change occurred inside me . . . . I didn't bring it about, it happened automatically as I thought over this whole complex, the whole war complex, the whole nation complex, nationalism and all that. Up until May 8 1945, I rejected and despised it, because I couldn't break my oath and my only alternative would have been to shoot myself.

Commentator: Despite his talk about suicide, Eichmann did his best to avoid dying for Führer, Folk, and Fatherland. He went to great lengths to survive the Third Reich. He denies that he disappeared at the end of the war, but this is only his way of implying that he did not feel guilty. Of course he knew that the victors would put him on trial. Allegedly, he despised his friends who at the collapse went underground with forged papers. But he himself went underground in Germany, with forged papers and an assumed name, and remained there until the spring of 1950. In the spring of 1945 he made his way from Aussee to Ulm under the identity of Adolf Barth, a corporal in the Luftwaffe. He was captured by the Americans but when US Army Intelligence began to question him, he managed to escape. He did not go far. As SS Oberscharführer Adolf Barth, he landed in another American POW camp at Weiden in the Palatinate. There he transformed himself into SS Untersturmführer Eckmann, who again escaped, and under the name of Otto Heninger took refuge with a peasant in Prien on the Chiemsee in Bavaria. In March 1946, this Otto Heninger, born in Breslau (where the records had presumably been destroyed), registered as a forestry worker with the police in the Lower Saxon town of Eversen, and soon found work. His employer was bankrupted by the currency reform, but Eichmann stayed in the region. In Altensalzkoth near Celle, he leased a piece of land, on which he raised chickens. By the spring of 1950 he had saved enough for his long-planned ocean voyage. He slipped across the border from Austria to Italy and there obtained a passport in the name of Ricardo Klement. Obtaining a visa from the Argentine consul in Genoa, he set sail for Buenos Aires on July 14 1950. In the land of the dictator Juan Perón, where many of his fellow National Socialists had already sought refuge, he felt safe from pursuit.

Less: Would you please take a look at this photograph? Is it your picture?

Eichmann: Yes. It was taken in Argentina.

Less: In what year?

Eichmann: Hmm, that must have been . . . in Tucuman, I think . . . . Yes, I can tell by the suit, in Tucuman. That would make it about . . . 1951 or 1952. No, not 1952. Yes, '51 I think. '50 or '51.

Less: And you wrote this? The handwriting is yours? 'Adolf Eichmann, SS Obersturmführer, Ret.'

Eichmann: Oh yes. I can't remember for whom I wrote that. Maybe for Geller. Maybe he wanted it.

Less: Who was Geller?

Eichmann: Geller—I went over with him—was another SS man, a Standartenführer. But now it occurs to me, it wasn't necessarily Geller. It may have been someone else. A close friend. Not a

195

female, no, it was a . . . male, and I remember vaguely, he absolutely wanted me to . . . write my rank underneath.

Less: [ironically] I see.

Eichmann: I can't remember aut / . . autographing this picture like a movie star. No, I can sooner see myself writing my name on the back. This is a picture I had to have taken, I think, for the Capri Company personnel records; the original wasn't as big as this reproduction.

Less: But the picture does date approximately from 1950 or 1951?

Commentator: The tribunal is in possession of a second photograph of Eichmann. It shows him and two other men in civilian clothing leaning against the railing of the ship that was taking these fugitive SS men to South America. The Capri Company worked for the Argentine government, prospecting for water-power sites and planning hydroelectric plants. Most of its employees were Germans who had left Germany after the war. Now provided with an Argentine passport, the experienced organizer Ricardo Klement supervised a crew of native workers and was soon making enough money to send for his family. At the end of June 1952, Vera Eichmann, resident in Aussee, and her sons Klaus, Dieter, and Horst, set out for Genoa, Buenos Aires, and Tucuman. At first Eichmann's sons knew him as Uncle Ricardo. They kept their family name, and their mother used her maiden name. When the Capri Company failed for want of government commissions, Ricardo Klement moved with his family to a suburb of Buenos Aires—and took up lodgings in a house whose owner, Francisco Schmidt, a Jew, when questioned later on, had only good to say of his tenant. Successively, Eichmann operated a small laundry, worked in an office, and managed a rabbit farm. Finally, he was employed by Daimler-Benz where he rose in a few months to be a department head. He was soon well enough off to buy a piece of land and build a house.

Less: Your work in the war was top secret?

Eichmann: Since I haven't been a bearer of secrets for a long time, I am in no way bound by the oath I took long ago and observed to the letter until May 9 1945. From that time on, I have felt inwardly free, regardless of what happens to my person. I no longer feel bound by any moral constraint. So I see no reason whatever for refusing to testify.

Less: So you're concealing nothing?

Eichmann: One might be tempted to say that I admit everything, as long as—let's say—as long as it's not too damaging, but that in certain points, let's say, where the crux as such is concerned, I take refuge in lapses of memory. I must reject this supposition for conscientious reasons, because in my opinion that would be tantamount to a cowardly evasion.

Less: So you haven't glossed anything over?

Eichmann: About a year and a half ago, a friend who had come back from a trip to Germany told me that among certain sections of the German youth a sense of guilt was being felt; certain guilt complexes had emerged about all those events. To me this fact was a boundary stone, so to speak, the same as when I heard about the first human rocket landing on the moon. It became a cardinal point in my inner life, with many thoughts circling around it. It was this realization that made me refuse to escape prosecution by flight when I couldn't help seeing that I was surrounded by spies and, so to speak, that the noose around me was drawing tighter and tighter. First I read in the paper how Israeli Prime Minister Ben-Gurion had issued the order to look for me. Secondly, I heard about a commando making inquiries in my neighbourhood about building a sewing-machine factory. They wanted to buy land. But in that particular area there was neither electric current nor fresh water. And then I found out that —to judge by their language at least—they were probably North American Jews. I had a marvellous way of going underground again. But I didn't do it; I just went on with my work and allowed fate overtake me. With the certificates and papers I had, I could easily have found employment in some Argentine government institution, in Patagonia, for instance. I rejected that idea, because I said to myself that I no longer had the right to disappear, especially after being so impressed by what I'd heard about the guilt felt by the German youth.

Commentator: Various people have claimed the glory of having discovered Adolf Eichmann's hiding place and bringing him to justice. One is Simon Wiesenthal, who describes himself as an 'Eichmann hunter'; for many years he followed various trails and came out with a number of conjectures. But he went to Argentina too late. Another was the journalist Tuvia Friedmann, who had been persecuted by the Nazis in his native Poland and sent to a concentration camp. The fact is that before the end of 1959 agents of the Israeli Secret Service had begun to shadow Ricardo Klement in Olivos, a suburb of Buenos Aires. It was Fritz Bauer, the late Frankfurt prosecuting attorney who first directed his Israeli colleagues to Argentina; but it was not until March 1960 that they had proof that this man was really Adolf Eichmann. Preparations had already been made for the kidnapping when the family moved into their newly built house in the outskirts. There, between his house and the nearest bus stop, Klement was dragged into a car, taken to a hiding place, and asked: 'What is your name?' He replied: 'I am Adolf Eichmann. And you are Israelis?' That was on May 11 1960. For the next few days he was held prisoner, most of the time under heavy sedation. On the evening of May 20, he was driven to the airport, placed in a wheelchair, represented as a wealthy invalid who wished to die in the Promised Land, and rolled aboard an Israeli commercial aircraft, which had flown to Buenos Aires expressly to take delivery of Adolf Eichmann. On May 23 1961 an Israeli magistrate read him the indictment, accusing him 'of having in the years from 1938 to 1945 caused the deaths of millions of Jews in the occupied territories.' He was asked: 'Do you plead guilty?' He replied: 'I have nothing to say except that I am not responsible for the events of which I am accused. I shall prove it in due time.'

Less: I would now like to read you a few passages from the German periodical *Stern*. The issue of July 9 1960 contains an article about you. I'll only read you a few bits. Here it says: 'And so he writes'—meaning you—'on the title page of Dr Fritz Kahn's book, *The Atom*: "I mentally digested this book and found it a magnificent confirmation of the National Socialist religion and theism; and because this faith is remotely related to the Communist doctrine of matter, that is, to Leninist materialism, I warned my children against lumping them all together. Leninist-Marxist doctrine teaches materialism. It is cold and lifeless. Theism, on the other hand, is loving, natural, and always alive. But unfortunately I must fear that considering the ignorance of my three sons all this will be no more than empty chaff."' Do you remember anything like that?

Eichmann: My house must have been searched after I was dragged away. That's what I infer. I know I wrote that thing. Because my sons were so absolutely uninterested in their . . . their . . . let's say faculties for spiritual development; I wrote that as a warning to them.

Less: The article goes on to say: 'He told them the excuse and justification he had prepared for himself. He said their father was wanted, that he was accused of hideous crimes, but that the accusation was not true. He has only been a conscientious official, who did what he was ordered to do but never killed anyone.' It continues: 'With friends he admits who he is, engages in endless conversations, and reads everything that has been published since the war about his field of activity, the "Jewish question". He clings desperately to the one remaining justification for his actions: his oath to the flag, his sense of duty and obedience. And everyone who in the last hours of the Thousand Year Reich put human feeling above unconditional obedience is the object of Eichmann's irreconcilable hatred. He has read Gerhard Boldt's book *The Last Days of the Reich Chancellery*, and discovered that Boldt, the author, was not obedient to his Führer down to the last comma. The blurb begins with the words: "In January 1945, a young front-line officer. . . ." Eichman crosses out "front line officer" and writes in "scoundrel", "traitor", "skunk". Wherever

Boldt's name appears in the book, he adds "scoundrel", "traitor", or "skunk". Where Boldt writes that in the last days of the National Socialist Reich high SS leaders, who had been haughty and arrogant up until then, suddenly shrivelled and appealed to anyone who would listen for sympathy, Eichmann makes the marginal note: "The author is a stupid ass-hole. The swine's name is Boldt."

'In another passage Eichmann writes: "The author should be skinned alive for his treachery. With scoundrels of his ilk the war was bound to be lost." And finally, on the last pages of the book, Eichmann's resumé:
1. "Every man is entitled to live as he pleases.
2. But then he has no right to call himself an officer, because
3. Officer = fulfilment of duty as specified in the soldier's oath."

'There we have it again, "fulfilment of duty", that straw he clings to and in defence of which he develops a passion and a vocabulary with which he was not yet familiar in the days when he was coldly and with murderous precision helping to solve the "Jewish question".'

Did you make such marginal notes?

Eichmann: I did. But it's disgusting of the man to speak of a straw with which he was not yet familiar at that time. It has always been familiar to me. In fact it's my norm. I have taken Kant's Categorical Imperative as my norm; I did long ago. I have ordered my life by that imperative, and continued to do so in my sermons to my sons when I realized that they were letting themselves go. In view of their laziness, their *désintéressement* about the future of their education, I tried to make them see reason with strong words . . . . Sometimes when reading a book . . . I was seized with righteous indignation, and in that mood I reached for a pencil and wrote what seemed significant to me at the moment.

Less: The *Stern* article goes on: 'Friends and acquaintances who spoke with him in Argentina at that time describe him as a man who had gone to pieces, who recognized his unspeakable guilt, but who, instead of confessing it to himself, cast about with an obstinate rage for formal justifications, to avoid having to condemn himself.'

Eichmann: That's not true. That's . . . that's . . . journalistic rubbish.

Less: And now this: 'Eichmann's conscience . . . . "I'm getting sick and tired," he writes, "of living the life of an anonymous wanderer between two worlds. The voice of my heart, which no man can escape, has always whispered to me to look for peace. I would also like to be at peace with my former enemies. Maybe that is a part of the German character. I would be only too glad to surrender to the German authorities, if I were not obliged to consider that people may still be too much interested in the political aspect of the matter to permit a clear, objective outcome. Far be it from me to doubt that a German court would arrive at a just verdict, but I am not at all clear about the juridical status that would be accorded today to a former receiver of orders, whose duty it was to be loyal to his oath and to carry out the orders and instructions given him. I was no more than a faithful, decent, correct, conscientious, and enthusiastic member of the SS and of Reich Security Headquarters, inspired solely by idealistic feelings towards the fatherland to which I have the honour of belonging. Despite conscientious self-examination, I must find in my favour that I was neither a murderer nor a mass murderer. But to be absolutely truthful, I must accuse myself of complicity in killing, because I passed on the deportation orders I received and because at least a fraction of the deportees were killed, though by an entirely different unit. I have said that I would have to accuse myself of complicity in killing, if I were to judge myself with merciless severity. But I do not yet see clearly whether I have the right to do this vis-à-vis my immediate subordinates. Therefore I am still engaged in an inner struggle. My subjective attitude toward the things that happened was my belief in the necessity of a total war, because I could not help believing in the constant proclamations issued by the leaders of the then German Reich, such as: 'Victory in this total war or the German nation will perish.' On the strength of that attitude, I did my commanded duty with a clear conscience and a faithful heart.'"

Eichmann: Exactly!

Less: Did you write those things or . . . .

Eichmann: I can't remember where I wrote them, but the words are mine. I recognize the words . . . . Where they come from . . . I can't explain.

Less: And *Stern* goes on to say: 'This Eichmann was neither depraved nor unfeeling. According to his own credible testimony, he was rather sensitive. And yet, consciously and with open eyes, this man signed the deportation orders which for many hundreds of thousands meant death. He was a bureaucrat of murder and he knew it. At that time he had no inhibitions or any desire to plead the constraint of his oath. He must bear full responsibility.'

Eichmann: That last is journalistic rubbish. My attitude was that I should loyally obey my oath . . . that can't be changed and it can't be interpreted. Journalists, yes, journalists can do it. And novelists, they can do it too.

Less: Do you subscribe to the notations in your books?

Eichmann: With regard to the quotations I wrote in my books, I take the point of view that no one has a right to take an interest in what I write in my private books unless I lend him the books. And I never lent anyone those books.

Herr Hauptmann, may I, in conclusion, make some personal remarks and announce a personal decision I have made. I have stated here as much as I could recall in spite of the fifteen years that have meanwhile elapsed. Fundamentally—or so at least I believe—nothing worth mentioning remains to be said. But there must be, of that I am sure, any number of details which, if released by some stimulus, will rise up in images before my eyes. I wish to say that I am prepared to divulge everything, absolutely everything known to me concerning the events in question. I have long been inwardly prepared to make a general statement of this sort, but I did not know where fate would call on me to make it. As early as January of this year someone told me that I would appear in court before the year was out. I was also told that I would not survive my fifty-sixth year. One of these prophecies has already come true and the other—I believe—is inexorable. This alone gives me an unstinting inner readiness to tell of my own free will everything I know, spontaneously, without regard for my own person, which no longer matters to me. All my life I have been accustomed to obedience, from early childhood to May 8 1945—an obedience which in my years of membership in the SS became blind and unconditional. What would I have gained by disobedience? And whom would it have served? I never, at any time, played an essential, decisive role in the events from 1935 to 1945; for that my rank and functions placed me in far too low a position. Nevertheless, I realize of course that I cannot wash my hands in innocence, because the fact that I was an absolute receiver of orders has undoubtedly ceased to mean anything. Though there is no blood on my hands, I shall certainly be convicted of complicity in murder. But be that as it may, I am inwardly prepared to atone for the terrible events. I know the death penalty awaits me. I am not asking you for mercy, because I am not entitled to it. In fact, if it seems to be a greater act of atonement, I am prepared, as an example and deterrent to all the anti-Semites of the earth, to hang myself in public. But let me first write a book about these horrible events as a warning and example for the young people of the present and future, and then let my life on earth end. May I, Herr Hauptmann, give you this statement for your records?

Commentator: Eichmann shares the wish to write his memoirs before being executed with Rudolf Höss, the Commandant of the Auschwitz death camp, and Dr Hans Frank, who as Governor-

General of occupied Poland was responsible for countless executions. These two got their wish. Others, such as Dr Robert Ley, head of the National Labour Front, and Julius Streicher, the most primitive of all the anti-Semitic agitators, were not given time enough. Eichmann, it is true, left written confessions of sorts, but they are sparse and fragmentary, avoid concrete details, and were obviously intended to justify him to his family. Thus the record of his hearings in Israel becomes the most important and complete document concerning the character and acts of a man whose name, throughout the world, is mentioned immediately after Hitler's when the destruction of the Jews by the Nazis is discussed. But basically Eichmann—as the trial itself subsequently showed—was not much more than a receiver of orders. His acts were inspired less by his anti-Semitism than by conscientiousness, careerism, and love of power. It came as a bitter disappointment to him that he never rose above the middle echelons of the SS hierarchy, that he never had anything more on his collar patch than four stars and a stripe, the insignia of an Obersturmbannführer, the SS equivalent of a lieutenant-colonel. It never dawned on him that even despots tend to leave their executioners in the shade.

Two months after the last hearing, on April 11 1961, the trial opened in Jerusalem. The court for this special case was established by a new law. A number of Jews who had played leading roles in the Jewish communities of Berlin, Vienna, Prague, and Budapest appeared as witnesses for the prosecution. Eichmann confessed a large part of his deeds, but tried to justify them on the strength of orders from above. If he secretly hoped to be convicted only of complicity in murder and so escape with his life, the scope of his activities, if nothing else, made this impossible. It was a fair trial as far as the feelings of the judges toward this defendant permitted. The trial went on for seven months and in every session the sufferings and deaths of Jews were re-enacted. On December 11, the presiding judge handed down the death sentence. Six months later, on May 31 1962, Adolf Eichmann was hanged. His body was burned and the ashes strewn into the sea.

Edited and collated by Jochen von Lang and Claus Sibyll
Translated from the German by Ralph Mannheim

PETER WEISS
1916 to 1982

THE AESTHETICS OF
RESISTANCE

A s we walked back through the court-yard of the municipal buildings in Valencia, we were watched from above by the Empecinado, the Espoz y Mina, and the Priest Merino. They were the champions of the heroic eight-year war against Napoleon's armies: huge papier mâché statues propped up in carts that were filled with dried flowers. This year, they had not been wheeled out to the *fallas* on March 19th. That was the day of the great carnival that normally took place in the town amid the din of kettle-drums, whistles, pipes, squibs, pop-guns, and rockets. And, in this coming year, none of these grotesque puppets, put together in hidden court-yards, would pass rocking down through the streets in a clamouring torchlit procession to the Plaza Castelar. They would not go up in flames while the crowd danced and sang. Fire-works and explosions of a different kind would fill the night. Left behind here, the statues towered above us with their large staring eyes in a gloomy desperation. With swords and banners leaning against them—vain, splendid—they seemed to sneer at us as we left the Baroque hall. We were feeling beaten and disappointed: we had just been turned down by the military commission of the Republic because it could no longer accept foreign volunteers. There was no time left to train them; the brigades had to leave the region within a month. Again we understood the inconceivable: that this civil war might end without our victory. And yet despite everything, suddenly, on this bewildering day in the second week of September, we were not to be used. Unless we came up with something else to do, we were totally useless. At the Party office, we were ordered to take the transport back to Denia that evening and once there to try to board one of the ships for Marseilles. I found myself wandering aimlessly through the town, filling in time before reporting to the departure point of the truck convoy. And, as so often happens in Spain, I witnessed an event that belonged to the past and that was also strangely timeless. Off the Plaza de la Virgen, throngs of people gathered together by a side entrance to the Cathedral. I went over and found I stood before the regional tribunals who held their public sitting there every Thursday. To the left of the door, under the stone figures of the Saints, the judges, quaint in their capacious black jackets, sat on high chairs behind a semi-circular barrier of green wrought-iron. A brass plate was fixed on the back of each chair indicating the name of each water-district: Mislata, Favara, Rovella, Pautahar, and Rascania. The hearing dealt with disputes arising from the use of ditches and canals in the rice-fields on the low-lying land around Lake Albufera. The judges could easily have been sitting there centuries before: the same tanned faces—some of them old and wrinkled, some bearded—all of them attentive, shrewd, experienced, and full of dignity. Often, to the hilarity of those standing around, the judges showed their humour in answering a plaintiff or defendant, or in passing a judgement. 'And yet even today,' said a voice at my side, 'despite all their evident superiority, they still have to take the old property laws into account in every decision. Of course, jurisdiction in these matters is traditionally left in their hands: they are, after all, the only ones who know every wall and furrow. But, even so, the State, whether feudal or republican, is merely insuring that these judges will see to the preservation of the old regulations.' It was Ayschmann who spoke. A bandage was strapped round his neck, forming a cross over his chest and shoulders. 'Just a broken collar-bone,' he said, 'a few broken ribs, a concussion, a torn liver.' An exploding mine had hurled him five metres through the air against a wall. He was carrying one or two books under his arm. As if reporting back from some reconnaissance mission, he pointed out the exact place where they were purchased: in a second-hand bookshop between the Plaza de Toros and the long brick-work façade of the North Station. He dragged me away, eager to show me the illustrations in his books. We passed the alabaster gate of the Palace des Marqués de Dos Aguas with its dolphins, lions, and Titans. We walked through the city gate—its round towers potted with firing-slits—and across the Serranos Bridge over the broad, dried out river-bed. Flocks of sheep grazed along the sides of the Turia, which was now little more than a trickle. On the far side, beyond the high wall of the river bank, were fields and orange plantations. Ayschmann's gait was stiff in his bandages: he was heading for the orange woods beyond the outskirts of the town. We took a path that led among the trees, and sat down on a slope. Ayschmann opened a magazine, *Cahiers d'Art*, containing reproductions of the painting 'Guernica' in its different stages: the preliminary studies for it and the final version. The black and grey tones of the magazine's fold-out supplement gave us a good idea of the painting, which itself contained no other colours. The original was about three and a half by eight metres in size and had been shown for the first time last year in the Spanish Republican Pavilion at the Paris World's Fair. At first, the picture we held stood out oddly against the bright, unbelievably phosphorescent blue-green leaves of the orange trees. The picture revealed something new, something totally unique. The shadows and cones of light, the intersecting two-dimensional, elephantine limbs and faces, the severe diagonals and perpendiculars contrasted coarsely and violently with the deep, still density around us. The air was filled with the metallic singing of the crickets. Not a single sound could be

heard from the town. After a while, the composition—with its central pyramid and towering shapes—came into perspective. Without fully comprehending what was before us, we saw what was happening in Spain. In the picture, destruction and regeneration, despair and hope were forged into a spare language of symbols. The bodies were naked, battered to bits, and deformed by the forces bearing down on them: arms stretched out of the jagged tongues of flames; beneath the arms, a chin reared up in protest; the neck was elongated, the facial features distorted by terror, and the torso shrivelled to a peg: charred, flung up by the heat of the furnace. The stooping woman in the bottom right of the painting was struggling upwards out of the darkness and into the wedge of light: she was

just able to drag the stone-weight lumps of her legs and feet, and her hands flapped helplessly as if blown back by a strong current of air; her face, in contrast, was raised, and looked up toward the glowing lamp held into the room, clasped in a knotted fist on a swollen arm. The woman in the bottom left of the painting was a cowering bundle; one puffy hand hung down at her side, and in her other arm she held a dead child: its toes tiny and miserable, the palms of its hands stretched out flat. Above her screaming profile, a bull, with a pointed tongue sticking from its mouth, kept watch and under whom the woman had sought refuge: it stood there huge and snorting; its tail whipped the air violently; its head was turned and from it human eyes stared out to the front. Above the toppled statue of the warrior was the horse. The statue was a plastercast with frighteningly life-like hands: one was opened showing the lines of its palm, the other clamped round the handle of a splintered sword. The horse—although reduced to slabs of muscle, wounded with a huge gaping gash, pierced through by a lance, and forced down onto one knee—continued to paw the ground, and was, bellowing from its angry mouth, still dangerous. Extending from its swirling mane was a cloud-like arm; in a bunched-up fist it held a miserable paraffin-lamp of the sort you find in peasant houses. There was, moreover, something special about this ancient lamp: it was thrust in through the narrow skylight by a Nike whose other hand rested between her breasts in the form of a star. Her dominating face, swirling out of the infinite, flowed from the inside of a building and then made its way ouside under a tiled roof and past a white-washed wall. But it was precisely this outward motion that brought it back into the interior of the bare oblong room in which the apocalyptic event was taking place, illuminated by the electric sun of a kitchen light, against whose cold naked rays the flame of the pathetic oil-lamp was burning gently, undisturbed in its glass. Roughly speaking, it was these features of the picture which initially suggested themselves to us, although our understanding of them could easily have been quite different: every detail of the picture was ambiguous. Wasn't the gesture of the woman struggling towards the centre of the picture more humble than anything else? Didn't her empty hands hanging loose at her side reveal that she had just laid her dead to rest? And didn't the position of the hacked-off arms of the statue lying in front of her recall the bearing of Him who was lifted from the cross? Growing from the clenched hand with the sword was the blurred and flimsy stem of a flower. On the table,

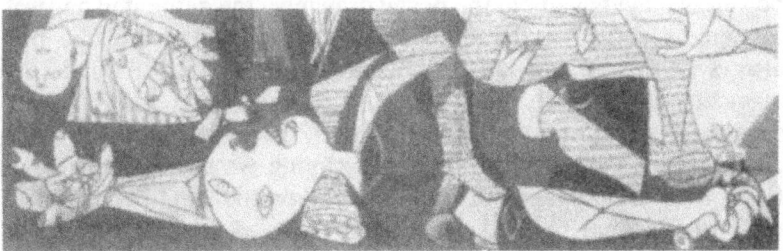

whose dark outline could be made out in the background, a bird fluttered—perhaps a dove—but it was deformed, with its bill turned upwards. The lines on the palm of the fallen warrior recurred as leitmotiv in the palms of the women and the child and again in the hoof of the horse. Everything was interrelated, linked together and subjected to the same governing principle, the same destiny on the stage of this barn, this kitchen, this banality fixed under the spell of unnatural forces. The initial versions of the picture and the sketches and drawings in the magazine revealed that the bull and the hand

rushing forward with the emergency lamp had dominated the vision from the very start. And since, with each version, the bull had become progressively more human and the horse more and more bestial, we concluded that portrayed in the Taurus we saw the permanence of the Spanish people, and in the rigid severity of the narrow-eyed stallion we saw the hated war begun by the Fascists. There was, moreover, a preliminary series of engravings that prefigured the thematic content of the painting, in which the horse was depicted as a loathsome monstrosity with facial features that recalled the Generalissimo, and the bull as the supreme, overriding power. And yet again, in the pencil drawings, the demented nag was repeatedly shown as battered and hacked down, while the bull always remained intact in all its triumph. A full study of the magazine did reveal, however, one or two rough drafts which suggested an alternative interpretation. In one, a small winged charger was shown flying from the gaping wound in the horse's torso, only to reappear gracefully situated on the tamed and saddled bull. In the final painted version, the winged charger was either entirely left out or else transformed into the dove. The wound itself,

on the other hand, was so disturbingly colossal that we were forced to focus on it over and over again. With a hole of that size in its side, the beast could hardly stay up and must already have given up the ghost. When we considered how impressed we were by the drawings with the Pegasus figure, we wondered if it wasn't precisely through its absence, through the alarming gap it left, that the artist intended to stress one of the main themes of the painting. It was tempting to take into account the general development of these accompanying pictures and thus to regret the disappearance of the Pegasus in the face of this universal suffering. But if we gave in to this temptation, wouldn't we also have to admit that those critics who demanded that a work of art inspire people to action would be right in censuring this picture for obscurantism and lack of unity? This, according to Ayschmann, was the clash of two different interpretations of realism. The agonizing disfigurement of a humanity burdened by destruction contradicted the Party belief that those involved in the struggle must maintain their energy and unity at all times. These drawings were grotesque. They were almost childlike scribbles, and were thus, it would be said, unsuited to represent the cause of the proletariat. The picture's antagonistic forces combined in this manner to make for a violent conflict in the mind of the beholder even before he had a chance to understand what Picasso was really trying to express. The outer skin of reality had been peeled away. Oppression and violence, class-consciousness and partiality, fear of death and heroic courage were revealed functioning in their full elemental dynamism. But, for us, what seemed torn apart, came together to form a new whole, and, in so doing, it set up an invincible resistance against the enemy. Even if the picture, with its horrible scar, attacked every form of life and thereby seemed to question the future existence of art itself, its effect was in no way undermined. In the final version, nothing remained of the Muse's spirit in this torture chamber: the artist had suppressed the initial inspiration—evident in his preliminary sketches—and had thus rendered the event more starkly and openly as a result. Nevertheless, our belief that the Pegasus was an invisible part of the picture was confirmed in a remark by Picasso we found that left no doubt about his working methods and stated that nothing, not even a preliminary sketch, was to be seen as lost or discarded. His whole life, he had declared while still at work on this painting, was nothing less than a continual struggle against the backwardness of thought and the killing of art. He was referring to the repression of the Spanish people and the restrictions of their freedom exercised by the forces of reaction. Picasso was putting the struggle for truth in art on the same level as the revolt against demagogy; the work of the artist was inseparable from social and political reality. The destructive forces that had been let loose in Spain were set to exterminate not only people and towns but also the power of artistic expression. In a different work, for instance, the picture series called 'Sueño y Mentira de Franco', we see Claudillo—portrayed as a molluscous figure with snouts—first attack the 'image' of the arts with a pick-axe, then, surrounded by barbed wire, offer a sacrifice to the god of money. Next we see him tossed on the horns of an enraged bull while those around him—their faces streaming with tears—follow the different stages of his duel between life and death, until ultimately only a woman crouched before the burning ruins of

213

Peter Weiss

her house remains, holding her dead child in her arms. There was much, however, that was still concealed, much that was still to be explored. The bombing by German planes of the Condor Legion of the Basque town of Guernica in the afternoon of April 26 1937 signalled that what was happening in the crammed space of this two-dimensional kitchen merely prepared the way for even greater devastation. A page of prophecy was held here under a dazzling glare. And since it was obvious that the bulb in the roof with its

twisted filament might soon burn out, the other, more reliable oil-lamp had been brought in as well—in it was the light of conscious-ness, the light of understanding. The initial sketches showed that the bull originally dominated all the other figures in the painting, but in later versions it gradually lost ground to the horse. The horse initially began as a felled beast, but later it gradually struggled back to an upright position, although always exhibiting its mortal wound. So as the war had progressed, the Spanish bull moved closer and closer to the possibility of retreat, while the horse remained in the centre, pierced through by a spear and bellowing rage in a hail of arrows. We felt compelled in our first impression of the picture to take it apart, examining it from different view-points so as to understand it fully by reconstructing it ourselves. This compulsion confirmed what I had felt since my earliest artistic inquiries. As with the crystalline shapes of Léger's 'Nudes in the Forest', here again I felt that the sharply edged objects that jutted against each other conveyed a power which forced the visual understanding to construct and reconstruct itself over and over again. Léger's language of green and violet cubes, cones, and cylinders representative of the wood, stone, and bodies in the forest suggested an existence wedged in between the roots and stumps of trees. Even so, the violent strain of this labour and the piston-like sinews invoked a world outside the painting. Viewing these cyclopses trapped in the earth, we couldn't help but see ourselves in the pictures—ourselves as cogs functioning in the machine. In the same way, the extended base-lines of Feiniger's houses suggested a whole town, and the flashing, comet-like shapes in the 'Tower of the Blue Horses' introduced a vitality that conventional representation could never achieve. Works of this kind, relying on surprising ambiguities instead of certainties predetermined by a specific point of view, disclosed considerably more about the mechanics of our existence than was ever possible in any static arrangement. They invited the imagination to look for connections and comparisons. It was perfectly comprehensible to me that the destruction of Guernica should take place on the square flagstones of a kitchen. It was in fact in the same kind of room that I myself had realized that there could be no division between the essence of art and social and political phenomena. 'But didn't you always feel handicapped beside the other students who had nothing in the way of their studies?' asked Ayschmann. His question took me by surprise and upset an intellectual equality between us that was, on my part, a pretence. I had no solid intellectual background. My learning had been acquired in bouts of sporadic reading. I had no school or univeristy diploma. On the other hand, I had proved my worth in factories, workshops, and warehouses. For a moment, I felt hostile towards Ayschmann, who had naturally taken full advantage of his easy access to an academic training. Inwardly, I revolted against his world, but I also felt ashamed by what I was feeling as Ayschmann's question obviously arose from a spirit of mutual fellowship. 'We didn't see ourselves as inferior at all,' I said. 'In fact with our practical experience, we often felt above the other students. After all, what they learned from books was not beyond our reach, whereas they had none of our basic training.' We understood the notion of the intellectual in a much wider sense. When we spoke of the intelligentsia at home, we referred to anybody who had the ability to think independently. Nevertheless, Ayschmann was quite right: there was an abyss between us. I was self-educated. Had I come from a family with money, my development would have been different. For that reason, my parents' determination to make literature a natural part of my surroundings had to be regarded as important and special. At school, until I was twelve, I was at the mercy of a system intent on producing only factory-fodder. Not one of the teachers would have taken it upon himself to encourage the talent that each of us possessed. As working-class children, we were destined for nullity; the slightest suggestion of a questioning mind was beaten down with fists and canings. Yet even so, when my father came home tired from work, he still managed to sit down at the table and discuss various books with me. It was he who encouraged me to go to the library. And he himself would bring back books from the sections of the library that were closed to children. Reading and studying reproductions of art became an everyday part of existence. Literature was a necessity. I began to see that without it, life would be impossible. I couldn't say exactly when my interest in books had been awoken for the first time. There were always travelogues, biographies, and documents relating to important discoveries and historical events lying around in our kitchen. Page by page, I absorbed these books. Their content kept me company even in my dreams. Ayschmann felt my experience was probably exceptional. But he had always believed that it was possible to commit yourself fully to literature, philosophy, and art no matter where you came from. The capacity for thought was universal. It had always annoyed us that we were regarded as incapable of intellectual activity after the day's work. We were workers; we had set out to create our own cultural foundations. The suggestion that this could only be achieved under special conditions was, to us, discriminatory and patronizing. That we, no better or cleverer than anyone else, were capable of study and research was surely proof that anyone could do it. It was merely the motivation that was sometimes lacking—a motivation that was discouraged in schools and later discouraged by the trade unions which inculcated only a petit-bourgeois complacency. In conditions like these, we were forced to win what was rightfully ours only by the strength of our own exertions. That is what I meant when I said that it was nothing but my father's own initiative that had driven him to take the step from slavery to the Age of Science. His only help was in the firm knowledge that this was his right. Since his biggest concern was the understanding of art and literature, he often became violently angry with the populist material that had been edited and simplified to suit our demands. Ayschmann asked whether it really had arisen from our most deeply held convictions. The best reply was in remembering that I, along with a few close friends, had realized that this was indeed the right approach. At the same time, we had received some assistance: we attended a progressive school, even if it was only for a short time, which we considered a privilege. All the same, it was certainly excruciating to have to depend on help of that kind. The kitchen lamp had lit up a world for us in which everything we imagined took on concrete shape; our thoughts took us far away to a *Finisterre* where meetings took place with mythological phenomena. It was in much the same way that we found that the connection between Picasso's war-horse and the shattered, plaster-cast warrior led us to other thoughts, other metamorphoses: the horse and warrior had begun, in the preliminary studies, as separate entities, but had by the end, perished together as one body, battered into pieces, with the form of the woman and her dead child torn from the wound. Male and female merged into one here, and we were reminded of Pegasus springing from Medusa's body. We could recognize Medusa's dreadful visage and petrifying look, in the face of the horse as well as in that of the warrior. Perseus had killed the Gorgon by keeping his head turned from her, only looking at her distorted features in a mirror, and this was a device that Picasso had adopted for his own use. The source of the violence—the attacker—was invisible in Picasso's picture. Only the subjugation could be seen; only the sufferers were revealed. Naked and unprotected, they were delivered into the hands of an invisible enemy with immeasureable power. Perseus, Dante, and Picasso remained unscathed while handing down what their mirrors had caught—the head of Medusa, the circles of the Inferno, and the rout of Guernica. The imagination would continue to live for as long as human resistance continued. But the invisible enemy would not simply be content with material destruction; it demanded the total annihilation of the moral foundations as well. It is important that the aggressor does not remain hidden in a vacuum but that he is recognizably portrayed—on this we both agreed. This did not mean, however, that the medium of artistic expression shouldn't represent complexity. We, for instance, were still unable to grasp fully the extent of the catastrophe that had fallen on these faces and bodies. These forms and gestures, squashed flat by the pressure of the blast, had been projected onto the screen by a light that no human eye could endure. Any attempt to explain what was portrayed there would obliterate the sense of the work. The more we were prepared to open ourselves unconditionally to this monument to Guernica, the more powerfully it affected us. The way its roughly hewn elements were put together gave us fairly quickly an approximate idea of what was taking place in the picture. Everything was firmly in place with every relationship simply and sharply defined. But as we began to understand what was really there in the picture—and the powerful forces it released—we felt we were looking at our own lives in which opinions and loyalties held us together on the outside, but in which we were helpless deep inside, beset by confusion, fear, and doubt. No matter how much we analysed our circumstances, we never got further than hypotheses, none of which lasted long before being abandoned. This lack of inner security, this instability, was the source of a type of thought that would disappear along with the last vestiges of bourgeois society and which had infected us despite the political alternative we had found. We had expended a great deal of energy in the fight against lethargy and bitterness in Spain. But when the collapse at the front came, febrile memories were dredged up: how initiatives taken by earlier workers' movements had fallen to pieces, how the struggle against the profiteers had been lost again and again, and how this ultimately served only to exacerbate the drastic dependency of the exploited. The number of the resistance was still not large enough, and for that reason hundreds of thousands had had to pay with their lives. All the same, what took place today in Spain was begun by the insurgents of Madrid in 1808, the French revolutionaries in 1830, the Communards, and the October revolutionaries. All of this—the powerful advances made, their collapse, the regaining of strength for a new leap forward—all of this was in the great painting of 'Guernica'. The workers in our countries had allowed the power to be wrenched from their grip two decades earlier. The reformists had merely helped to strengthen the position of the profiteers whose dominion had led to the most horrific perversions. The swollen, burst-open corpses, and disarranged facial features in Picasso's picture bore witness to this epoch. The painting screamed out in memory of every past period of oppression. The vision recalled another painting across whose centre was stretched a flying black horse mounted by a woman in a torn, flapping dress carrying a torch and a sword. Under the horse's hooves lay the naked and shattered bodies of the fallen. This was war—envisaged by Rousseau over half a century before—leaping over land-formations and pale, greying bodies. The face of the woman rider with its large, heavily rimmed eyes and gaping mouth, radiated the same horror that paralysed the inhabitants of Guernica. Picasso's painting could be traced back to the 'Pietà's of Mantegna and the Master of Avignon, to Beatus of Liebana's 'Apocalypse', and even to the Stone Age cave drawings. The fallen warrior in the foreground of 'Guernica' bore a strong similarity to the dead figure stretched out on his back in the 'Burial at Avignon'. The eleventh-century miniature of Beatus revealed that Picasso had taken elements of its composition for his own work. But the original eleventh century work was set in a landscape that was still natural: Picasso's was not: the fallen warrior, the horse, and the woman with her child are already preparing the way for mannerism and abstraction, while the dove, invested with the inscription 'Columba '— hope, light, peace—had flown from Beatus' olive-tree to the corner of Picasso's kitchen. His painting left no doubt about its origins. But the restraint with which his predecessors had expressed grief had disappeared. In this painting, no torment was hidden from sight. The tears had become needles and arrows that left cuts in the flesh. What was new and unorthodox became all the more significant, the more we were able to discover its foundations and origins. Ayschmann's books and magazines revealed the history of art to us as a history of human life in which the decisive stages of social development were visible. We found associations with our own development. Our thought had been considerably influenced by paintings and literary works. Times of change were often linked with particu-

and literary works. Times of change were often linked with particular artistic themes. Bearing this in mind, we found ourselves now, at a time when political struggle was all-decisive, thinking about the child in Picasso's 'Minotauromachia'. Unflinching, it raised its light up to the shadows; it embodied something beyond poetry; in its fragility, it represented a form of wisdom without which the monstrous rampage of reality could never be grasped. Paintings like this stood like sign-posts in the chaos of historical descent. Several other pictures caught our attention too. Delacroix's 'Liberty on the Barricades' was, like 'Guernica', composed with a central pyramidal structure which held all its disparate elements together to form a whole. The colours were reduced to leaden shades, to a gloomy umbra: even the red blaze of the tri-colour was subdued by screens

of smoke. The people's leader, this strong, half-naked washer-woman, rose up over paving-stones, wooden planks, and the flattened wax corpses of the fallen. She was carrying a gun and a flag, and her partly turned face was reminiscent of the Nike whose immense profile stretched across Picasso's painting. The fullness of the washer-woman's flesh, her fist clenched tightly around a sharply outlined gun, her strong thigh planted firmly forward—all these pointed to the moment when the idea becomes material force. The three elements of the proletariat stood around her: the workers, intellectuals, and youth. Ayschmann pointed out the man wearing a black hat, coat, and a broad necktie round his collar: Delacroix's self-portrait. We appreciated the picture even more with this biographical detail, for it revealed an aesthetic choice forced on the artist by the pressure of the times. Delacroix, who was more conservative than radical, nevertheless pictured himself right in the forefront of revolutionary activity—a role for which he was hardly suited. He was on his knees and turned partly away as if feeling behind him for some sort of support. He held his gun somewhat nervously in his hands, awkwardly fingering the trigger—a moment representative of his attitude throughout his entire life. This picture rendered a kind of wish-fulfilment, giving it, in turn, a strange dream-like quality. You could see by the astonished look on the artist's face that he didn't really belong there: against the intensely realistic background of the painting, he seemed hardly aware of his own actions and looked, in any case, to be on the point of contradicting them. Delacroix's vision anticipated the developments in the future. In the foreground of the picture was a street-urchin. Brandishing a pistol in each hand, the street-urchin had managed to surge one step ahead of protecting Liberty. The standard-bearer herself seemed invulnerable, and—while the statuesque figures behind her maintained a more detached, attentive attitude—the whole energy, spontaneity, and heroism of the scene concentrated on this child. As he raised his foot to jump over the dead—his oversized ammunition pouch slung from his hip—it was as if the revolution were already won. At the same time, this heroic confidence was precisely what made the whole scene so horrific. There was no doubt that this boy, so totally defenceless against the enemy, would be shot down a moment later to land on the very heap of corpses that seemed already about to envelop him. But, worse, the events of July 28 1830 were well known. The people gathered under the banner of Liberty had already been betrayed. Four years earlier they had completed the labour of revolt only to find that their martyrs had opened the way for more powerful classes. This time they were to be excluded once again as a new monied aristocracy and monarchy forced their way to the front. By the time revolution and counter-revolution had replaced the Jacobin dictatorship with the Napoleonic throne and had re-established the royalty amid the rubble of the Empire, large scale capital had established its unlimited power—was already entrenched in opposition to the barricades. In future phases of the revolution, the struggle would continue. But despite this picture's obvious claim to celebrating the grandeur of a bold historical leap forward, it nevertheless conveyed a sense of paralysis. The artist himself held back from this regenerative 'leap'. Weighed down by the burden of a Romantic and allegoric mode of perception, he remained behind in what was essentially an intermediate stage in the development of a politically conscious art. The future of these people, here seen pulling themselves together once again after having been ripped apart by enemy fire, lay before the bastions of 1831, 1834, 1848, and 1871; it lay in the conquests in the field of art that found form through Courbet, Millet, Daumier, and Van Gogh. Delacroix wished to emphasize that his own place was among the mutineers, but instead he recoiled in fright. He was closer to the bourgeoisie than to his heroes and was quite prepared to turn his hand against the uprising. It was, however, precisely this weakness that characterized the situation on the barricades. His pale features, the red band around his waist, a lop-sided top hat which gave him an air of insolence and then the nervous way he took his position among the others: these all showed him to represent that class which even in the heat of battle kept a sharp eye on its own interests. Like Picasso, he had succeeded in visualizing a moment in history, an instant of conflicting hopes. While the people under the goddess of Liberty bled to death, our dark and melancholy 'fellow-traveller' saw the end of his dream. The dream was replaced by betrayal. This was precisely what happened on that day in Paris. The workers had begun the struggle for their rights. Standing in their way, obstructing their path and tying them down were the oppressive forces of reaction. The climb to a more advanced historical stage was an endless toil. Once the heap of torn-up paving stones had been crossed, scientific socialism would be born, only to be viciously attacked, slandered, and undermined in the following century by a bourgeoisie who were

armed to the teeth. Delacroix's picture was greatly appreciated by
the self-named 'bourgeois monarch'. It had become the apotheosis
of his road to power, and had made its creator a well-paid servant.
In contrast Géricault's 'The Raft of the Medusa', which took the
Academy by storm twelve years earlier, had constituted a dangerous attack on the establishment. Seven metres by five, its huge size
alone threatened to overpower all the other paintings in the Salon.
Its subject, however—the selfishness of the government revealed in
the corruption and cynicism of those in its service—was intolerable
to the authorities. On July 2 1816, the 'Medusa', flagship of a
French naval task force bound for Senegal, had run aground near
Cap Blanc because of the incompetence of its commander and the
negligence of the marine authorities. The life-boats could barely
hold half the roughly three hundred soldiers and settlers on board
who were bound for the colonies. The captain, high-ranking
officers, and the influential passengers had taken possession of the
life-boats by force. The other castaways had crammed themselves
together on a makeshift raft put together from planks and bits of
mast, which the life-boats had been meant to tow: the rising storm,
however, had severed the tow-rope and the raft drifted away.
Twelve days later, a mere fifteen of those hundred and fifty were
still alive, the rest having perished from thirst and starvation or from
the fights that broke out. Although this disaster had occurred three
years before the painting was first exhibited, the authorities prohibited the mention of the name 'Medusa' in the title and hung the
work, described as a shipwreck scene, in bad light, high above all
the other pictures. The moment captured by the artist—showing the
mast of the rescuing frigate that appeared over the horizon—was
loaded with such provocative despair that representatives of the
Bourbon Restoration had rightly seen it as the first step in a revolt
against the régime. The reproduction of the painting in our book
was indistinct enough to put us in the position of those who had
attempted to decipher something of the work's authenticity despite
bad lighting and the height at which it had been hung. The survivors
on the raft were united in a motion that swept upwards and away
from the dead in the foreground. Each of them had heaved himself
into a more upright position than the man behind him so that the
whole grasping movement culminated in the dark back of the most

dominant figure at the far side of the raft. In this figure's waving hand, a scarf was blown to the side in a crosswind. The underlying

principle of the composition was the double diagonal. The current of excitement that spread through the group carried the interwoven figures from the bottom left of the painting to the top right, where the tiny mast was on the point of being hidden by an approaching wave. The other diagonal began in the bottom right where the arm of one of the dead hung overboard and drew violently up to the top left by the billowing sail, so that the direction of the throng of figures formed a cross with the direction in which the raft was being blown. The result was a feeling of vertigo. The raft was not drifting towards the distant ship, but beyond it. The sense of alarm derived from this perception was intensified by the sight of a huge wave that towered unnoticed over the bow of the vessel about to crash down on the survivors. Delacroix had placed his figures facing the spectator—only his own partly hesitant, partly coquettish attitude put a damper on the appeal to join in the struggle. Géricault had abandoned this form of direct agitation. Most of the castaways had their backs turned, were separated, wrapped up in themselves. The castaway facing the front sat with his arm slung around one of the dead, sunk in grief and exhaustion. It was as if the raft were seen from the standpoint of someone drowning; rescue was such an unlikely prospect that it hardly seemed to exist in the imagination. This sudden image of help to which every last reserve of energy on the raft had turned was so much a part of the future, so far removed from the world of the onlookers that it might easily be mere self-deception, a hallucination. A single catastrophe had become the symbol for a way of life. With their backs turned in contempt on those who had tempered their ways to suit the times, the castaways represented the casualties of a generation that had experienced the Fall of the Bastille in their youth only to be delivered into the hands of their oppressors. They leaned and clung to one another, and the sources of conflict that had probably brought them together on the ship in the first place had disappeared: the struggle, hunger, thirst, death on the high sea—all were forgotten. They emerged now as one mutually supportive unity, determined either to survive together or perish one and all. The fact that the one who was waving, the strongest of them, was an African—probably taken on board the Medusa to be sold as a slave—directed our thoughts to the universal liberation of the oppressed. Ayschmann had suddenly grown pale. He slumped forwards and the book fell from his hand. I laid him out on his back on the ground. 'Just a fainting spell, it'll go in a minute,' he said, sitting up again. Each picture we had been looking at for the last hour was informed by an awareness of the violence and speed with which life can be extinguished. We saw figures in these paintings who, like ourselves, fought not to be annihilated, who lay, kneeled, and crawled over mountains of corpses. Ayschmann said death was constantly at his side. These artists had managed to wrench an instant of continued existence from the overwhelming forces of destruction and to translate it into a timeless image. The effort involved must have been so great that it left an echo in their painting: something uncanny—the silence of held breath. I asked Ayschmann if he wanted me to take him to hospital, but he had opened the book again—this time to Goya's picture of the execution of the rebels. 'And yet,' he continued, looking at those faces with their jaws clenched in hatred and wide staring eyes, 'I feel no horror at the thought that everything which is precious to us can so easily be lost for ever in an instant. These feelings of closeness we have, which are so incredibly important to us, are only there as long as we live. It all disappears when we die. What I mean,' he went on, 'is that we only cling to life as long as we are aware of it. We can hardly feel pain at the loss of our own existence since we're not there to feel it anyway. You can only fear death if you are alive yourself and then you haven't any reason to fear it precisely because you are alive. The fear disappears with death which is why fear of death is absurd. If there's only one thing I've learned from life, it's never to allow my sense of awareness to slacken, never to forget that I *am* alive.' Those condemned to death on the third of May 1808 had but a tiny fraction of time left. The guns were already raised. Pools of blood glimmered in the light of a lantern which had been set down nearby. In front of the kneeling cluster of figures lay the shredded corpses of those who had already been slaughtered. A densely crowded procession of prisoners was being led up the slope. Some had clenched fists, others covered their faces with their hands. Those thronged together in the foreground,

however—workers, peasants, a monk—stood directly opposite the muzzles of their executioners' guns, staring back in wild defiance. One of them, wearing an open white shirt, stretched out his arms wide to embrace death. The tension, waiting for this salvo, was unbearable, because endless. The prisoners were pouring out through the yawning arch of the gate of a town which jutted out behind in dark silhouettes. The heavy brown-green of the night sky was taken up again in the coats of the grenadiers whose fingers were curled round the triggers of their guns. In the muddy darkness of the hour before dawn, the livid yellow wedge of a hillside penetrated the scene from the left to be sliced through by the bayonets. Though help was nowhere to be seen and though there could be no doubt but that the guns would resound with a crash a moment later, a feeling of victory emanated from the band of insurgents while the backs of the soldiers, lined up like automatons, were bent in anticipation of coming defeat. 'And why should we be afraid of death anyway?' said Ayschmann. 'After all, the fact that we don't exist before our birth doesn't disturb us.' Then, pointing out the man with the wide open arms, he said, 'Don't you think he expresses everything that can be achieved during the short span between birth and death? Isn't his gesture full of pride and superiority, leaving everything he knows behind him, offering up his body to meet his end in the full certainty of not having lived in vain? They all have the some look in their eyes. I've seen these eyes over and over again. At Teruel and Caspe, at Vinaroz, Benicasim, and Castellón, and I suppose my eyes had the same stare as I flew through the air before everything went black.'

Translated from the German by Iain Galbraith

GRANTA

MILAN KUNDERA
THE STORY OF A
VARIATION

1

When in 1968 the Russians occupied my small country, all my books were banned, and at a stroke I was unable to earn my living legally. Numerous people wanted to help me. One day a theatre director came to see me to suggest that I write, under his name, a dramatic adaptation of Dostoevsky's *The Idiot*.

So I re-read the book and found that though I might die of hunger, I couldn't do the job. The novel's world of excessive gestures, obscure depths, and aggressive sentimentality repelled me. I felt at once an inexplicable nostalgia for *Jacques le Fataliste*.

'Would you not prefer Diderot to Dostoevsky?' I asked my theatre director.

He didn't, but I, on the other hand, was unable to extricate myself from the sudden, strange desire to stay as long as possible in the company of Jacques and his master, and so began to imagine them as the characters of a play of my own.

2

Why this sudden aversion to Dostoevsky?

An anti-Russian reflex of a Czech traumatized by the occupation of his homeland? No, because I never stopped liking Chekhov. Doubts about the aesthetic value of his work? No again: I couldn't claim the slightest objectivity for a distaste that had taken even me by surprise.

What really irritated me about Dostoevsky was the *climate* of his books, a world where everything becomes sentiment. To put it another way: a world in which sentiment is raised to the level of a value and a truth.

On the third day of the occupation I was driving from Prague to Budejovicz—the town where Camus set his play *Le Malentendu* [*The Misunderstanding*]. Along the roads, in the fields, in the forests, everywhere Russian infantrymen were encamped. They stopped my car. The officer in charge ordered three soldiers to conduct a search. When they finished, he asked me in Russian: '*Kak tchuvstvuyetyese?'* which means 'How are you feeling?' or 'What are your sentiments?' The question was intended to be neither provocative nor ironic; on the contrary, for he continued: 'This whole thing is nothing but a big misunderstanding. But it will straighten itself out. You must know we love the Czechs. We love you all!'

The countryside has been ripped apart by thousands of tanks, the future of the nation compromised for centuries, Czech statesmen rounded up and arrested—and an officer of the occupying army declares his love for you. Please understand me: the man had no desire to criticize the invasion, far from it. They all talked a little like that; their attitude was founded not on the sadistic delight of rapists, but on quite another archetype: unrequited love. Why do these Czechs (whom we love so much!) not want to live with us, and live like us? What a pity we must use tanks to teach them the nature of love!

3

Sentimentality is indispensable to man, but is of doubtful quality when it begins to be considered as a value in itself, as a criterion of truth, or as a justification for a form of behaviour. The most noble national sentiments stand ready to justify the worst horrors; his breast inflated with lyrical sentiment, man commits the lowest deeds in the sacred name of love.

The replacement of rational thought by sentimentality produces ignorance and intolerance; this kind of sensibility grows into what Jung called 'the superstructure of brutality'.

The elevation of sentiment to the level of a value dates far back, perhaps from the moment when Christianity separated from Judaism. 'Love God and do what you will,' said St Augustine. The famous phrase is revealing: the criterion of truth is being shifted from exterior to interior—into the arbitrary sphere of subjectivity. The vague sentiment of love ('Love God'—the Christian commandment) replaces the clarity of the Law (the Judaic commandment) and becomes the uncertain criterion of morality.

The history of Christian society is a millennium-long school of sensibility: Jesus crucified taught us to adulate suffering; courtly verse discovered profane love; the bourgeois family made us feel the nostalgia for the home; political demagoguery succeeded in 'sentimentalizing' the will to power. This long history shaped the richness, the strength, and the beauty of our feelings.

But from the Renaissance onwards, western sentimentality has been balanced by the complementary spirits of reason and doubt, of playfulness and the understanding of the relativity of human affairs. It was then that the West came into its own.

In his celebrated lecture at Harvard, Solzhenitsyn put the beginning of the crisis of the West exactly in the Renaissance. Russia in particular among civilizations is expressed and revealed by this judgement, for it is precisely the historical absence of the Renaissance and the spirit that resulted that distinguishes it from the West. This is why the Russian mentality knows a different balance between rationality and sentimentality; in this different balance (or imbalance) is to be found the famous enigma of the Russian soul: its profundity as well as its brutality.

When this heavy irrationality fell on my country, I felt the instinctive need to take deep breaths of the modern West. It seemed to me to be nowhere more concentrated than in the feast of intelligence, humour, and fantasy which makes up *Jacques le Fataliste*.

(You might object: after all, wasn't it *rationality*, of the totalitarian variety, rather than irrationality which fell on Prague? Absolutely not; the rationality of Descartes and Diderot, that personal *cogito* which doubts and questions, has little to do with what is called totalitarian rationality, which is nothing but a system of impersonal syllogisms created to veil the naked irrationality which is the will to power.)

4

If I had to define myself, I would say that I am a hedonist trapped in a world politicized in the extreme. This is the situation described by the stories of *Laughable Loves*, my favourite of the books I've written because it reflects the happiest period of my life. A strange coincidence: the last of these tales, whose creation was threaded through the sixties, I completed three days before the arrival of the Russians.

When the French edition appeared in 1970, critics brought up the tradition of the Enlightenment. Amazed at this comparison, I repeated, with rather childish eagerness, that I did like the eighteenth century. To tell the truth, it isn't the eighteenth century as such that I like, it's Diderot. More accurately, the novels of Diderot. And to be still more precise: I like *Jacques le Fataliste*.

This view of the work of Diderot is certainly personal to a fault, but perhaps not unjustified: you may ignore Diderot the dramatist; at a pinch you may understand the history of philosophy without reading the essays of the great encyclopedist; but I insist that without *Jacques le Fataliste* the history of the novel remains obscure and incomplete. *Jacques le Fataliste* has suffered from being examined exclusively as part of the *oeuvre* of Diderot rather than in the international context of the novel: its true greatness is only perceptible when it is placed beside *Don Quixote* or *Tom Jones*, *Ulysses* or *Ferdydurke*.

You might object that compared to Diderot's other activities, *Jacques le Fataliste* was nothing but an entertainment, and that it was very strongly influenced by its great model: Laurence Sterne's *Tristram Shandy*.

5

I have often heard it said that the novel has already exhausted all its possibilities. I have the opposite impression: that in four hundred years of existence the novel has missed many of its opportunities: it has left many great opportunities unexploited, many roads forgotten, many calls unheard.

Tristram Shandy is one of the great lost directions. The development of the novel has exploited almost completely the example of Samuel Richardson, who discovered the psychological possibilities of the epistolary form. It has paid, by contrast, very little attention to the perspective contained in the work of Sterne.

Tristram Shandy is a game-novel. Sterne dwells at length on the conception and birth of his hero only to abandon shamelessly the story of his life almost immediately afterwards; he jokes with his readers and leads them into endless digressions; he begins an anecdote and never finishes it; he puts the dedication and preface in the middle of the book, and so on, and so on, and so on.

In brief, Sterne does not construct his novel around *unity of action*, the principle always considered inherent to the very notion of the novel. The novel, that great game with invented characters, is for him unlimited freedom of formal invention.

An American critic, in defence of it, writes that '*Tristram Shandy*, although a comedy, is a serious work, and it is serious throughout.' What in heaven is a serious comedy, and what is a comedy that isn't? The quotation is meaningless, but it betrays perfectly the panic that strikes literary criticism when faced by anything without a serious air.

Let me state this absolutely: no novel worthy of the name can take the world seriously. Moreover, what does it mean to take the world seriously? It certainly means this: to believe what the world would have us believe. From *Don Quixote* to *Ulysses*, the novel disputes what the world wants us to have.

But, you may say, a novel can dispute what the world wants us to have and still keep the faith of its own truth; it need not take the world seriously to be serious itself.

But just what is 'being serious'? 'Being serious' is to believe what you would have others to believe.

Certainly none of this applies to *Tristram Shandy*; to quote the American critic once more, it is non-serious 'throughout'; it requires us to believe in nothing: neither in the truth of its characters, nor in the Truths held by its author, nor in the truth of the novel as a literary genre: *everything* is in question; *everything* is doubtful; *everything* is the object of the game; *everything* is entertainment (without shame in being entertaining)—with all the consequences this implies for the form of the novel.

Sterne discovered the immense possibilities of *playfulness* in the novel and thus opened a new route for its evolution. But no one heard his invitation to the journey. No one followed him. No one that is, but Diderot.

He alone was alive to this call of the new. It would therefore be absurd to deprecate his originality for this reason. No one disputes the originality of a Rousseau or a Laclos or a Göethe, because of the debt they, and the whole evolution of the novel, owe to the discoveries of old, naive Richardson. If the resemblance between Sterne and Diderot is so striking it is because their common enterprise has remained so completely isolated in the history of the novel.

6

The differences between *Tristram Shandy* and *Jacques le Fataliste* are, besides, no less important than the resemblances.

There is, first of all, *a difference of temperament*: Sterne is slow; his method is deceleration; his instrument is the microscope (with which he is able, as is James Joyce later, to stop time and separate out a single second of life).

Diderot is fast; his method is acceleration; his instrument is the telescope (I cannot think of a more fascinating beginning to a novel than the opening pages of *Jaques le Fataliste*: the virtuoso shift of registers; the sense of rhythm; the *prestissimo* of the first sentences).

There is also *a difference of structure*: *Tristram Shandy* is the monologue of a single narrator, Tristram himself. Sterne follows minutely all the capriciousness of Tristram's bizarre trains of thought.

Diderot uses five narrators, interrupting each other, to tell the stories that make up the novel: the author himself (talking to the reader); the master (talking to Jacques); Jacques (talking to his master); the inn-keeper (talking to his audience); and the Marquis des Arcis. All these individual stories are told mainly in dialogue, of unequalled virtuosity. But the narrators narrate these dialogues while participating in the dialogues themselves (dialogue, that is, is framed within a dialogue), so that altogether the novel resembles a gigantic conversation in raised voices.

There is also *a difference of spirit*: Parson Sterne's book is a compromise between the libertine and sentimental spirits, a nostalgic invocation of Rabelaisian gaiety in the antechamber of Victorian modesty.

Diderot's novel is an explosion of impertinent liberty without self-censorship, an eroticism unhampered by sentimental inhibitions.

There is, finally, *a difference in the degree of realistic illusion*: Sterne reverses chronological sequence, but the events of *Tristram Shandy* are firmly rooted in time and place. The characters are bizarre, but furnished with everything needed to make us believe in their real existence.

Diderot created a kind of space never seen before in the novel: that is, *a scene without décor*. Where did the characters come from? We don't know. What are their names? It doesn't matter. How old are they? Diderot does nothing to make us believe that these are real people existing in a specific moment. In all of the international history of the novel, *Jacques le Fataliste* represents the most radical refusal of the illusion of realism and of the aesthetic of the 'psychological' novel.

7

The literary practice of the *Reader's Digest* reflects faithfully the profound tendencies of our time and makes me think that one day perhaps all culture of the past will have been completely rewritten and completely forgotten behind its condensed version. Adaptations of the great novels for film and theatre are by their nature really no more than a kind of 'reader's digest'.

It isn't a matter of defending the untouchable virginity of works of art. After all, Shakespeare himself rewrote works devised by others. But he did not make *adaptations*: he used a work as a theme for his own *variation* of which he was the sole and absolute author. Diderot borrowed from Sterne the whole sequence of events in which Jacques is wounded in the knee, carried away on a cart, and nursed by a beautiful woman. He neither imitated nor adapted, but wrote a variation on a theme by Sterne.

On the other hand, the transpositions you see in versions of *Anna Karenina* made for film or the stage are adaptations: that is, reductions. The more the adaptor tries to hide discreetly behind the novel, the more he betrays it. In this reduction of a novel, the adaptor removes not only its charm, but its sense.

Tolstoy (to continue with the example) questioned the nature of human actions in a way that was radically new for the novel: he discovered the fatal importance of causes that are rationally unknowable in the making of a decision. Why does Anna kill herself? Tolstoy used an almost Joycean interior monologue to demonstrate the extent of *irrational* motivations which influenced his heroine. Thus each adaptation of this novel tends necessarily, by the nature of 'reader's digest' itself, to try to make Anna's behaviour clear and *logical*, to *rationalize* its causes; and so the adaptation becomes the negation, pure and simple, of the novel's originality.

You could put it the other way around: if the sense of the novel survives the rewriting, you have indirect proof of the novel's mediocrity. There are in the literature of the world two novels which are absolutely irreducible, totally unrewritable: *Tristram Shandy* and *Jacques le Fataliste*. How could you simplify this genial disorder and actually be left with something? *What* would have to be left behind?

It would be possible, it's true, to dramatize or film separately the story of Mme de La Pommeraye (in fact, it's been done) but the result would be a banal anecdote stripped of all its charm. In effect, the beauty of this story is inseparable from the *way* in which Diderot tells it: *one*, a woman of the people narrates events that take place in a social world outside her experience; *two*, all melodramatic identification with the characters is impossible since the narration is continually and incongruously interrupted by other anecdotes and remarks—each of which is, *three*, analysed, discussed, and commented upon unceasingly; but, *four*, each commentator draws a different conclusion, since Mme de La Pommeraye's story is an *anti-morality*.

Why should I say all that? Because I want to cry out along with Jacques' master: 'Death to all those who permit themselves to rewrite what's been written! May they be beaten and have their ears lopped off!'

8

And I also want to say that *Jacques and His Master* is not an adaptation; it's my own play, my own 'variation on Diderot', or rather, since it was conceived in admiration, my 'homage to Diderot'.

This 'variation-homage' is a multiple encounter: of two writers, but also of two centuries. And, of course, of the novel and the theatre. The form of a dramatic work has always been much more rigid, more standardized than that of the novel. The theatre has never had its Laurence Sterne. I was therefore writing not only a 'homage to Diderot' but also a 'homage to the novel' as I tried to lend my comedy the formal liberty that the novelist Diderot had discovered and Diderot the dramatist had never known.

That is its architecture: on the fragile base of Jacques and his master's journey rest three love stories: the master's, Jacques', and that of Mme de La Pommeraye. While the first two of these are loosely fixed (the second very loosely) in the plot of the journey, the third, which fills the whole second act, is from the technical point of view an episode pure and simple, unintegrated into the principal action of the play. Just here, in this obvious transgression of the 'laws' of dramatic construction, I saw the gamble I should take: the renunciation of strict unity of action, and the creation of coherence of the whole by more subtle means: by the techniques of polyphony (the three stories are not told successively but mingled) and variation (the three stories are in fact each variations of the others). And thus this play that is a 'variation on Diderot' is, at the same time, a 'homage to the act of variation' itself, as was my novel *The Book of Laughter and Forgetting* written seven years later.

9

For a Czech writer in the seventies it was strange to think that *Jacques le Fataliste* (written in the seventies of another century) was never published in its author's lifetime, and so could be circulated confidentially only in manuscript copies among a limited intimate public. What in Diderot's time was exceptional has become, in Prague two hundred years later, the common lot of every important Czech writer, who, banned from the printing presses, can only see his books distributed in typescript. This state of affairs began with the Russian invasion, has gone on to the present day, and by the look of things, will last.

I wrote *Jacques and His Master* for my private pleasure, and perhaps with the vague idea that it could one day be performed in a Czech theatre under a pseudonym. As a kind of signature, I spread through the text (another game, another variation!) several remembrances of my previous work: Jacques and his master evoke the two friends of 'The Golden Apple of Eternal Desire' (*Laughable Loves*); there is an allusion to *Life Is Elsewhere* and another to *The Farewell Party*. These are indeed remembrances: the whole play was a farewell to my life as a writer, a 'farewell in the form of a divertissement.' Yet I lived through this time without the bitter taste of personal defeat, for my private farewell was so much confused with another, greater one which went far beyond my own: faced by the endless Russian night, I witnessed the violent death in Prague of that western culture conceived at the dawn of the modern age, founded on the individual and his rationality, on pluralism of thought, and on tolerance. In a small western country, I saw the end of the West. That was the great farewell.

10

With an illiterate peasant for a servant, Don Quixote set out one day from his house to do battle with his enemies. A hundred and fifty years later, Toby Shandy transformed his garden into a great mock-up of a battlefield; there, he gave himself over to memories of his warlike youth, faithfully assisted by his valet Trim. And he limped, just like Jacques, who ten years later entertained his master on a journey. He was as talkative and stubborn as Private Schweik, who in the Austro-Hungarian army a hundred and fifty years after that, amused and horrified his master, Lieutenant Lukăc. Thirty years later, waiting for Godot, Vladimir and his servant already find themselves alone on the empty stage of the world. The journey is over.

Servant and master have made their way across the whole of the modern history of the West. In Prague, city of the great farewell, I heard their disappearing laughter. With love and anguish I clung to that laughter, as you cling to fragile, perishable things, things condemned.

Translated from the French by Francis Spufford.

Milan Kundera's play *Jacques et son maître,* 'inspired' by Diderot's *Jacques le fataliste,* was first performed in Zagreb in autumn 1980. The first English language production opens this year in Boston, Massachusetts.

GRANTA

ARIEL DORFMAN
HOW TO READ THE
COMICS

Ariel Dorfman

U ntil 1973 I lived in Santiago de Chile, the capital of Chile. And every Wednesday during my final year in that country, I purchased a copy of a children's magazine called *Mampato* that I took home to read to my six-year-old son before putting him to bed. In many respects, there was nothing special about the magazine. Like so many children's publications, it printed a number of features that were meant to be both entertaining and instructive: nature studies, vignettes of Chilean history, puzzles, cut-outs, do-it-yours games, mazes, and a number of comic strips reprinted from abroad. The main feature of the magazine, however, was the adventures of the comic-book character Mampato from which the magazine derived its name and which appeared in a four-page full-colour section in the centre of the publication. Unlike the other comic strips in the magazine, 'The Adventures of Mampato' was conceived, illustrated, and entirely produced in Chile.

For Chile, 1973 was a special year. The Allende government was fighting for its life. So, too, was my family. We were desperate and confused, and had little time to spare—certainly not for idle entertainments. But every Wednesday I made a point of buying my copy of *Mampato*. For by that time, the comic strip was no idle interest. It was an obsession.

The obsession developed out of a sense of alarm. Mass-media fiction is probably our most dogmatic form of communication. The stories of romantic novels, the *Reader's Digest*, and comic strips— from the Lone Ranger to Donald Duck to Babar the Elephant—are hardly meant to occasion debate. The points they make are simple and unambiguous; the interpretations they demand are straight-forward and inflexible; and the readers they entertain are asked to be nothing more than uncritical and passive consumers. And it is for this reason that *Mampato* was so disturbing. As I read more and more of it, I began to realize the implications of its narrative extended far beyond the comic book itself. While Mampato went about the business of overthrowing his comic-book tyrant in the year four thousand, another far less comic force was setting out to perform an act that was strikingly similar: the overthrow of a man also branded as a tyrannical dictator—Salvador Allende.

In the episodes that appeared during 1973, Mampato has a girl friend living in a distant land thousands of years in the future whom he decides to visit. Her name is Rena; always dressed in the latest fashion, she is a slim, blond, attractive Caucasian with bright green eyes. She is, by the standards of Chile's affluent Caucasian upper classes, the ideal woman. Rena, like the other inhabitants of this distant land, is a peaceful telepath. Telepathy is a recent and significant advancement in human psychology because now 'all minds think in a united way,' and because for all the new insights it occasions, it hasn't destroyed the natural spontaneity and charm of her or her people. Unfortunately these people are unable to defend themselves against their neighbours who are 'malign beings' out to 'dominate the earth'. Like Rena, Ferjus, the tyrant of the neighbouring country, can also read minds. But unlike Rena, who never abuses this power ('It's not nice to invade private thoughts without asking permission first'), Ferjus uses his capacity in order to destroy his victims.

Both countries represent, in their respective ways, various aspects of Chile. Rena's country suggests the Chilean topography: high mountains, cultivated valleys, and a number of trees and birds indigenous to this part of South America. Ferjus's country suggests the shape: he reigns over a mammoth tree, as elongated and as slender as Chile itself, with its different floors (or regions) interconnected by a system of lifts. With its bucolic tranquillity, Rena's country is representative of the utopia Chile might become (or else reminiscent of the utopia it, supposedly, once was). Ferjus's country, on the other hand, suggests the more contemporary and infernal image of a house ferociously divided against itself. And this division is clearly the result of 'foreigners' and their foreign influences. Ferjus's disciples are yellow-skinned usurpers of power, with many of the physical attributes traditionally associated with villains: fang-like teeth, protracted jaws, small heads, and over developed, muscular bodies. These attributes are also, it should be pointed out, typical of representations of the working-class.

Moreover, the members of this yellow race have two other traits that are specific to Chile: not only do they look like South American Indians but they can be identified with one particular group: they wear helmets that are in fact those worn by the construction crews commonly seen among Allende's working-class followers.

Ferjus and his 'yellow' race have enslaved the industrious, peace-loving 'Little People'—who, competent and intelligent, manufacture the country's goods and till its land—and to succeed in this tyranny, they have had to rely on the help of the spying 'Rat People' (whose thoughts are so repellent that not even the mind-reading Rena can account for them) and the 'Anthroposaurus', a prehistoric monster of colossal strength renowned for his hankering for slaves. Most of the time, however, Ferjus has little need of either the Rat People or the Anthroposaurus as he can always count on the support of the armed forces, a mutant race of warrior giants led by their befuddled but good-natured commander, Gor.

In addition to his army, Ferjus also has two weapons: the primitive spears with which he originally conquered the inhabitants of the mammoth tree and an arsenal of more modern instruments: hand-held paralyzers produced by the Little People against their will. Around the time of Mampato's visit, Ferjus is about to embark on a particularly threatening enterprise: he is in the midst of forcing the Little People to start building an immense paralyzer so large that it will enable him to subjugate not only Rena's civilization but, ultimately, the entire planet.

With Mampato's arrival, the scene is clearly established for a traditional comic book confrontation, but the confrontation that develops is in fact hardly traditional. Mampato sets to leading the Little People in a protracted struggle for freedom, but, with the threat of Ferjus's invasion becoming more and more imminent, Mampato must work quickly. Intending to trick Ferjus, Mampato encourages the Little People to agree to the building of the immense paralyzer so as to give them the time necessary to plan a proper mutiny. Mampato is found out, taken prisoner, and escapes only when one of the otherwise peaceful Little People overcomes his own disgust of violence and uses a gun to free his friend.

Reunited, the outlaws (babes?) meet in the woods to discuss a new strategy:

'Those who have not accepted the rule of Ferjus are
many .... But Ferjus is very powerful, and the only thing
we know how to do is work.'
'That's it,' Mampato exclaims. 'Work will be your
weapon.'

The next episode depicts an event that is unprecedented in
mass-media comics: a general strike. In a sub-literature that can be
shown consistently to defend threats to the status quo and to reinforce
the dominant ideology of a country's established classes, a strike is
simply inconceivable. Never, in the history of children's literature,
has a strike ever been presented favourably. But it is precisely this
strike that brings the great tree to a stand-still. The Yellow men yawn
and complain. 'There are no slaves to milk the cows;' 'Nobody is
collecting fruit;' and—the effect that is most debilitating—'The lifts
are no longer working:' all vertical communication in this long
country has been cut off.

Ferjus responds in two ways. First he seeks a political solution.
The Rat Men, intending to spy on their opposition, ask for a meeting
to discuss the possibility of a truce. 'Peace and friendship,' they
murmur, brandishing a dirty white banner. They offer the Little
People assistance, but ask that they be allowed to keep at least some
of their slaves. They are given the boot. Next, Ferjus seeks a military
solution, and sends Gor on a surprise attack. But Gor is beaten by
Ogú, Mampato's friend, and while retreating is captured by a Zorko,
a vegetable mutant who 'surrounds and devours its victims.' The
rebels, however, being fundamentally pacifists, take pity on their
enemy and decide to free him, but before doing so, they offer Gor a
lesson in political ethics:

Gor, the mutants have saved your life. Remember that
you are one of them. In spite of that, you serve the tyrants
who have enslaved your very own people. Now, you may
leave.

It is clear, that in any future confrontations, Gor will join the
resistance.

**We interrupt this story to bring the reader a special announcement.
The issue carrying this heart-warming reconciliation went on sale on
Wednesday, September 5. One day before the next issue was due to
appear—Tuesday, September 11 1973—the Chilean armed forces
staged one of the bloodiest coups in the history of Latin America.**

Meanwhile back in the fortieth century, Ferjus is now forced to enlist the help of the Anthroposaurus who, after trapping Mampato, is about to devour him and his entire group of followers. But then the change comes. Gor, having learned his lesson,

has a change of heart and leads the other giants against their former masters. They are called traitors but the charge no longer has any significance; their loyalties are with their own people: 'We are also slaves and have been used against the other mutants.'

Stripped of his military support, Ferjus takes refuge at the top of the magnificent tree, swearing: 'We shall overcome. We shall overcome and enslave you in conditions worse than ever before.' It is perhaps worth observing that 'We shall overcome' is a direct translation of *'venceremos'*: the most important phrase of the Left in Chile and the slogan most insistently identified with the Allende regime from 1970 to 1973.

Protected in his tree, Ferjus is invulnerable and the resistance is, for the moment, at a loss. The possibility of emigration is rejected ('Search for new lands where we can live without being slaves'), and the Little People decide to carry on, somehow, with their struggle: 'This is our land and we'll fight for it. The Yellow race has come to enslave us and it must go.' At last, a solution is suggested. The giant tree, already weakened by the tunnels burrowed by the Rat Men,

allows the Mutants the chance of reaching the roots and destroying them: 'Ferjus and his cronies will have to surrender.'

But Ferjus never has the chance. A devastating tempest uproots the tree and knocks it down, killing—against the pacifist intentions of the good Little People—Ferjus, the Yellow race, and the Rat men; there is solace only in the fact there were no women or children in the tree. Justice is meted out—impersonally, inevitably, and unquestionably—by nature itself. Ferjus has, in his way, merely chosen the crazy path of self-elimination, and is rightly punished for his own evil.

Once again, utopia is possible: 'The tempest is over and the sun shines.' Mampato waves good-bye, and, with a crowd consisting of the Little People and the repentant giants, offers his victory speech:

> Mutant friends. The tyranny is at an end. You shall never more be slaves. Now, you must all work together: the little people, the workers, the giants, and the cat people. By labouring together as a united people, all mutants will have a future that is free, prosperous, and happy.

The end.
The end?

I have just summarized a comic that, between May and October 1973, told the story, week after week, of how an oppressor was overthrown by an industrious and peace-loving populace. That during the same period the same story was also being enacted, week by week, in the streets makes it difficult to dismiss the possibility that infant literature can have political implications. It makes it difficult to regard the relationship between story and history as a mere coincidence. The parallels are simply too striking to be ignored.

Allende was not in power one day, and ousted the next. To recover the executive branch of the government, the former ruling classes of Chile undertook three years of intense social mobilization, reinforced by an economic blockade from abroad and sabotage from within, and further assisted by many errors and divisions inside the Popular Unity parties. When, at last, the military changed its sympathies from the government to the rebels, major shifts in society had already taken place that invited its intervention. By then, Allende had already lost every potential ally that he needed to carry out his political program of liberating his land: the same allies whose tolerance, if not support, he had counted on when coming to power.

From every possible perspective—economic, political, and ideological—the working class, that had constituted the main inspiration of the revolution, had become increasingly and dramatically isolated. Every other group necessary for a united and democratic national front—the middle classes, the Christian-Democrats, the Christians, and finally the armed forces—had already gone over to the other side.

This tremendous shift was largely the result of the media and the cultural machinery in Chile, through which Allende was portrayed as if he were Ferjus and the Chilean people mutinous mutants.

A popular revolution or a *coup d'état* is not inspired by foreign companies eager to recover their mines and factories or by industrialists determined to retrieve their banks and monopolies or by a feudal aristocracy that has witnessed impoverished peasants take over its land. A *coup d'état* can only be carried out in the name of morality, freedom, and the preservation of the fatherland—the eternal values undermined by 'corruption' and international 'communist conspiracies'.* The crusade of ethical surgery can only be declared to be at the service of the silent people, the little folk, the peaceful, humble inhabitants of all social sectors yearning for the return of the 'good old days' when it was possible to work together without the interference of an alien hatred imported from abroad. But it is important to note: the elected government did not jail or torture anybody. It allowed complete freedom of the press. It obeyed every judicial order even when most were decreed by judges who, defending private interests, twisted the meaning of the law in their favour. It staged every scheduled election and won most. But it was precisely this elected government that was labelled illegitimate, unjust, vindictive: in other words, a dictatorship.

The former administrators of Chile's economy, the perennial

---

*To understand the full extent of the ideological offensive, see the anthology *Cultura y comunicación de masas: materiales de la discusión chilena, 1970–73*, edited by M.A. Garretón and H. Valdés (1975); also F. Castillo, J. Larraín, R. Echeverría, 'Etapas y perspectivas de la lucha ideológica en Chile,' *Cuadernos de la Realidad Nacional* (July, 1972), pp. 114–52; and Ariel Dorfman, *Ensayos quemado en Chile, inocencia y neo-colonialismo* (1973).

owners of its institutions, scrambled back into power by first projecting the image of a noble country and a pure race besieged by malignant anti-Chileans bent upon taking over the work with the assistance of satanic international forces. The image combined primitivism with modernity, stupid brutality with devious calculations. It required constant manipulation so the public would be insistently reminded of the potential terrors of the future: the monster within the working-class who, once released, would provoke violence, occasion a blood-bath, and mark the end of civilization. This primeval beast, merely waiting for an opportunity to attack, could be defeated only by the miraculous intervention of the army, the navy, and the air force: the only institutions left to safeguard the national continuity and identity.

The only way to deal with cancer is to cut, doctor, cut deep and never mind the patient's screams. Allende's downfall was ultimately perceived not as the result of a counter-revolution that would abolish democracy. It was not the result of a 'destabilization' orchestrated by Kissinger. It was made to be seen as the consequence of Allende's blind obstinacy. Or it was the product of tragic forces unchained from beyond. It was, in short, of the very nature of things.

The adventures of Mampato in the fortieth century must be read in the context of this ideological war. The comic strip represents not what happened in Chile between May and October 1973, but what the Chilean ruling class would have understood and now understands of those months. Mampato's struggle is the dream, the self-justifying, idealized way: the best possible account—for the ruling class and its children—of the destruction of democracy. Their objectives could not have been more honorable or more disinterested. But *Mampato* is remarkable not only as an expression of the aspirations and fears of the reconquering class, or as the perfect interpretation for the young; it is also important as a program virtually reproducing the same tactics used against Allende elsewhere in the media. The summary of one strategy easily serves for the other. Such a summary might include the following:

A government, with a transitory monopoly on military strength, has to be deposed. Insubordination begins weakly and doubtfully, at first. Passive civil disobedience is followed by appeals to the authorities to change their policies. Negotiations with the government allow time for the revolt to spread. Partial confrontation follows which the government surmounts due the loyalty of the military. A strike, led by the transport workers, paralyzes the country. The government's call for a truce is rejected. Finally, after invocations of unity, liberty, and the preservation of the fatherland, the armed forces break with their superiors and join the other side. The insurrection succeeds. Members of the deposed government have not only disappeared, but their very roots have been eradicated. The head of state's efforts to avert the obvious outcome are useless: each week he is more and more alone. Abandoned, he believes himself to be more powerful than he is, threatens everybody with an untapped, monumental force he has kept in reserve, accuses his armed forces of betrayal, takes refuge in a last sanctuary, and is ultimately killed in a moment of tempestuous and sudden violence.

We have just listened to the story of Ferjus. It is also the story of Allende.

Once a young reader, or an older one, identifies these two stories at whatever subconscious or involuntary level, he has been prepared to interpret the prolonged and bitter struggle to oust Allende from the point of view of the rebels. The identification is reinforced by a series of overt and suggestive parallelisms: the words 'venceremos' in the overlord's mouth; Mampato's almost verbatim renditions of the anti-socialist slogans of the time; the description of the presidential guard in a way that recalls the caricatures in the Chilean right-wing press of the Popular Unity partisans; even the Anthroposaurus—the ultimate threat—recalls the 'cordones industriales' in Chile: the regional clusters of workers surrounding the Santiago metropolitan area whom the Left threatened to unleash and the Right appears to have genuinely feared. I would not be adding an inessential detail if I note that Ferjus's labelling of his giants as 'traitors' and his retreating to his tree-top reminds us of Allende going to die in La Moneda (the presidential palace), which he then ordered the women to leave, and from where he conveyed his last defiant message. Once the good mutants are seen as the people of Chile and once the yellow race assume the role of the enslaving foreigners every other equivalent parallel falls into place.

These similarities between corresponding structures are not so surprising. Chile was, after all, being created, as if it were a distorted work of art in the hands of a social class and its allies, a work of clay on a relief-map in the National Security Council. And Chile itself was being modelled by the same forces producing the magazine. The reader's first intuition (rebels are good, government is bad) would have been confirmed in the measure that he or she was able to gauge an identical division in Chile's contemporary history. The ideological offensive within which *Mampato* was produced is part of an on-going struggle in the streets, the barracks, and the banks. If we can assert that Chilean history causes *Mampato*, we can also assert the reverse: Allende's downfall was orchestrated by countless acts such as the writing of this comic. Story and history overlap and mutually reinforce each other.

These observations have some bearing on the discussion of the genesis of the Mampato adventures. It is tempting to surmise that we are in the presence of a full-fledged conspiracy intent on using infant literature as propaganda to brainwash children and make a bloody putsch look like a patriotic endeavour. The arguments for such a view are persuasive. *Mampato* was published by the Lord Cochrane Company, the same enterprise which publishes *El Mercurio*, the most important newspaper in Chile. Since it was founded in the nineteenth century, *El Mercurio* not only has defended foreign and domestic interests of the ruling class, but has always been a constant counsellor to all Chile's governments. I should add that the Lord Cochrane Company is owned by the Edwards family, perhaps the most powerful oligarchy in Chile, with connections among many multinationals (Agustín Edwards himself was international vice-president of Pepsi-Cola). *El Mercurio* not only received funds from the CIA during the Allende period, but the media attack it waged against the Left was, it has been stated, directed by North-American propaganda-experts, specialists in graphic design and disinformation.* What could be more natural than to extend the ideological coverage to include the

---

*See Fred S. Landis, *Psychological Warfare and Media Operations in Chile, 1970–1973*, mimeo (Washington, 1975). For *El Mercurio* and its relationship with the Chilean oligarchy, see Ricardo Lagos, *La concentración del poder económico* (Santiago, 1969), and

inventing of a fable which would win the minds of the children? These suspicions are further reinforced by a curious incident. In late July, Mampato's adventures in the fortieth century were suddenly interrupted, and, for one issue, Mampato was dropped as a character. In his place, Ogú was offered in a self-contained episode involving a journey to prehistoric times. The episode bore no relationship to current events or the narrative that either preceded or followed it. It is possible that an unprecedented interruption of this sort was merely the result of unforeseen technical difficulties or delays. There is, however, another possibility. Several days before this issue was scheduled for publication, Raul Henriquez, the Chilean Cardinal, called for national reconciliation and, to avoid civil war, asked for a meeting between the Christian-Democrats and the Left. There were rumours that much of the opposition would enter the government by way of a coalition. In the end, nothing happened. But under these circumstances, it is possible that the publishers of Mampato's rebellion against tyranny chose to wait before committing themselves further to a strategy that would then have to be modified.

I would not be surprised to discover that the adventures of Mampato *was* part of a preconceived campaign. So many 'campaigns', among activities that have no obvious political implications, have arisen out of conscious, rational planning. It is not impossible that this children's story is yet another instance. But although the conspiracy theory is attractive, I feel it is flawed. It is not simply that it would be impossible to prove. There is no way we can confirm the North American or Chilean influences. There is no way that we would hear from Themo Lobos, author and artist of the comic-book series, anything but heated denials of the charge that he was working with others. But it is merely that ultimately, the conspiracy theory is just too simple. It is too easy, too reductive, almost intellectually slothful to suggest that each ideological expression, each new set of ideas, each manifestation of culture

---

Peter Schenkel's 'La estructura de poder de los medios de comunicación in cinco países latinoamericanos,' in *Comunicación y Cambio Social*, edited by Peter Schenkel and Marco Ordóñez (Quito, 1975), pp. 13–56.

proceeds from some Machiavellian, all-powerful, calculating entity that programs our lives down to the last detail. It is true—especially of the complex chain of production involved in the mass-media—that some planning is always involved. But this planning does not necessarily assume an overt and unremitting control over the contents of what is produced. It is much closer to the truth to regard stories like *Mampato* as representative of nothing more than the immediate and possibly involuntary response of artists, already equipped with the mechanisms of expressions and interpretation, to the new conflicts around them—the conflicts that they, like their readers, are trying to understand and make comprehensible. Indeed, the freedom to create without outside interference is essential to the survival of the system. The less an author believes he is part of a strategy that he does not control, the better his performance will ultimately be. The more his relationship to unbridled power is cloaked and velveted, the easier it will be to develop his own ideas and characters without restraint. And meet the deadlines.

The man who conceived *Mampato* was not that different from others then living Chile. Everyone was under stress; each day was painful, confusing, and disorientating. Many looked for the most traditional and reassuring ways out; there is comfort in conservation. For someone working in the media, this possible way could be objectified and communicated to others, and surely brought its author a satisfaction analogous to what others were forced to derive from other sources. His creation, that is, was merely another expression of hope, dread, and anxiety: because, ultimately, it is impossible to determine an author's intentions. He may have been imitating real events when he seemed to be translating the lorry drivers' strike against Allende in October 1972 into the lift operators' strike against Ferjus in the issue of *Mampato* that appeared in June and July 1973. Then again, he may not have. Alternatively he may very well have been anticipating future events when, a week before Allende was crushed, the armed forces in *Mampato* shifted sides. Then again, he may not have. It is impossible to know. We will never learn intentions; we can only witness effects.

I can illustrate the problem in two other *Mampato* adventures that appeared in the same year. The first, published between January and March, recounts the capture of Ogú's tribe. A 'red monkey man' has taken over Ogú's magic stick, the instrument and symbol of his power. Without his stick, Ogú feels helpless and is unable to reconquer his birthright, even though he is scolded by Mampato: 'Forget your stupid superstition and remember that it is your obligation to liberate your people.' As Ogú wanders helplessly through the jungle, he learns that his son has been captured and is about to be devoured by (yes, here we go again) a gigantic primeval serpent. It is then that Ogú regains his strength and saves his son. 'You don't,' Mampato observes, 'need your magic stick after all.' 'If I'm this strong without it,' Ogú replies, 'imagine what I'll do now that I have it back.' To which Mampato comments: 'Nothing is too difficult if you love your children.'

This episode appears during the winter of 1973, during the same time of the parliamentary elections that the Right was confident of winning. Their intention was first to win a majority in Congress and from there go on to impeach the President: a palatable way of overthrowing the government without the use of the military. Their confidence was in part derived from the turmoil of the previous months involving large-scale student mobilization against the government. In this context, Ogú's episode seems to be suggesting that, even though the 'red' barbarians have stolen the executive office—the main instrument of power—the youth, by going out into the streets, are showing the way toward recovery. There is no reason to feel helpless; soon the 'instrument' will be returned.

However, the next episode, appearing in the instalments published between March and May, is filled with panic. Allende did not lose the election. On the contrary, gainsaying the trend evident in not only Chile but most other countries (in which a new government invariably loses some support by the time of its first congressional test), the Left took forty-five per cent of the vote—nine per cent more than it received in the presidential elections of 1970. The effect among the Right was immediate despondency.

This feeling of despondency is evident in *Mampato*. Shortly before the election, and at the end of the Ogú episode, it was announced that Mampato's struggle against the dictator would be resumed—the narrative most obviously appropriate for the period following the Right's projected congressional victory. But instead, a different episode appears. Mampato sets out on a journey to Atlantis where he comes upon an endless series of disasters: a volcano is about to erupt and, while a number of other catastrophes beleaguer the natives, Mampato and many of the inhabitants can think only of escaping. Everything is lost; paradise is about to be destroyed by fire; it is best to emigrate. It is perhaps worth observing that a story depicting a hero defeated by natural disasters and hounded by fears of apocalyse is unprecedented in children's mass literature.

We seem to be confirming the conspiracy theory.

But there is a problem. There is no question that this episode corresponds to the mood of Chile's dominant class, but it is extremely unlikely that it represents its members' interests or (as history has shown) their intentions. Or, to put it another way: it is doubtful that Chile's most powerful class of people was preparing for defeat, and that the Atlantis episode was therefore used to adjust the hopes of the Right to a more realistic relationship with the political possibilities of the day. Emigration was not, after all, the alternative chosen.

The man faced with writing the script and drawing the characters of *Mampato* was caught up in not a conspiracy but the mood of the times. His work was a symptom of contemporary crisis; he was part of not a plan but a larger collective effort to imagine, to determine, even to conjure up a different future. Working within the dominant economic system, he was, therefore, in the position to show its strengths. His responses to current events were his own, but—safe, sanitized, and virtually pre-ordained—they were also the responses of the system within which he worked.

Explicit political control, I am suggesting, was not required because powerful economic interests made it unnecessary. What is seen as appropriate to the dominant system is retained—published, reproduced, broadcast—and what is seen as inappropriate is simply discarded. If, for instance, the story of Ferjus were published in Chile today, the matter would be entirely different. The story would seem incoherent and slightly irrelevant. There is, for example, no lorry drivers' strike against Pinochet and the President's thugs are hardly construction workers. Even so, most of the population would see *Mampato* as an attack on the dictatorship. More important, the owners of the magazine or the individuals responsible to the ownership would insure that *Mampato* was simply not published. It is only when a work strays too far from the frontier of tolerance, when it conflicts too explicitly with the existing web of beliefs, when it cannot be rewritten or otherwise accommodated that the real authority of ownership emerges.

Intervention of this sort, however, is usually unnecessary. In most respects, a work's success is directly measured by its lack of obvious purpose, its inconspicuousness. If self-censorship does not prevail, the genres of mass communication—their techniques, practices, and traditions—end up influencing the producer and keeping him or her within limits. It is important to remember that even here, these stories, while full of political implications, do not explicitly betray a direct, causal relationship with society. To go against the grain is political; to flow with it is entertainment. That is how the cards are stacked.

These forms of fiction ask to be seen only as instances of fun, and the serious issues inevitably expressed by them are not meant to be registered—at least not explicitly. By its nature as entertainment, infant literature is a guardian of the dominant values, a defender of the status quo: it is, after all, what the consumer has been led to expect. Like every other mass-media comic, *Mampato* is an example of conservative entertainment. But what makes *Mampato* interesting is the time in which it appeared; history required it to assume an unusual responsibility: a tactical role. The crisis in Chile was of such dimensions that it threatened to overturn and revolutionize the prevailing conditions of power and property, and the media, in its own interests, was encouraged to abandon its enforced voice of 'neutrality': it was no longer guarding the dominant values; it was arguing for them. And it is at such a moment that the relationship between culture and society becomes manifest and is laid bare. Manipulation was always a feature of *Mampato*, as it is in all mass-market entertainment; during the crisis in Chile, the manipulation was, by necessity, explicitly revealed. The magazine had drifted—either consciously or unconsciously—into the arena of everyday politics.

Mampato is different from most other possible examples of popular culture because, in this case, historical circumstances have revealed the giddy moment in which a whole

257

chain of mass-market production was forced to adapt and change to specific and identifiable challenges. This change under the stress of history is not, however, unique. What *Mampato* is forced to do with such urgent transparency is evident on a different scale in virtually every other media product in the world. Each has originated among cultural uncertainties as important as those that gave birth to *Mampato*; but because these uncertainties are not, as a rule, tantamount to a national crisis, a mass-media product's relationship to the society in which it is produced is not nearly as obvious. Whether we are speaking of Disney cartoons or Babar the Elephant or the Lone Ranger, it is difficult to identify the processes of the genesis. Their origins are obscured, and they appear like orphans set loose in the universe. But they are not orphans, and it is imperative that their parents be identified.

E ven though it is possible to identify and examine the origins of *Mampato* in 1973, an enterprise of this sort is nevertheless fraught with methodological risks. If it were possible to proceed in a similar fashion with every work of mass-market culture we would still have many pitfalls to hurdle. Is it not possible, for instance, that I have merely come upon what I was determined to find? Have I only disinterred those structures which I wanted to reveal in the first place? Indeed there are many people who will not only disagree with my interpretation of the struggles in Chile in 1973, but who also will reject the premises that I work from as absurd, arguing that children's literature, unless outright propaganda, has nothing to do with social issues. The only way I can denounce mass-market fiction of this sort as limiting people's capacity for understanding the world is, an observer might assert, because I have proceeded from the assumption of a dominant system that functions persuasively to victimize its members. The conclusions of my study, therefore, are suspect because they derive from a specific position that has led me as a critic to detect, perhaps even to reconstruct, in the works I am examining, precisely the ideological configuration I set out to find.

Accusations of this sort hold enough truth to worry me. I feel that my observations on children's literature and the 'infantile assumptions' of adult mass-media production reveal the machinery from which their ultimate effects are produced. But I also believe that

I have not gone far enough into the complexities of the incestuous association between culture and society; that I am not taking fully into account that I, too, am a product of what I am studying; that I, too, occupy a mobile place in both history and the field of knowledge. It is outside the range of this essay to develop a proper, scientific sociology of culture. Nevertheless I am still able to recognize that my methodology has implications that question my conclusions and that therefore limit their impact.

I am also troubled by another aspect of this debate. By stating that mass-media entertainment—not just *Mampato* but every other analogous work—is inimical to the freedom and humanity of those who read it, I am probably scaring off the very people I want to reach most. For while it is obviously important to develop a discussion of this sort among those who concur with my belief that the present economic and political structures are culturally repressive, I would much prefer to extend my audience beyond the circle of the initiated and the already convinced. But it is inevitable that those who innocently and insistently devour the products of the mass media will regard my re-interpretation of them as not only a disgusting and biased exercise but a threatening one. My only answer is that I, too, am a historical subject, as much a product of history as *Mampato* or Donald Duck or Babar the Elephant or the *Reader's Digest*. As much as the reader or non-readers of these pages. As much as any other author who might read these works as archetypes, myths, psycho-analytic manifestions, or simply entertainments.

There can, however, be no retreat from holding a position. For me, the only way to make contact with reality, to break the idols and the icons and discover the secrets they hide, is bring to them a view that is, in many respects, alien or even blasphemous. To be politically committed may prejudice my research, but this research is also an instrument that allows us to penetrate the deceptive appearances of our experience and to reach the truth that lies behind them. There is, I believe, no other way to advance our knowledge.

Mampato shows how readers were living a history as it was depicted in narrative; how the division between history and representation was not merely blurred but rendered non-existent. As such, they were made to understand that the death of Chilean democracy, the massacre of thousands, the denationalization of the economy, the assassination of the President were in fact part of an epic struggle for justice and freedom. They were not aware of the extent to which they were being indoctrinated because, like the millions of others who are consuming mass-media messages of less obvious origins, they were not able to consider that their innocence—and the innocence of their entertainment—was profoundly fraudulent.

If they had been willing to risk that innocence, they would have been able to see that it was Mampato who helped plan the coup, Ogú who was pulling the trigger, and Rena who was whitewashing and absolving us all.

It would have changed them beyond their softest dreams.

But that, of course, would have been another story.

Or do I mean another history?

GRANTA

UWE JOHNSON
AN UNFATHOMABLE
SHIP

I n the Thames two miles north of the Isle of Sheppey, there is a curious cluster of parallel slanting stakes. They are visible mainly at low water but they are also noticeable in an eighteen-foot flood tide, for behind them the surface of the water ripples away to the horizon in rapidly changing lights and shades. The visitor to the town of Sheerness at the north-west corner of the island may at first take these slanting stakes for eel traps—their poles leaning away from a strong west wind. Distances are difficult to judge over open water and the black triangle appearing between the stakes at ebb tide can easily be mistaken for the owner's fishing boat. Anyone attracted to the spot will need binoculars. He will be wrong about the eel traps. They are not moved once a fortnight and, moreover, the stakes, of unequal length, are at strangely regular intervals. Besides they are too close to the central waterway of the Thames itself.

The inhabitants of Sheerness are only too willing to tell a stranger. As if imparting a piece of confidential good news, they say: 'However dark the cloud it still has a silver lining.'

The cloud under which these people live along this stretch of the Thames is the memory of the flood of February 1953; it submerged wide areas of the island together with the town of Sheerness. Moreover it could come back, resulting in houses awash, sheep drowned, telephone junction boxes flooded, electrical short-circuits, burst gas mains, and the uncharitable responses of the insurance companies. After 1953, the possibility of a second flood was thoroughly discussed—the best plans were expressed — but when the flood returned to the island again in January 1978 neither the sea wall nor the warning system had been completed. People had to suffer just as they had twenty-five years before, except that this time there were no directly attributable human casualties. Such is the future prospect for this area.

The second prospect, the precious 'lining' to this dark cloud, is called *Richard Montgomery*. It is the name of an Amerian ammunition ship which went aground in the summer of 1944; as a result the ship sank, since which time only the tips of its derricks and masts and a corner of the bridge are visible. The ship is referred to simply as 'the wreck' or 'our wreck' or more respectfully 'the Grand Old Lady of the Thames'. To the unspoken pride of its admirers it appears as 'our only spectacle': either we go to the grave by flood or we go skyhigh in a fireball.

It is, pending this dénouement, well worth investigating this piece of flotsam and assembling the accumulated store of ideas which flow from it in various historical, cultural, and political fields.

Richard Montgomery was born in 1738, and he can hardly have seriously expected his name to be remembered two hundred years after his death. He was an Irishman who enlisted in the British service at the age of eighteen and did not sell his services to the American rebels until he was thirty-four. When appointed Brigadier-General by George Washington in 1775, therefore, he was hardly one of the most senior of his rank in the American army. Montgomery made his name at the capture of Montreal on November 13 1775, but on December 31st he made a fool of himself by attacking the fortress of Quebec with a mere 1,675 semi-trained men against a garrison of British regulars. The enterprise ended in complete defeat and his own death. Even so, this turn-coat mercenary had already become a General whom men would follow. Nevertheless, his fame was some time arriving: he had to possess his soul in patience until, during the Second World War, ships were being named after the fathers of the American revolution. The Liberty ship series started in 1941, but the *Richard Montgomery* did not go down the slips in Jacksonville, Florida, until 1943. Barely a year later it was a wreck off Sheerness, Kent.

There might be a subject to pursue here—the magic of a name.

A ship for liberty. The name 'Liberty Ship' was intended to be evocative of a national emergency, to be a symbol like the Liberty Bell hung in Pennsylvania State House in 1753 for the jubilee of William Penn's constitution, carrying the inscription 'Proclaim liberty throughout all the land unto all the inhabitants thereof' (Leviticus 25.10). The bell's first casting, however, was a failure and the tone was faulty. Though recast several times, it still got on the inhabitants' nerves, and as early as 1772 they were complaining to their new authorities that the solemn sound was heard too often. Nevertheless it was rung on July 8 1776 for the public reading of the *Declaration of Independence*. In 1777 the British occupied the city and the bell had to be hidden out in the country. It was eventually brought back to Chestnut Street and did its patriotic duty until finally in 1835 it split in half during the funeral of a Minister of Justice. In 1941 liberty, American style, was threatened by the German and Italian U-boats as once it had been threatened by troops from the city of London. Roosevelt's answer to the sudden loss of his freedom at sea was a massive ship-building program in the name of victory, of liberty.

(The story of the Liberty Bell has an Old World sequel. In 1950, after the victorious Red Army had called off the blockade of West Berlin, some seventeen million American citizens subscribed for a copy of their Liberty Bell to be hung in the Rathaus of Berlin-Schöneberg. Its inscription reads: 'That this world under God shall have a new birth of freedom.' Since then it has rung for two minutes every day at midday (as well as on solemn occasions). In the winter of 1965 the faithful press of West Berlin called upon the inhabitants to subscribe for miniature copies of the Schöneberg Liberty Bell (17.25 Deutschmarks a time) to be sent to the dependants of American citizens who had given their lives in military service in Viet Nam or whose death might be anticipated in the future. Clearly such a recompense for the gift of 1950 was intended to spread abroad an image—at least for the mourning Americans—of everything for which their men were dying in Southeast Asia: liberty dispensed or preserved under God and symbolized by a little bell—from a Berlin china factory—that was placed alongside the black-draped photographs on American mantelpieces).

The ships named after the genuine Liberty Bell of Philadelphia's Chestnut Street also made their contribution to a somewhat dark chapter in American trade-union history. They were standardized freighters and as early as spring 1942 could be constructed in sixty to seventy days (the original plan had envisaged one hundred and five days). Eventually the ship-yard of a certain Henry J. Kaiser in Richmond, California, needed a mere four days and fifteen hours to build one of these 10,490-ton, 440 foot-long ships. Adherence to a standard pattern, simplification of construction, and use of prefabricated parts attracted to the ship-yard workers who had never seen the inside of a factory. Wartime emergency and increased production brought the chronic unemployment to an end for the rest of the war. Since many of the wives went to work in factories the standard of living of the average family seemed higher than ever. In fact wages were frozen and heavily taxed while prices rose steadily. Strikes were illegal as a result of a voluntary wartime commitment by the trade unions themselves (it is worth noting that one-third of the members of the War Council itself thought that the trade unions were making agreements which must inevitably alienate them from the workers). The trade unions were responsible for renouncing their members' established right to double time for work on Sundays and holidays and they also supported Roosevelt's decree binding workers to their place of work for the duration of the war. If there was a strike, the government sent troops into the factory where work had stopped and threatened the strikers with immediate conscription into the army. By 1941 the trade unions had formally expressed their disapproval of any form of action on the part of the workers. By June 1943 a strike became illegal as soon as the State became involved. For their passivity, the trade union leaders were rewarded by a clause in the standard contract that required a worker to remain in the trade union until his contract was terminated. Finally management relieved the trade unions of the tiresome business of collecting their members' dues as they were simply deducted from wages and paid direct into the account of the workers' representatives, whose isolation inevitably increased as a result. The Communists acted no differently, at least from June 1941 onwards. They were the most zealous supporters of the strike ban, declaring strikers to be traitors and branding them members of a 'Sixth Column'. They preached 'speed-up': the acceleration of production; they advocated piece-work and a wage freeze; they even proposed continuance of the no-strike pledge for an unlimited period, outlasting the war. So the situation of the workers' movement in the United States at this time was the very antithesis of 'liberty'.

The Liberty ship at the bottom of the Thames also stands as a warning sign of another aspect of American liberty: the liberty to profit from other people's labours. Henry J. Kaiser is literally the incarnation of this system of liberty. He began his rise in the business world by running away from school in 1895 at the age of thirteen and working in a dry-goods store for $1.50 a week. When he died in 1967 he owned one hundred and eighty factories that produced three hundred different products in forty-one countries. He was worth nearly three billion dollars. On his way to the top, he had constructed miles upon miles of roads and motorways (two hundred miles and five hundred bridges in Cuba alone, all completed in four and a half years instead of the planned seven), dams, pipelines, automobiles, hospitals, and one thousand four hundred and ninety of the total of two thousand six hundred and ten Liberty ships which made his name famous. The Liberty ship program was exactly suited to a man whose motto was that there was no money in a job carried out slowly. One of Roosevelt's biographers says of Kaiser that he 'grabbed all the tools and materials he could lay his hands on, hired untrained workers recklessly on the theory that he could teach them, and was denounced for pirating labour and priority supplies.' Kaiser, he adds, had instinctively grasped Roosevelt's motto rule that 'energy is more efficient than efficiency'. This author also refers to the 'happy protection of cost-plus': the guarantee to reimburse production costs plus the customary profit in all government contracts. During the war Bethlehem Steel, Kaiser's leading competitor at the time, received 1,246 billion dollars for ship-building alone. It is obvious that Henry J. Kaiser Company acquired in the end a still larger sum.

Kaiser's view of the matter was: 'I'm a builder and if you call yourself a builder, you ought to be able to build anything.' Eventually he was running six ship-yards on the Pacific coast and one on the Atlantic with, on top of everything else, fifty-eight slipways. As a result he was accorded a fitting obituary in the *New York Times* containing no hint that he had acquired a fortune of inordinate size. Admittedly the 1975 *Encyclopedia Britannica* is too refined to mention him, whereas it does say something about Richard Montgomery. However, Kaiser lies in state beneath two columns; and, in any case, he and his trade are remembered in England to this day by a ship in the Thames.

The war memorial Britannia in front of Sheerness railway station has room on her plinth only for the dead of World War I; those of World War II are commemorated in a Roll of Honour in the abbey church in the middle of the island. Sheerness and Sheppey have their memorial of the 1939–45 war in the water instead of on land; it is a 'horrid plagiarism' since all Liberty ships unfailingly carried as their official designation the symbols EC-2: the '2' because the American version of an original British draft was so numbered and 'EC' for *economy* because of the ship's parsimonious construction. In the case of the Liberty ships this parsimonious construction was evident mainly in a new welding technique that was used in place of riveting: the design provided for five holds and derricks and so accommodation for the crews of the ship and its AA guns (in a three-storey erection amidships) was spartan in the extreme; no attempt at beautification was made and no gyro-compass or radar were provided. The sole purpose of these vessels was the movement of freight, escorted and protected by the convoy watchdogs, and no affection or respect for these work-horses, however fancy their names might be, could turn them into white swans. These shapeless, efficient Liberty ships were the first to break through to an England besieged by German U-boats, and provide it with weapons, equipment, food, and ultimately the troops for the invasion on D Day, June 6 1944. There are in fact, no dead men in the *Richard Montgomery*, but this was the time when anyone boarding a Liberty ship risked becoming victim to German torpedoes.

The legal basis for these deliveries without payment was the law of 'Lease-Lend' of March 11 1941, accepted by the American House of Representatives and Senate only after bitter argument with the isolationists and the rather less than fraternal majorities. The main beneficiaries of Lease-Lend were Great Britain and the Commonwealth. Great Britain recognized its contribution to the outcome of the war and repaid about two per cent of the thirty billion or so dollars-worth of the goods it had received. By November 7 1941 Roosevelt had contrived to legalize these deliveries to the Soviet Union as well: they were made by way of Murmansk, Archangel, Vladivostok, and Iran. The significance of this aid for the survival of the USSR is a matter of controversy, and invites discussion in the light of historical materialism. In the official *Dictionary of History* compiled 'specially' by the East German 'Institute for Marxism of the Central Committee of the SED' (Germany and German Workers' Movement), Lease-Lend is not mentioned as an entry on its own or in an article entitled 'The Great Patriotic War of the Soviet Union', nor under 'Second World War'. Under 'Anti-Hitler Coalition' is the following statement: 'The Anti-Hitler coalition was further developed by, for instance . . . the agreement of June 11 1942 between the USSR and the USA on principles of mutual assistance.' However closely these words are studied they hardly lead one to suppose that the value of American deliveries to the Soviet Union reached a total of 10.6 billion dollars—a figure, it should be noted, representative of only those goods that arrived direct from the United States and not representative of the goods that arrived by British and Canadian deliveries. One suspects that the silence still maintained today about the arrival in three Soviet ports of American ships loaded with lorries, petroleum products, food, and railway equipment is due to dialectical considerations—perhaps also considerations of *realpolitik* and simple emotional mortification. For the time being, however, the Allies delivered merely inanimate objects. Furthermore, they insisted somewhat tactlessly on an acknowledgement of their deliveries: for instance in March 1943 when the United States Ambassador in Moscow referred to the 'ungrateful' attitude on the part of the Soviets to the official and private aid provided to their country. *Pravda* thereupon printed a fairly complete list of American deliveries made since the outbreak of war—such was the importance to Stalin of their continuance. Nevertheless he must have found it tactless that his allies should have compelled him to give his Nazi enemies information on certain of his reserves. As far as the controversial offensive is concerned, the reigning President of the National Defence Committee of the Soviet Union reported on November 6 1943: 'It should also be added that the Allies have regularly supplied us with a variety of war material and with raw materials, so that it can be said without exaggeration that they have contributed significantly to the success of our summer campaign.' Thus speaks the military historian Alexander Weith in his *Russia at*

War of the undisputed master in his lifetime, the Generalissimo who, by assuming this title, took upon himself responsibility for the success of his policy. At first his policy vis-à-vis the Allies was a failure. As early as July 18 1941, when things were going badly in his struggle with Hitler, he asked the British to open a second front against the traitor 'in the west (northern France) and in the north (the Arctic)': the Soviet Union signed the Atlantic Charter shortly thereafter. What Molotov intended to bring back from Washington in the summer of 1942 was something far more important than spare parts or tins of ham and it was spelled out in the communiqué agreed with Roosevelt: 'Full understanding was reached with regard to the urgent task of creating a Second Front in Europe in 1942.' This was read to a jubilant Supreme Soviet with the great man present. But then the Second Front did not materialize in 1942. The great man was made to look a fool in front of his own people. It was the great Stalin himself who admonished Churchill that the failure to act would deal 'a mortal blow to the whole of Soviet foreign opinion.' He was also made to look a fool to Hitler's soldiers on whom leaflets were dropped announcing the Second Front for 1942. No Second Front appeared in 1943 either; instead there were always fresh excuses based on the situation in the Mediterranean or Pacific theatres. Meanwhile Lease-Lend deliveries were curtailed, allegedly to allow for the build-up of supplies for the Second Front which nevertheless, still remained undetectable. For a man who was responsible year after year for a war waged in his own country for which his own people bore the burden, Stalin could easily have taken this dilatoriness on the part of his allies as evidence of a desire to see the Red Army and the German army bleed each other to death first—and then open a Second Front in France. In February 1945 mere expediency dictated some expression of gratitude, and Lease-Lend was described as 'one of the President's most remarkable and vital achievements.' Hardly was the war over, however, when the United States in May 1945, cancelled Lease-Lend arrangements: the foreign contributions to the feeding of the Red Army disappeared overnight and some ten million soldiers were thrown on the resources of an already under-nourished population. Not surprisingly the historian's comment is that 'the Russians had intended to make a suitable expression of gratitude to the United

States for the Lend-Lease assistance during the War, but the way in which the program had been halted made this impossible now.' So, comrades, we will take the words out of Roosevelt's mouth and call the affair a 'douche of cold water'. Even today there has been no negotiated termination of Lease-Lend between the Soviet Union and its allies. It was this process of fobbing the Soviet Union off with goods only for so long, which, in addition to the quarrel over Poland, must be regarded as one of the root causes of the Cold War. And so today, upstream in the Hudson River—'mothballed' but available within four weeks—lies a fleet, and in the Thames off Sheerness a single ship, of a series whose name has no place in Communist terminology (Stalinist version): Liberty.

Now for the cause of the mishap. At dawn on August 20 1944 in fair weather and good visibility the *Richard Montgomery*, en route to Cherbourg, turned west into the English Channel and headed into the broad estuary of the Thames where it was to await a convoy. When, in accordance with instructions, it veered towards a shoal, it was warned by a cacophony of sirens from other ships. In Southend, on the opposite bank, the Deputy Harbour Master had also noticed that this thirty-two-foot draught ship had been allotted a mooring where there was only twenty-four feet of water at low tide. He was just about to issue more appropriate instructions to the new arrival through pierhead control when his superior officer stopped him. The superior officer's professional knowledge told him that the *Montgomery* belonged to the place allotted to it and he overruled his subordinate's decision. (The subordinate requested confirmation of the order in writing, but two days later he was tranferred to another post and did not appear when a commission of inquiry, assembled at the end of the month, was trying to establish what had happened. The ship's First Officer, when asked why he had allowed the Captain to stay asleep, simply replied: 'I don't know'.) So the *Montgomery* dropped anchor off Sheerness. Then came a spring tide, throwing the ship hither and yon against the sand-banks until finally it stuck fast. The Captain was now either extracted from bed or was woken by the bumps. The Captain then refused assistance from tugs. About four hours later the tide went out and, as the stem of the ship was no longer waterborne, its steel plates began to bend and crack (they were welded, not riveted, it will be remembered). Two days later the ship broke in two and sank. Holds three, four, and five were successfully cleared, but when the British stevedores realized what had arrived in them, they demanded danger money. Many children in Sheerness were then kept at home.

The *Richard Montgomery*'s cargo was destined for the United States Air Force and according to the manifest there still remain in the wreck:

—2,893 tons of bombs containing about 1,200 tons of TNT.

—One hundred seventy-three tons of self-detonating anti-personnel bombs with built-in firing mechanisms.

—One hundred seven tons of containers of phosphorous which burst into flame on contact with oxygen.

The whole cargo was, of course, intended ultimately for the Germans. By non-nuclear standards the force of an explosion of this lethal mixture would be almost inconceivable. Taking the *Richard Montgomery* as the centre of a two-mile circle, the main areas of dry land to be affected would be the north-west corner of the island with the town and harbour of Sheerness. There all older buildings and unsupported walls would collapse and both gas and water mains would be ruptured. Broken windows and a collapse of rickety chimneys or dilapidated roofing would be likely within a radius of seven miles. This would include half the town of Sittingbourne, together with the oil terminal and refinery complex on the Isle of Grain west of Sheppey. The explosion could produce a fireball, the blast from which would hurl sizeable objects and debris for more than a mile, perhaps landing on some super-tanker with over 100,000 tons of oil in its belly (the *Richard Montgomery* lies close to the busy Thames waterway). Simultaneous explosion of the entire cargo would produce a tidal wave which would bore up the Medway and Thames destroying further built-up areas on the banks. The effect would be multiplied at low tide owing to reduced blanketing. Weather would be a decisive factor governing the area affected. If there was thick low cloud over the explosion, the blast wave would bounce back and the effects would then be felt as far upstream as Canvey Island, where there are tanks with a capacity of more than one million gallons of oil together with chemical and methane gas containers. A chain reactor or domino effect might produce greater or smaller damage on the eastern outskirts of London. It seems unlikely that the House of Commons or Whitehall would be affected, however.

In the autumn of 1977 Whitehall made a pronouncement: 'As you already know government explosive experts are firmly of the opinion that any attempt to salvage the wreck or its cargo is inherently more dangerous than leaving it in *situ*.' The United States government had already been told the same in 1948 when it proposed to remove its property and sink it in deep water. In 1967 the Americans again suggested that the bombs be salvaged but all assistance was politely refused.

For a long time, moreover, it was not clear which department of Whitehall would be held responsible in the event of a catastrophe. In 1952 a parliamentary question seemed to indicate that the *Richard Montgomery* was under the jurisdiction of the Port of London Authority. That organization, however, saw fit to receive this imputation in silence. Eighteen years later the Department of Trade acknowledge responsibility for the wreck. The Ministry of Defence, however, also has some connection with the *Richard Montgomery* and other warlike matters, for instance when it lends divers, launches, and equipment to the Department of Trade for an inspection. If there is a sociological implication in all this, it becomes lost in the bureaucracy.

The British hosts to this Liberty ship seem doubtful whether the Americans really know all about their own bombs. The extent of British knowledge emerges from an answer given to the M.P. for Gravesend by the Under-Secretary for Transport and Trade to the effect that the government did not know the state of the explosives and was not going to take the risk of finding out. The government adheres faithfully to this decision. The last time the bombs were officially inspected was in 1952. Since then the official line is that the more and the longer the bombs are exposed to sea water, the more harmless they will become, despite the fact that they are packed in water-tight steel containers and that scientists advise that TNT is unaffected by water. (So 'let sleeping bombs lie' although the dogs in the proverb have been known to wake up on occasions.) Since 1952 only the hull has been thought worthy of investigation and this only every four years. In September 1978 the big question was whether the wreck had meanwhile broken apart in another place. The second crack was not news in Sheerness as even divers sent down by the government drink a pint of beer after work and get talking. 'The Ministry of Defence says that it has known about a second crack in the hull for a number of years, although the Department of Trade has said that one of the objects of the present survey would be to establish whether, in fact, a second crack existed.' The current view of the Department of Trade about the *Richard Montgomery* was given in 1978: 'There is no significant change in the state of the wreck nor any additional spillage of explosives.' This comment refers also to bombs which have already spilled out through existing cracks.

The Ministry responsible admits that it does not know even the number of bombs left in the wreck of the *Richard Montgomery* in 1944. 'When some of the bombs were taken off the ship, the numbers were not closely recorded. It has been known for some years that the manifest was not recorded entirely accurately.' The Minister himself added: 'In other words the cargo may by now be perfectly safe or it may still be sensitive.'

The possibility of an explosion is not disputed. If there was one while an attempt at salvage was being made, the responsibility would be that of the government in office at the time; any such attempt is therefore to be avoided. Other possibilities are: collision of another ship with the wreck (the local coast-guard station has reported twenty-four near-collisions); the effects of flood water and collapse of intermediate decks allowing bombs stowed on them to fall on those below; spontaneous ignition of the explosives through denting of the bomb casings; even pressure waves from low-flying jet aircraft have been mentioned; finally there are potential suicides, fearful of solitude, or terrorists (there have been twenty-three individual acts of terrorism at sea since 1974) or students bent on testing the truth of the saying that anyone setting the Thames on fire is a miracle man.

However the problem may be handled, the administration is exemplary. There is a board carrying these words:

WARNING
DANGER
UNEXPLODED AMMUNITION
KEEP AT LEAST 5000 FEET FROM WRECK

There are two light buoys; at night there is a cheeping warning signal; access to the wreck is forbidden (law for protection of the wreck 1973); the Medway Port Authority has the problem-child on its radar screen, and its launches visit the wreck four times a day. Such are the security precautions. Further solutions are still being considered in official quarters: enclosing the *Richard Montgomery* in some solid construction, towing the bombs away under water, giving them a top covering of concrete and, finally, the construction of an airport opposite the wreck so that the take-off and landing-paths of jumbo jets would lead them over it, if necessary at low level.

The problem has given rise to a piece of literature in the form of a detective novel: *Blockbuster* by Stephen Barbay (New York, 1977).

Popular stories: Churchill wrote a letter to Roosevelt's successor to the effect that he ought to remove his bombs but the Americans refused, arguing that a gift was a gift. There is a firm in Holland which specializes in removing dangerous wrecks all over the world but it preferred not to touch this one—pardon, it was a Japanese firm; eventually we plucked up courage to ask the Germans for expert assistance but they took one look at the *Richard Montgomery* and made off; there is one advantage to the Common Market.

Little psychological implications: the people of this island face imminent danger daily; the *Richard Montgomery* is at present on everyone's mind until it has almost become part of the lingo. One of them said: 'I wish the damn thing would go up and then we'd be rid of it.' The people are attached to their island even though it is such a dangerous place. Very few school-leavers go to look for work on the mainland. People come back to spend their declining years face to face with a time bomb. Even strangers settle down here separated merely by a window-pane from a formidable potential explosion. A word in their ear might be: there seems to be a death-wish here.

Referring to the atom bomb a theologian has been heard to say: perhaps God is at last tired of mankind, but has it got to be all mankind at once? The *Richard Montgomery* fans might be enough to begin with.

The latest statement: 'It must be most reassuring for the inhabitants of Sheppey to learn that the wreck of the *Richard Montgomery*, and also its deadly cargo, is still the property of the United States of America. In a recent memorandum the Parliamentary Under-Secretary for Trade stated that, 'should the wreck explode, all claims for damages should be directed to the United States government.'

Local comment: 'So they are people we have to take action against. May be, but we're a long way from that yet.'

After the flood of January 1978 the inhabitants of Sheppey were promised by one of their elected representatives that the island would never again be flooded as long as he was in office and that, if it were, he would resign. They had nearly twelve months in which to observe that the sea front had been made passable again for the benefit of day tourists from London, although they wondered why the seawall was being reinforced in such secrecy that no change in it was visible even to the keenest eye. At eleven o'clock in the evening of December 25 1978, shortly before an abnormally high tide forecast in the official tide table, water was splashing over the much-discussed little wall. The authorities had learned their lesson only to the extent that the alarm was not given until two hours later and then by loud-speaker instead of the promised siren. Whipped up by a foreseeable storm, the water forced its way into the island, making itself at home in over five hundred houses and business premises, burning out fuses, bursting gas mains, swamping telephone junctions, and ruining a lot of things which might have come in useful for food and clothing. The flood had such an easy time that it came back on Boxing Day afternoon, nullifying all the pumping and clearance work done in the morning and contaminating ploughland and pasture more thoroughly. Once more some sheep were drowned. The insurance companies, however, beat a hasty retreat from an area where they had to pay so much whenever the weather so decided. The sufferers from this latest invasion have had to pay out of their rates more than forty million pounds. And once more a Commission of Inquiry asks itself how this could have happened, and a lot of people are promising really, this time, to learn something from it. The promised resignation did not materialize.

> Was I deceived or did a sable cloud
> Turn forth her silver lining on the night?

Murphy, the statistician, gives the answer with his unrivalled law: if there is the slightest chance that something will go wrong, it will go wrong. An expanded version of Murphy's law is: nothing is ever as simple as it seems. Everything lasts longer than one expects. If it is possible for several things to go wrong, the one that goes wrong first will do the most damage. Pressed to dilate further on his theory of inevitability, Murphy continues: 'The importance of a subject can be judged by the lack of interest in it.' From this it follows that as soon as some threat demands our attention and requires we take precautions, theoretical efforts will certainly be made, even if the threat is only a shattered ship in the mouth of the Thames.

Translated from the German by Lawrence Wilson

GRANTA

NADIME GORDIMER
CITY OF THE DEAD,
CITY OF THE LIVING

Nadime Gordimer

You only count the days if you are waiting to have a baby or you are in prison. I've had my child but I'm counting the days since he's been in this house.

The street delves down between two rows of houses like the abandoned bed of a river that has changed course. The shebeen-keeper who lives opposite has a car that sways and churns its way to her fancy wrought-iron gate. Everyone else, including shebeen customers, walks over the stones, sand, and gullies, home from the bus station. It's too far to bicycle to work in town.

The house provides the sub-economic township planner's usual two rooms and kitchen with a little yard at the back, into which his maquette figures of the ideal family unit of four fitted neatly. Like most of the houses in the street, it has been arranged inside and out to hold the number of people the ingenuity of necessity provides for. The garage is the home of sub-tenants. (The shebeen-keeper, who knows everything about everybody, might remember how the house came to have a garage—perhaps a taxi owner once lived there.) The front door of the house itself opens into a room that has been subdivided by greenish brocade curtains whose colour had faded and embossed pattern worn off before they were discarded in another kind of house. On one side of the curtains is a living-room with just space enough to crate a plastic-covered sofa and two chairs, a coffee table with crocheted cover, vase of dyed feather flowers and oil lamp, and a radio-and-cassette-player combination with home-built speakers. There is a large varnished print of a horse with wild orange mane and flaring nostrils on the wall. The floor is cement, shined with black polish. On the other side of the curtains is a bed, a burglar-proofed window, a small table with candle, bottle of anti-acid tablets, and alarm clock. During the day a frilly nylon night-gown is laid out on the blankets. A woman's clothes are in a box under the bed. In the dry cleaner's plastic sheath, a man's suit hangs from a nail.

A door, never closed, leads from the living-room to the kitchen. There is a sink, which is also the bathroom of the house, a coal-burning stove finned with chrome like a 1940s car, a pearly-blue formica dresser with glass doors that don't slide easily, a table and plastic chairs. The smell of cooking never varies: mealie-meal burning, curry overpowering the sweet reek of offal, sour porridge, onions. A small refrigerator, not connected, is used to store margarine, condensed milk, tinned pilchards; there is no electricity.

Another door, with a pebbled glass pane in its upper half, is always kept closed. It opens off the kitchen. Net curtains reinforce the privacy of the pebbled glass; the privacy of the tenant of the house, Samson Moreke, whose room is behind there, shared with his wife and baby and whichever of their older children spends time away from other relatives who take care of them in country villages. When all the children are in their parents' home at once, the sofa is a bed for two; others sleep on the floor in the kitchen. Sometimes the sofa is not available, since adult relatives who find jobs in the city need somewhere to live. Number 1907 Block C holds—has held—eleven people; how many it could hold is a mattter of who else has nowhere to go. This reckoning includes the woman lodger and her respectable succession of lovers behind the green brocade curtain, but not the family lodging in the garage.

In the backyard, Samson Moreke, in whose name tenancy of Number 1907 Block C is registered by the authorities, has put up poles and chicken wire and planted Catawba grapevines that make a pleasant green arbour in summer. Underneath are three metal chairs and matching table, bearing traces of white paint, which —like the green brocade curtains, the picture of the horse with orange mane, the poles, chicken wire, and vines—have been discarded by the various employers for whom Moreke works in the city as an itinerant gardener. The arbour is between the garage and the lavatory, which is shared by everyone on the property, both tenants and lodgers.

On Sundays Moreke sits under his grapevine and drinks a bottle of beer brought from the shebeen across the road. Even in winter he sits there; it is warmer out in the midday winter sun than in the house, the shadow of the vine merely a twisted rope—grapes eaten, roof of leaves fallen. Although the yard is behind the house and there is a yellow dog on guard tied to a packing-case shelter, there is not much privacy. A large portion of the space of the family living in the garage is taken up by a paraffin-powered refrigerator filled with soft-drink cans and pots of flavoured yoghurt: a useful little business that serves the community and supplements the earnings of the breadwinner, a cleaner at the city slaughter-house. The sliding metal shutter meant for the egress of a car from the garage is permanently bolted down. All day Sunday children come on errands to buy, knocking at the old kitchen door, salvaged from the city, that Moreke has set into the wall of the garage.

A street where there is a shebeen, a house opposite a shebeen cannot be private, anyway. All weekend drunks wander over the ruts that make the gait even of the sober seem drunken. The children playing in the street take no notice of men fuddled between song and argument, who talk to people who are not there.

As well as friends and relatives, acquaintances of Moreke —who have got to know where he lives through travelling with him on the buses to work—walk over from the shebeen and appear in the yard. Moreke is a man who always puts aside money to buy the Sunday newspaper; he has to fold away the paper and talk instead. The guests usually bring a cold quart or two with them (the shebeen, too, has a paraffin refrigerator, restaurant-size). Talk and laughter make the dog bark. Someone plays a transistor radio. The chairs are filled, and some comers stretch on the bit of tough grass. Most of the Sunday visitors are men but there are women, particularly young ones, who have gone with them to the shebeen or taken up with them there; these women are polite and deferent to Moreke's wife, Nanike, when she has time to join the gathering. Often they will hold her latest—fifth living—baby while she goes back into the kitchen to cook or hangs her washing on the fence. She takes a beer or two herself, but although she is in her early thirties and knows she is still pretty—except for a missing front tooth—she does not giggle or get flirtatious. She is content to sit with the new baby on her lap, in the sun, among men and women like herself, while her husband tells anecdotes which make them laugh or challenge him. He learns a lot from the newspapers.

Nanike was sitting in the yard with him and his friends the Sunday a cousin arrived with a couple of hangers-on. They didn't bring beer, but were given some. There were greetings, but who really hears names? One of the hangers-on fell asleep on the grass, a boy with a body like a baggy suit. The other had a yellow face, lighter than anyone else present, narrow as a trowel, and the irregular pock-marks of the pitted skin were flocked, round the area where men grow hair, with sparse tufts of black. She noticed he wore a gold earring in one ear. He had nothing to say but later took up a guitar belonging to someone else and played to himself. One of the people living in the garage, crossing the path of the group under the arbour on his way to the lavatory with his roll of toilet paper, paused to look or listen, but everyone else was talking too loudly to hear the soft plang-plang, and the after-buzz when the player's palm stilled the instrument's vibration.

Moreke went off with his friends when they left, and came back, not late. His wife had gone to bed. She was sleepy, feeding the baby. Because he stood there, at the foot of the bed, did not begin to undress, she understood someone must be with him.

'Mtembu's friend.' Her husband's head indicated the other side of the glass-paned door.

'What does he want here now?'

'I brought him. Mtembu asked.'

'What for?'

Moreke sat down on the bed. He spoke softly, mouthing at her face. 'He needs somewhere to stay.'

'Where was he before, then?'

Moreke lifted and dropped his elbows limply at a question not to be asked.

The baby lost the nipple and nuzzled furiously at air. She guided its mouth. 'Why can't he stay with Mtembu? You could have told Mtembu no.'

'He's your cousin.'

'Well, I will tell him no. If Mtembu needs somewhere to stay, I have to take him. But not anyone he brings from the street.'

Her husband yawned, straining every muscle in his face. Suddenly he stopped and began putting together the sheets of his Sunday paper that were scattered on the floor. He folded them more or less in order, slapping and smoothing the creases.

'Well?'

He said nothing, walked out. She heard the voices in the kitchen, but not what was being said.

He opened their door again and shut it behind him. 'It's not a business of cousins. This one is in trouble. You don't read the

papers . . . the blowing up of that police station . . . *you* know, last
month? They didn't catch them all . . . . It isn't safe for Mtembu to
keep him any longer. He must keep moving.'

Her soft jowls stiffened.

Her husband assured her awkwardly. 'A few days. Only for a
couple of days. Then'—a gesture—'out of the country.'

H*e never takes off the gold earring, even when he sleeps. He
sleeps on the sofa. He didn't bring a blanket, a towel,
nothing—uses our things. I don't know what the earring
means; when I was a child there were men who came to work on the
mines who had earrings, but in both ears—country people. He's a
town person; another one who reads newspapers. He tidies away the
blankets I gave him and then he reads newspapers the whole day. He
can't go out.*

The others at Number 1907 Block C were told the man was
Nanike Moreke's cousin, had come to look for work, and
had nowhere to stay. There are people in that position in
every house. No one with a roof over his head can say 'no' to one of
the same blood—everyone knows that; Moreke's wife had not
denied that. But she wanted to know what to say if someone asked
the man's name. He himself answered at once, his strong thin hand
twisting the gold hoop in his ear like a girl. 'Shisonka. Tell them
Shisonka.'

'And the other name?'

Her husband answered. 'That name is enough.'

Moreke and his wife didn't use the name among themselves.
They referred to the man as 'he' and 'him'. Moreke addressed him
as 'Mfo', brother; she called him simply 'you'. Moreke answered
questions nobody asked. He said to his wife, in front of the man,
'What is the same blood? Here in this place? If you are not white,
you are all the same blood, here.' She looked at her husband
respectfully, as she did when he read to her out of his newspaper.

The woman lodger worked in the kitchen at a Kentucky Fried
Chicken shop in the city, and like Moreke was out at work all day;
at weekends she slept at her mother's place, where her children
lived, so she did not know the man Shisonka never left the house to

look for work or for any other reason. Her lover came to her room only to share the bed, creeping late past whatever sleeping form might be on the sofa, and leaving before first light to get to a factory in the white industrial area. The only problem was the family who lived in the garage. The man had to cross the yard to use the lavatory. The slaughter-house cleaner's mother and wife would notice he was there, in the house; that he never went out. It was Moreke's wife who thought of this, and told the woman in the garage her cousin was sick; he had just been discharged from hospital. And indeed, they took care of him as if he had been— Moreke and his wife, Nanike. They did not have the money to eat meat often but on Tuesday Moreke bought a pluck from the butchery near the bus station in the city; the man sat down to eat with them. Moreke brought cigarettes home—the man paid him—it was clear he must have cigarettes, needed cigarettes more than food. And don't let him go out, don't ever let him go to the shop for cigarettes, or over to Ma Radebe for drink, Moreke told his wife; *you* go, if he needs anything, *you* just leave everything, shut the house—go.

I wash his clothes with our things. His shirt and pullover have labels in another language, come from some other country. Even the letters are different. I give him food in the middle of the day. I myself eat in the yard, with the baby. I told him he should play the music, in there, if he wants to. He listens to Samson's tapes. How could I keep my own sister out of the house? When she saw him I said he was a friend of Samson—a new friend. She likes light skinned. But it means people notice you. It must be very hard to hide. He doesn't say so. He doesn't look afraid. The beard will hide him; but how long does it take for a beard to grow, how long, how long before he goes away?

Every night that week the two men talked. Not in the room with the sofa and radio-and-cassette player, if the woman lodger was at home on the other side of the curtains, but in the room where the Morekes slept. The man had a kitchen chair Moreke brought in; there was just room for it between the big bed and the wardrobe. Moreke lay on the bed with a pillow stuffed under his nape. Sometimes his wife stayed in the kitchen, at other times she came in and sat with the baby on the bed. She could see Moreke's face and the back of the man's head in the panel mirror of the wardrobe while they talked. The shape of the head swelled up from the thin neck, a puff-ball of black kapok. Deep in, there was a small patch without hair, a skin infection or a healed wound. His front aspect—a narrow yellow face keenly attentive, cigarette wagging like a finger from the corner of his lips, loop of gold round the lobe of one of the alert pointed ears—seemed unaware of the blemish, something that attacked him unnoticed from behind.

They talked about the things that interested Moreke; the political meetings disguised as church services of which he read reports but did not attend. The man laughed, and argued with Moreke patiently. 'What's the use, man? If you don't stand there? Stand with your feet as well as agree with your head . . . . Yes, go and get that head knocked if the dogs and the *kerries* come. Since '76, the kids've shown you how . . . . You know now.'

Moreke wanted to tell the man what he thought of the Urban Councils the authorities wanted to set up, and the Committees people themselves had formed in opposition. As, when he found himself in the company of a sports-promoter, he wanted to give his opinion of the state of soccer today. 'Those Council men are nothing to me. You understand? They only want big jobs and smart cars for themselves. I'm a poor man, I'll never have a car. But they say they're going to make this place like a white Jo'burg. Maybe the government listens to them . . . . They say they can do it. The Committees—eh?—they say like *I* do, *those Council men are nothing*—but they themselves, what can they do? They know everything is no good here. They talk; they tell us about it; they go to jail. So what's the use? What can you do?'

The man did not tell what he had done. 'The police station' was there, ready in their minds, ready to their tongues; not spoken.

The man was smiling at Moreke, at something he had heard many times before and might be leaving behind for good, now. 'Your Council. Those dummies. You see this *donga* called a street, outside? This place without even electric light in the rooms? You dig beautiful gardens, the flowers smell nice . . . and how many people must shit in that stinking hovel in your yard? How much do you get for digging the ground white people own? You told me what you get. 'Top wages': ten rands a day. Just enough for the rent in this place, and not even the shit-house belongs to you, not even the mud you bring in from the yard on your shoes . . . .

Moreke became released, excited. 'The bus fares went up last week. They say the rent is going up . . . .'

'Those dummies, that's what they do for you. You see? But the Committee tells you they don't pay the rent, because you aren't paid enough to live in the 'beautiful city' the dummies promise you. Isn't that the truth? Isn't the truth what you *know*? Don't you listen to the ones who speak the truth?'

Moreke's wife had had, for a few minutes, the expression of one waiting to interrupt. 'I'll go to Radebe and get a bottle of beer, if you want.'

The two men gave a flitting nod to one another in approval.

Moreke counted out the money. 'Don't let anybody come back with you.'

His wife took the coins without looking up. 'I'm not a fool.' The baby was asleep on the bed. She closed the door quietly behind her. The two men lost the thread of their talk for a moment; Moreke filled it: 'A good woman.'

W*e are alone together. The baby likes him. I don't give the breast every time, now; yesterday when I was fetching the coal he fed the bottle to her. I ask him what children he has? He only smiles, shakes his head. I don't know if this means it was silly to ask, because everyone has children.*

Perhaps it meant he doesn't know, pretends he doesn't know — thinks a lot of himself, smart young man with a gold ring in his ear has plenty of girl-friends to get babies with him.

The police station was never mentioned, but one of the nights the man spent describing to the Moreke couple foreign places he had been to—that must have been before the police station happened. He told about the oldest city on the African continent, so old it had a city of the dead as well as a city of the living—a whole city of tombs like houses. The religion there was the same as the religion of the Indian shopkeepers, here at home. Then he had lived in another kind of country, where there was snow for half the year or more. It was dark until ten in the morning and again from three o'clock in the afternoon. He described the clothes he had been given to protect him against the cold. 'Such people, I can tell you. You can't believe such white people exist.If our people turn up there . . . you get everything you need, they just give it . . . . And there's a museum—it's out in the country—they have ships there their people sailed all over the world more than two thousand years ago. They may even have come here . . . . This pullover is still from them . . . full of holes now . . . .'

'Look at that, hai!' Moreke admired the intricately-worked bands of coloured wools in a design based upon natural features he did not recognize—dark frozen forms of fir forests and the molecular pattern of snow crystals. 'She'll mend it for you.'

His wife was willing but apprehensive. 'I'll try and get the same colours. I don't know if I can find them here.'

The man smiled at the kindness of his own people. 'She shouldn't take a lot of trouble. I won't need it, anyway.'

No one asked where it was that the pullover wouldn't be needed; what kind of place, what continent he would be going to when he got away.

After the man had retired to his sofa that night Moreke read the morning paper he had brought from an employer's kitchen in the city. He kept lowering the sheets slowly and looking around at the room, then returning to his reading. The baby was restless; but it was not that he commented on.

'It's better not to know too much about him.'

His wife turned the child onto its belly. 'Why?'

Her face was innocently before his like a mirror he didn't want to look into. He had kept encouraging the man to go on with his talk of living in foreign places.

The shadows thrown by the candle capered through the room, bending furniture and bodies, flying over the ceiling, quieting the baby with wonder. 'Because then . . . if they question us, we won't have anything to tell.'

H*e did bring something. A gun.*
       He comes into the kitchen, now, and helps me when
       I'm washing up. He came in, this morning, and put his
hands in the soapy water, didn't say anything, started cleaning up.
Our hands were in the grease and soap. I couldn't see his fingers but
sometimes I felt them when they bumped mine. He scraped the pot
and dried everything. I didn't say thanks. To say thank you to a
man—it's not man's work, he might feel ashamed.

He stays in the kitchen—we stay in the kitchen with the baby
most of the day. He doesn't sit in there, anymore, listening to the
tapes. I go in and turn on the machine loud enough for us to hear it
well in the kitchen.

B y Thursday the tufts of beard were thickening and knitting
       together on the man's face. Samson Moreke tried to find
       Mtembu to hear what plans had been made but Mtembu did
not come in response to messages and was not anywhere Moreke
looked for him. Moreke took the opportunity, while the woman in
whose garden he worked on Thursdays was out, to telephone
Mtembu's place of work from her house, but was told that workshop employees were not allowed to receive calls.

He brought home chicken feet for soup and a piece of beef
shank. Figs had ripened in the Thursday garden and he'd been given
some in a newspaper poke. He asked, 'When do you expect to hear
from Mtembu?'

The man was reading the sheet of paper stained with milky sap
from the stems of figs. Samson Moreke had never really been in jail
himself—only the usual short-term stays for pass offences—but he
knew from people who had been inside a long time that there was
this need to read every scrap of paper that might come your way
from the outside world.

'—Well, it doesn't matter. You're all right here. We can just
carry on. I suppose Mtembu will turn up this weekend.'

As if he heard in this resignation Moreke's anticipation of the
usual Sunday beer in the yard, the man suddenly took charge of
Moreke and his wife, crumpling the dirty newspaper and rubbing his
palms together to rid them of stickiness. His narrow yellow face was
set clear-cut in black hair all round now, like the framed face of the

king in Moreke's pack of worn cards. The black eyes and earring were the same liquid-bright. The perfectly-ironed shirt he wore was open at the breast in the manner of all attractive young men of his age. 'Look, nobody must come here. Saturday, Sunday. None of your friends. You must shut up this place. Keep them all away. Nobody walking into the yard from the shebeen. That's *out*.'

Moreke looked from the man to his wife; back to the man again. Moreke half-coughed, half-laughed. 'But how do I do that, man? How do I stop them? I can't put bars on my gate. There're the other people, in the garage. They sell things.'

'*You* stay inside. Here in this house, with the doors locked. There are too many people around at the weekend. Let them think you've gone away.'

Moreke still smiled, amazed, helpless. 'And the one in there, with her boy-friend? What's she going to think?'

Moreke's wife spoke swiftly. 'She'll be at her mother's house.'

And now the plan of action fell efficiently into place; each knew his part within it. 'Oh yes. Thank the Lord for that. Maybe I'll go over to Radebe's tonight and just say I'm not going to be here Sunday. And Saturday I'll say I'm going to the soccer.'

His wife shook her head. 'Not the soccer. Your friends will want to come and talk about it afterwards.'

'*Hai, mama*! All right, a funeral, far away . . . .' Moreke laughed, and stopped himself with an embarrassed drawing of mucus back through the nose.

W *hile I'm ironing, he cleans the gun.*

I saw he needed another rag and I gave it to him.

He asked for oil, and I took cooking oil out of the cupboard, but then I saw in his face that was not what he wanted. I went to the garage and borrowed Three-in-One from Nchaba's wife.

He never takes out the gun when Samson's here. He knows only he and I know about it.

I said, what happened there, on your head at the back—that sore? His hand went to it, under the hair, he doesn't think it shows. I'll get him something for it, some ointment. If he's still here on Monday.

Perhaps he is cross because I spoke about it.

Then when I came back with the oil, he sat at the kitchen table laughing at me, smiling, as if I was a young girl. I forgot—I felt I was a girl. But I don't really like that kind of face, his face—light-skinned. You can never forget a face like that. If you are questioned, you can never say you don't remember what someone like that looks like.

He picks up the baby as if it belongs to him. To him as well, while we are in the kitchen together.

That night the two men didn't talk. They seemed to have nothing to say. Like prisoners who get their last mealie-pap of the day before being locked up for the night, Moreke's wife gave them their meal before dark. Then all three went from the kitchen to the Morekes' room, where any light that might shine from behind the curtains and give away a presence was directed only towards a blind: a high corrugated tin fence in a lane full of breast-high khakiweed. Moreke shared his newspaper. When the man had read it, he tossed through the third-hand adventure comics and sales promotion pamphlets given away in city super-markets Nanike Moreke kept; he read the manual 'Teach Yourself How to Sell Insurance' in which, at some stage, 'Samson Moreke' had been carefully written on the fly-leaf.

There was no beer. Moreke's wife knew her way about her kitchen in the dark; she fetched the litre bottle of coke that was on the kitchen table and poured herself a glass. Her husband stayed the offer with a raised hand; the other man's inertia over the manual was overcome just enough to move his head in refusal. She had taken up again the cover for the bed she had begun when she had had some free time, waiting for this fifth child to be born. Crocheted roses, each caught in a squared web of a looser pattern, were worked separately and then joined to the whole they slowly extended. The tiny flash of her steel hook and the hair-thin gold in his ear signalled in candle-light. At about ten o'clock there was a knock at the front door. The internal walls of these houses are planned at minimum specification for cheapness and a blow on any part of the house reverberates through every room. The black-framed, bone-yellow face raised and held, absolutely still, above the manual. Moreke opened his mouth and, swinging his legs over the side, lifted himself from the bed. But his wife's hand on his shoulder made him subside again; only the bed creaked slightly. The slenderness of her body from the waist up was merely rooted in heavy maternal hips and thighs; with a movement soft as the breath she expelled, she leant and blew out the candles.

A sensible precaution; someone might follow round the walls of the house looking for some sign of life. They sat in the dark. There was no bark from the dog in the yard. The knocking stopped. Moreke thought he heard laughter, and the gate twang. But the shebeen is noisy on a Friday; the sounds could have come from anywhere. 'Just someone who's had a few drinks. It often happens. Sometimes we don't even wake up, I suppose, ay, Nanike.' Moreke's hoarse whisper, strangely, woke the baby, who let out the thin wail that meets the spectre in a bad dream, breaks through into consciousness a response to a threat that can't be defeated in the conscious world. In the dark, they all went to bed.

A city of the dead, a city of the living. It was better when Samson got him to talk about things like that. Things far away can't do any harm. We'll never have a car, like the Councillors, and we'll never have to run away to those far places, like him. Lucky to have this house; many, many people are jealous of that. I never knew, until this house was so quiet, how much noise people make at the weekend, I didn't hear the laughing, the talking in the street, Radebe's music going, the terrible screams of people fighting.

On Saturday Moreke took his blue ruled pad and an envelope to the kitchen table. But his wife was peeling pumpkin and slicing onions; there was no space, so he went back to the room where the sofa was, and his radio-and-cassette player. First he addressed the envelope to their twelve-year-old boy at mission school. It took him the whole morning to write a letter, although he could read so well. Once or twice he asked the man how to spell a word in English.

He lay smoking on his bed, the sofa. 'Why in English?'

'Rapula knows English very well . . . . It helps him to get letters . . . .'

'You shouldn't send him away from here, baba. You think it's safer, but you are wrong. It's like you and the meetings. The more you try to be safe, the worse it will be for your children.' He stared quietly at Moreke. 'And look, now I'm here.'

'Yes.'

'And you look after me.'

'Yes.'

'And you're not afraid.'

'Yes, we're afraid . . . but of many things . . . . When I come home with money . . . three times *tsotsis* have hit me, taken everything. You see here where I was cut on the cheek. This arm was broken. I couldn't work. Not even push the lawn-mower. I had to pay some young one to hold my jobs for me.'

The man smoked and smiled. 'I don't understand you. You see? I don't understand you. Bring your children home, man. We're shut up in the ghetto to kill each other. That's what they want, in their white city. So you send the children away; that's what they want, too. To get rid of us. We must all stick together. That's the only way to fight our way out.'

That night he asked if Moreke had a chess set.

Moreke giggled, gave clucks of embarrassment. 'That board with the little dolls? I'm not an educated man! I don't know those games!'

They played together the game that everybody knows, that is, played on the pavements outside shops and in factory yards, with the board drawn on concrete or in dust, and bottle-tops for counters. This time a handful of dried beans from the kitchen served, and a board drawn by Moreke on a box-lid. He won game after game from the man. His wife had the Primus stove in the room, now, and she made tea. The game was not resumed. She had added three completed squares to her bed-cover in two nights; after the tea, she did not take it up again. They sat listening to Saturday night, all round them, pressing in upon the hollow cement units of which the house was built. Often trampling steps seemed just about to halt at the front or back door. The splintering of wood under a truncheon or the shatter of the window-panes, thin ice under the weight of the roving dark outside, waited upon every second. The woman's eyelids slid down, fragile and faintly greasy, outlining intimately the aspect of the orbs beneath, in sleep. Her face became unguarded as the baby's. Every now and then she would start, come to herself again. But her husband and the man made no move to go to bed. The man picked up and ran the fine head of her crochet hook under the rind of each fingernail, again and again, until the tool had done the cleaning job to satisfaction.

When the man went to bed at last, by the light of the cigarette lighter he shielded in his hand to see his way to the sofa, he found she had put a plastic chamber-pot on the floor. Probably the husband had thought of it.

All Sunday morning the two men worked together on a fault in Moreke's tape player, though they were unable to test it with the volume switched on. Moreke could not afford to take the player to a repair shop. The man seemed to think the fault a simple matter; like any other city youngster, he had grown up with such machines. Moreke's wife cooked mealie-rice and made a curry gravy for the Sunday meal. 'Should I go to Radebe and get beer?' She had followed her husband into their room to ask him alone.

'You want to advertise we are here? You know what he said.'

'Ask him if it matters, if I go—a woman.'

'I'm not going to ask. Did he say he wants beer? Did I?'

But in the afternoon she did ask something. She went straight to the man, not Moreke. 'I have to go out to the shop.' It was very hot in the closed house; the smell of curry mixed with the smell of the baby in the fug of its own warmth and wrappings. He wrinkled his face, exposed clenched teeth in a suppressed yawn; what shops—had she forgotten it was Sunday? She understood his reaction. But there were corner shops that sold essentials even on Sundays; he must know that. 'I have to get milk. Milk for the baby.'

She stood there, in her over-trodden slippers, her old skirt and cheap blouse—a woman not to be noticed among every other woman in the streets. He didn't refuse her. No need. Not after all this past week. Not for the baby. She was not like her husband, big-mouth, friendly with everyone. He nodded; it was a humble errand that wouldn't concern him.

She went out of the house just as she was, her money in her hand. Moreke and the baby were asleep in their room. The street looked new, bright, refreshing, after the dim house. A small boy with a toy machine-gun covered her in his fire, chattering his little white teeth with rat-a-tat-tttt. Ma Radebe, the shebeen-keeper, her hair plaited with blue and red beads, her beautiful long red nails resting on the steering wheel, was backing her car out of her gateway. She braked to let her neighbour pass and leaned from the car window. '*My dear*'—in English—'I was supposed to be gone from this place two hours ago. I'm due at a big wedding that will already be over . . . . How are you? Didn't see your husband for a few days . . . nothing wrong across the road?'

Moreke's wife stood and shook her head. Radebe was not one who expected or waited for answers when she greeted anyone. When the car had driven off Moreke's wife went on down the street and down the next one, past the shop where young boys were gathered scuffling and dancing to the shop-keeper's radio, and on to the purplish brick building with the security fence round it and a flag flying. One of her own people was on guard outside leaning on a hand machine-gun. She went up the steps and into the office, where there were more of her own people in uniform, but one of *them* in charge. She spoke in her own language to her own kind, but they seemed disbelieving. They repeated the name of that other police station, that was blown up, and asked her if she was sure? She said she was quite sure. Then they took her to the white officer and she told in English—'There, in my house, 1907 Block C. He has been there a week. He has a gun.'

I *don't know why I did it. I get ready to say that to anyone who is going to ask me, but nobody in this house asks. The baby laughs at me while I wash him, stares up while we're alone in the house and he's feeding at the breast, and to him I say out loud: I don't know why.*

A week after the man was taken away that Sunday by the security police, Ma Radebe again met Moreke's wife in their street. The shebeen-keeper gazed at her for a moment, and spat.

GRANTA

ANTONIO LOBO

ANTUNES

SOUTH OF NOWHERE

Antonio Lobo Antunes

If you and I were ant-eaters, instead of a man and a woman talking to each other in this corner of the bar, perhaps I would then be able to accustom myself to your silence. Perhaps we would understand each other through the complicity of our restless snouts sniffing the pavement nostalgically for non-existent insects. We might join, under the cover of darkness, in coitus as sad as the nights of Lisbon. Maybe then you would finally tell me something about yourself. It is possible that behind your Cranach forehead is a secret tenderness for rhinoceros. And perhaps, if you were to touch me, you might suddenly discover the unicorn in me. We could buy tickets to ride the little train that circles the zoo, going from animal to animal, waving, for example, to the white bears of the Arctic grotto. We could observe the anal conjunctivitis of the baboons, their eyelids inflamed with haemorrhoids. We could kiss in front of the cage of lions, moth-eaten like old coats, rolling their lips over stripped gums. You could buy me a popsicle near the corner where the clowns, arching their eyebrows, buffet each other to the tragic tune of a saxophone.

Do you remember the stone eagles at the entrance to the zoo? My parents lived not very far away. From the window of my brother's room you could see the camels and their bored expressions. Sitting on the toilet, I listened to the complaints of the seals who were impeded by the width of the moat from swimming down the sewage canals and emerging in a jet of water through the spigots in my bathroom. The

---

In the sixties, the Movement for the Liberation of Angola (MPLA) began its war for national independence from Portugal. The war lasted for fourteen years, and Portugal—first under the leadership of Antonio Salazar, the prime minister from 1932 until shortly before his death in 1970, and subsequently under the leadership of Marcello Caetano—sent over a million and a half troops to fight in Angola. In 1974, Caetano was overthrown in a bloodless coup, and, in the following year, Portugal declared Angola independent. Shortly before then, PIDE—the International and State Defence Police famous in both Portugal and Angola for its repressive methods—was officially disbanded.

Antonio Lobo Antunes was among the troops sent to fight in Angola. He served as a medic for twenty-seven months.

one-armed peanut vendor set up her basket industry in the shade of our veranda, and she would relate her husband's drinking sprees to my grandmother with epic zeal.

In every building there along the Rua Barata Salgueiro lived an old relative amid debris of Chinese vases and mouldy cabinets. In kitchens, ageless servants, all named Albertina, prepared salt-free broths while mumbling fragments of rosary as seasoning for the white rice. My aunts used to approach me, jerking like music-box figurines, to poke my ribs with their canes, observe the lining of my jacket disdainfully, and proclaim: 'You're so skinny.' My pronounced clavicles were more shameful than lipstick on a man's collar. My aunts would then settle with difficulty on the edge of their arm-chairs decorated with crocheted doilies; they would pour tea from ornate services, delivering a torrent of comments while pointing with their teaspoons at photographs of furious generals who, after glorious combats of backgammon and billiards in depressing mess-halls, died before I was born.

'Fortunately the army will make a man of him.'

This vigorous prophecy, transmitted during my childhood and adolescence through false teeth, prolonged itself in strident echoes at the canasta tables, where the women of the clan countered the Sunday Mass with the pagan game at two centavos a point. The pompous solemnity of the men of the family fascinated me even before my first communion, when I still didn't understand that their hushed, reverent conferences were simply about the soft merits of the maid's back-side. These men gravely agreed with my aunts' plans for me, hoping to rid themselves of a future rival who might also cop feels and pinches while the table was being cleared.

The spectre of Salazar, our glorious leader, hovered over the white washbasins, protecting us from the gloomy and suspect idea of socialism. The PIDE carried on courageously with its valiant crusade against the sinister notion of democracy. The framed picture of Cardinal Cerejeira, childhood friend of our leader, zealous guardian of the purity of the Portuguese Catholic Church, guaranteed the perpetuity of the Conference of St Vincent de Paul, and by extension, of the poor servants. The print, picturing the people shouting for joy around a libertarian guillotine, was permanently exiled to the attic, along with old bidets and broken chairs.

When I embarked for Angola, on a ship full of troops, finally to become a man, my tribe, grateful to the government for giving me the opportunity for my metamorphosis, appeared *en masse* at the docks, consenting, in a transport of patriotic fervour, to be elbowed by a restless crowd that came there impotently to witness its own death.

Luanda was Angola's shabby port, its warehouses shimmering in the humidity and heat. The water was like turbid sun-tan lotion glistening on dirty old skin. Blacks squatted in small groups and watched us with timeless distraction. Thin white birds dissolved into the palms along the bay. In the distance was the island to which whores—tired of the men from Lisbon who had forgotten about tenderness—went to drink the last of the soda-pop champagne. Short, bespectacled second lieutenants, with the scrupulous manner of students, led us in the direction of the cattle-cars that waited for us near a barge covered with trash and slime, like the barge near *Cruz Quebrada*, you'll remember, where the sewage spreads out in stagnant pools at the feet of the city, and where old dogs vomit garbage. Wherever we drop anchor, we announce our adventurous presence with our standards and our empty jam tins. I have always thought that we Portuguese should erect a monument to spit in—a spit-poet, a spit-tomb of the unknown soldier, a spit-equestrian— something in honour of the perfect Portuguese male who boasts of his most recent fornication and then spits.

Our train finally rolled from the station near the port and was full of suit-cases and the timid fear of foreigners in an unknown land. The colourful misery of Luanda's slums—the slow thighs of the women and the swollen bellies of the children—awoke in me a strange sensation of the absurd. It was a discomfort I had been feeling since leaving Lisbon, perhaps shared by one of the priests on the boat who was preoccupied with finding a justification for the massacre of the innocents. We would meet, sometimes, on the bulwark—he clutching his books and I with my hands in my pockets—to look at the same black opaque waves. I lost touch with that priest, but I remember his expression: a perplexed Noah forced to board an ark full of animals suffering from stomach aches—dragged from their jobs, their billiard tables, and their clubs—and launched, in the name of strident ideas, into two years of anguish, insecurity, and carnage.

As to the carnage, there was no doubt: huge crates of coffins filled a part of the ship's hold, and we played the macabre game of trying to guess their future occupants. Him? Me? Both of us? The fat major over there talking to the communications officer? Whenever you examine people closely they start to acquire, subtly, a posthumous profile dignified by our fantasy of their death. Sympathy, friendship, even a certain tenderness, become easier.

The train that took us from that African *Cruz Quebrada* ended up dumping us near Luanda in a barracks of sorts. The sweat tingled on our skin. At the officers' quarters, mosquitoes penetrated the window screens to produce a sharp insistent harmony in the dark. Outside, unfamiliar constellations surprised me. We had dinner in the city in sordid esplanades full of soldiers. Fat white men, briefcases under their arms, exchanged Portuguese money for Angolan currency with the measured pace of seagulls. The streets, all looking like Lisbon's Morais Soares, joined and separated in a labyrinth that wound its way to the fort. Provincial neon lights were reflected on the sidewalks in blinking orange pools.

The closeness of death makes us more wary, or at least, more prudent. In Luanda, waiting for a few days before entering the combat zone, we exchanged metaphysics for the degenerate cabarets of the island—whores at our sides, buckets of cheap Raposeira champagne before us, and the little cross-eyed strip-tease artist taking her clothes off on stage with the tired detachment of an old cobra shedding its skin. A few times I woke up in the rooms of slick pensións without knowing how I had got there, and dressed myself in silence looking for my shoes under a black lace brassière, trying not to disturb the sleep of the shape rolled up in the sheets, of which I could see only a confused mass of hair on the pillow. In fact, fulfilling my family's prophecy, I had become a man: a type of cynical and sad avidity. Despair and egoism had supplanted the fragile pleasures of childhood, the laughter without reservation or cryptic meanings—which I think I can hear, you know?—sometimes at night, on my way home in a deserted street, echoing behind me, as a cascade of ridicule.

The Gago Coutinho outpost was our first destination: near the Zambian border, three hundred kilometres south of Luso, two thousand kilometres east of Luanda, the Gago Coutinho comprised a mound of dusty red earth between two eroded plains; a barracks; several tribes led by chieftains forced by the Portuguese government to wear carnival costumes with ridiculous stars and ribbons; the PIDE station; the administration building; Mete Lenha's Café; and the lepers' colony. Once a week I rang a bell, and dozens of deformed larvae would emerge, limping, dragging themselves, loping from the bushes, the trees, the grass huts—larvae of all ages on whose shoulders rags flapped like feathers—advancing toward me and extending the remains of their arms for bottles of medicine. Senhor Jonatao, the black nurse from the public health delegation, distributed pills with the macabre majesty of a priest engaged in a eucharistic ritual for the living dead, some of whom, already blind, had eyes that had been reduced to a cloudy-blue mucus. Mute, frightened children, without fingers, and tortured by flies, huddled together, as women with gargoyle features whispered among themselves. Senhor Jonatao would treat the lepers with a tincture of iodine, while I circulated randomly from tribe to tribe frightening skeletal old women squatting at the entrance to the huts. I smelled manioc drying on matting and humidity, rain, dry excrement, and obese rats rummaging in the garbage. I saw the plain in the distance and a narrow, sinuous river and bats waiting for sunset in the ruins of a colonialist's home, overgrown by colourless grass.

Gago Coutinho also had Mete Lenha's Café. Mete Lenha, who lisped and whose efforts to talk twisted his face into the grimaces of someone straining to shit, was married to a kind of petrol tank, adorned with strident necklaces; who always complained to the officers about the pinches with which the soldiers paid homage to her massive thighs—difficult, in fact, to discern in a woman who looked like an immense rolling gluteus, whose jowls had something anal about them, and whose nose looked like a painful haemorrhoid. This café was for innocent refreshment on impossibly long Sunday afternoons, and it was there that, for the first time, the lieutenant confidentially opened his wallet to show me the picture of his maid, and, leaning back in the wrought-iron chair that was too narrow for his enormous scapula, uttered the grand synthesis of a lifetime of reflection: if the man of the house doesn't give the cook a little stir, the household will never have any love.

After dinner the officers would drive frantically in their jeeps from hut to hut in search of cheap, quick love in stuffy rooms, lit by tentative oil lamps that cast chapel-like illusions on the mud walls. We would arrive with contra-VD ointment that we applied to our cocks sticking through our open zippers, under the indifferent gaze of women with sharp triangular teeth who, squatting on make-shift beds, offered profiles resembling certain Picasso portraits. Often lying beside them were sleeping children, chickens, or some decrepit forebear lost in mummy nightmares, snoring out the hieroglyphics of his dreams. The lieutenant fornicated with the visor of his cap twisted around to the back of his head and with his pistol still strapped to his waist, ever on the alert; the operations officer ordered a sewing machine from Luso and sewed the hems of his trousers at dawn, sitting next to a splendidly energetic black woman with pendulous breasts; and the captain, with whom I played checkers, sat at the wheel of his jeep and asked prepubescent girls to masturbate him, offering them little packages of mint candy. 'The white man came with the whip,' sang the sergeant with the guitar. 'The white man came with the whip and beat the chieftain and the people. The white man came with the whip and beat the chieftain and the people.'

Most of the chieftain's people, however, had already fled to the bush. Forbidden to fish and hunt, dispossessed, hemmed in by barbed-wire fences, fed handouts of dried fish, spied on by the PIDE, tyrannized by the black bodyguards of the officers, they had fled to where the MPLA, our invisible enemy, was hiding. We were forced to fight a hallucinatory war. With every wound from an ambush or a mine, the same distressing question occurred to me—product of the Portuguese youth movement, Catholic journals and the monarchist tabloids, nephew of catechists and an intimate of the Holy Family that visited us at home in a bell jar—who is killing us? The guerrillas or Lisbon? Lisbon, the Americans, the Russians, the Chinese, the whole fucking lot? Who is shitting on us in the name of interests that escape me? Who stuck me in the ass-hole of the world full of red dust and sand, to play checkers with an old captain who was promoted from sergeant and who smelled like a menopausal book-keeper patiently suffering from chronic colitis? Who will explain the absurdity of this to me—of the letters I receive that tell me of a world that distance has rendered strange and unreal, of the calendars I mark with crosses to count the days until my release, as I see before me only the endless tunnel of months into which I have hurled myself?

Then, we were in Ninda.

Ninda: dry corn stalks growing next to the barbed wire rustled all night. The witch doctor sucked blood from the necks of decapitated chickens. And the captain and I played chess at the dining-room table, amid disarray. We would talk outside, sitting in the dark in curved barrel-backed chairs, guessing each other's location from our voices. The captain had introduced me to Marx and Marx then observed me from a distance muttering unintelligible economic theories; bewigged Lenin conspired amid a group of ardent men in frock-coats; Rosa Luxemburg limped in the streets of Berlin; Jaures, shot to death in a restaurant—a napkin around his neck, like a Chicago gangster—spun round and round as in a barber's chair, mirrors and bottles shattering. I imagined myself entering my house accompanied by these spectres as my frightened relatives ran to the safety provided by their own political and religious icons, threatening the socialist vampires with the adjuratory garlic braids of Our Lady of the Conception.

The platoon that went out at night to protect the barracks crouched amid scraggly bushes that grew yellow and gnarled in the sand. Returning in the dark, they passed in front of us, and dispersed silently into the cabins where the bodies of sleeping soldiers were strewn about. I asked the captain, 'What has our government done to my people? What have they done to us sitting and waiting in this oceanless landscape, imprisoned by three rings of barbed wire in a land that doesn't belong to us, dying from malaria and whistling bullets, waiting for supplies whose arrival is always threatened by accidents, ambushes and mines, fighting an invisible enemy, fighting impossibly long days that do not follow one upon the other, fighting homesickness, indignation, and remorse?'

Ninda. The attack began near the landing field, opposite the tribal village. There were moving lights that turned on and off pin the plateau in a kind of morse code. The enormous moon shone on our prefab barracks and sentry posts protected by sandbags and wooden logs. At the door of the health station, I, half-asleep and naked, saw soldiers running with their rifles toward the barbed wire. Then voices, the shouts, red spurts—all of that—the tension, lack of decent food, the precarious shelters, the undrinkable water, the monstrous cruelty of war, it all made me feel as if I were in an unreal place, a dream. Lying in my barracks, waiting for the attack to subside, looking at the stiff silhouettes of the eucalyptus trees with a useless G3 rifle in my sweaty palms and a cigarette stuck in my mouth like a toothpick, I thought of myself as a character from Beckett waiting for the hand grenade of a redemptive Godot. The novels I still had to write accumulated in the attic of my mind like old machines reduced to a heap of odd parts that I could never re-assemble; the women I would never sleep with offered their spreading thighs to others. My unborn child would be only the improbable material-ization of a distant afternoon in Tomar, in a room in the officers' quarters with the window wide open looking out on the park, and my wife and I celebrating our desire in bed.

Ninda.

Listen. Look at me and listen, I need you to listen to me. Listen to me with the same anxious attention we gave the radio appeals from the column under fire, the voice of the transmissions officer, calling, begging, forgetting the security code, the captain hurriedly climbing with half-a-dozen volunteers into his Mercedes that skidded in the sand on its way to the ambush. Listen to me the way I bent over our first corpse, desperately hoping that he was still breathing, the corpse I wrapped in a blanket and took to my room right after lunch, and as I closed the door I said, 'Have a nice nap,' as outside the soldiers looked at me in silence. This time there'll be no miracle, fellows, I thought, looking at them. 'He's taking a nap,' I explained to them, 'he's taking a nap and I don't want you to wake him up because he doesn't want to wake up,' and then I went to treat the wounded who were writhing in stretchers, and never before had the eucalyptus of Ninda seemed as big to me as on that afternoon, big, black, high, frightening, and the medic who was helping me kept saying Shit, shit, shit, with his northern accent—we came from all points of our muzzled country to die in Ninda, from our sad country of stone and sea to die in Ninda—Shit, shit, shit, I repeated along with the medic in my sophisticated Lisbon accent, while the captain got out of the Mercedes with infinite weariness, holding his weapon like a useless fishing rod, and the people from the black compound peered at us anxiously. Listen to me as I listened to the throbbing of the blood in my temples, and through the spaces in the lattice work on the porch I could see the captain pacing back and forth pressing a glass of whiskey to his chest, talking to himself, everyone talking to himself because nobody was able to talk to anybody—'Let's drink to National Unity'—while the corpse grew in the room until it burst through the walls, dragged itself through the sand to reach the bush in search of the echo of the shot that had killed it, and then the helicopter transported it to Gago Coutinho as if they were sweeping shameful garbage under a rug, and the medic arranged the surgical instruments in the stainless steel box, the scalpels, pincers, the needles, and probes, and sat down next to me on the steps of the first-aid station, a type of small vacation cottage for ageing caretakers, virgin governesses—'Fuck it,' said the medic, polishing his boots with his fingers.

Listen: before that there was Ferreira's leg, that is, Ferreira's leg that an anti-personnel mine transformed into the absence of Ferreira's leg, and there was Corporal Mazunguidi's tattered thighs from which I extracted even the metal eyelets of his boots. I walked out to the porch of the first-aid station in my blood-stained shirt where the indifferent clarity of the day was an insult and the freshness of the morning a welcome relief. If the revolution is over, see, and in a way it really is, it is because the dead of Africa, their mouths full of dirt, cannot protest, and hour by hour the political Right kills more of them while we, the survivors, continue to doubt that we are alive, continue to be afraid that we will discover in some casual gesture that we are as dead as they. The burial urn of Corporal Pereira, Carpinteiro's urn, Macaco's urn, the man killed by a mine just fifty metres away from me, whose ribs were crushed by the sand bag against the steering wheel of the overturned car, and on whom I wanted to perform a cardiac massage but his chest was a soft, popping, boneless mass, and my palms pressed a pulp—it just took one explosion to turn Macaco into a rag-and-sawdust puppet. The captain disappeared into the pantry of the mess hall and came back with more whiskey in his glass, and the plain lost colour, announcing night, and the medic who kept saying Shit, shit, shit, squatted at our feet. We all said Shit, between our clenched teeth, the captain whispered Shit into his whiskey glass, the duty officer stood at attention in front of the flag and his fingers, adjusting his cap, shouted Shit, the stray dogs rubbing against our heels moaned Shit as they stared at us with eyes as imploring as those of the customers in this bar here, humid with resignation and stupid meekness, eyes bobbing up and down over glasses of Cognac.

Why the hell won't they talk about it? I'm beginning to think that the million and a half Portuguese who passed through Africa never existed and I am narrating for you a cheap contrived story composed of one-third bullshit, one-third alcohol, and one-third tenderness to persuade you to watch the sunrise with me in the pale blue clarity that pierces the blinds and reveals the curve of a thigh, the silhouette of a shoulder on the mattress, our bodies entangled in torpor. How long has it been since I was able to sleep? I enter each night like a furtive bum with a second-class ticket in a first-class car, a clandestine passenger of my depressions coiled in inertia, a walking dead man, deriving deceptive energy from vodka. Really, how long has it been since I have been able to sleep? Every morning in the mirror, I discover I have grown older: the foam of the shaving cream transforms me into a pyjama-wearing Santa Claus whose tousled hair modestly hides the wrinkles on his forehead.

On the afternoon of June 22 1971, I was in Chieme. It was then that they called me by radio from Gago Coutinho to announce the birth of my daughter by spelling, 'Gordo, Ira, Romeo, Lucky.' And with the walls lined with pictures of nude women for the siesta masturbation, enormous mammaries that suddenly began to advance and withdraw, I gripped the back of the corporal's chair and thought something crazy is going to happen me and I'm screwed.

I had got married, you know how it is, four months before leaving, in August, on a sunny afternoon of which I have confused and ardent memories. The sound of the organ, the flowers on the altar, and the tears of the family lent a certain soft and compassionate Buñuel touch. There were brief week-end encounters when we would make love with urgent anger, inventing a desperate tenderness in

305

anticipation of the anguish of our approaching separation, and we said good-bye in the rain, on the docks, dry eyed, locked in an embrace of orphans. And now, ten thousand kilometres from me, my daughter suddenly burst forth in the transmissions cubicle. My daughter. The National Women's Movement must have been thinking of us as its members sat under their hairdryers; the patriots of the National Union must have been thinking of us as they affectionately nurtured the heroes who would replace us; the businessmen must have been thinking of us while they manufactured war material at reasonable prices; the Government must have been thinking of us as it gave miserable pensions to the soldiers' wives; and we, ungrateful targets of so much love, left the barbed wire where we were rotting only to die perversely in a mine or an ambush, or else we simply abandoned fatherless children who had been taught to point at our pictures next to the television set in living-rooms where we had never been.

My place? I live behind the illuminated fountain in Picheleira, in an apartment with a view of the river, and every time I open the door and clear my throat, the echo of my cough bounces back from the end of the hall and I am overcome by a strange sensation, do you understand? Has it ever occurred to you to observe yourself when you are alone? Your eyes search for an impossible companionship in their own reflection. At moments like these I usually sit on the floor in my daughters' room. My girls visit me every two weeks spreading crumbs throughout the deserted rooms and I watch over their sleep with sentimental solicitude, tripping on dolls' legs and comic books. Or, from time to time, women I have casually found in the corner of a sofa at a friend's party, like unexpectedly finding change in the pocket of one's winter coat, come up with me in the elevator for the quick imitation of fascination and tenderness that I know by heart—from the first suggestive Scotch to the look of desire long enough not to be sincere, to the afterlife of love-making, the sluicings in the bidet where our effusions dissolve in soap, anger, and lukewarm water.

And how do you get along? You know, I imagine you in a scenario half-way between oriental philosophy and the judicious, lucid Left, for whom May '68 represented a kind of annoying childhood affliction that reduced the dream of a better life to the disillusioned, utilitarian, cynical Marxism of certain bureaucracies of the East: a lot of pillows on the floor, the smell of incense floating over the Indian bibelots, a Siamese cat disdainful as a prima donna, books by Reich and Garaudy promulgating their vehement prophecies on the shelves, the febrile voice of Leo Ferre on the record-player. Moustached architects with their studied rumpled look occasionally occupy your antique brass bed, filling your ashtrays with the butts of unfiltered cigarettes or scratching the shaggy hair on their chests. In the mornings, wearing slippers in the kitchen, you make the strong coffee that will propel you toward your job, as you sit at the steering wheel of a cream-coloured Renault 4, its back fender crushed by an irate taxi driver. Living in the same city, we can spend years and years near each other, but without ever meeting. We are, if I can express myself this way, contemporaries, and our parallel trajectories will finally meet in my house (because the smell of incense makes me sick).

The war in Africa? You're right, I'm wandering, I'm wandering like an old man on a park bench lost in the exquisite labyrinth of his past. What is certain is that, as Lisbon receded from me, my country became more and more unreal, my country, my house, my daughter with the clear eyes in her crib, became as unreal as these trees, these façades, these dead streets. Lisbon, understand, is an amusement park, a travelling circus set up beside a river, an invention of tiles that repeat each other: no, seriously, we live in a land that does not exist. It is only an eye, a name, not our country. Lisbon begins to take shape, believe me, only from a distance.

When my daughter was born I took a short leave and went to foggy Luanda. The windows of the pensión where I was staying opened out on the confused morning of Matamba, and I removed from my suitcase the picture of my daughter I'd been sent and put it between the telephone and a glass of water. In an anonymous room smelling of disinfectant, formica, and glue, I stretched out on the bed with my jacket and shoes on and fell asleep.

Night comes too soon in the tropics. I dined alone in a restaurant full of sleek men whose necks glistened with sweat, and whose fingers were studded with rings of red or black stones. A black hunchback went from table to table trying to hawk plastic dolls until the waiter swatted him with a grimy napkin. A juke-box shrieked with loud bullish suggestions in the background and I telephoned a stewardess I had met who was waiting for me on a third floor in the Bairro Prenda, stuffed into a pair of jeans so tight you could almost see the veins of her thighs.

'Hello Modesty Blaise,' I said. Her breasts, under a print t-shirt, were like two enormous pears under a Coca-Cola napkin: without her uniform, she didn't have the mystery I insist on attributing to angels. Her apartment smelled like dirty laundry and canned dog food. The African night came in through the open window in the guise of a thick stable odour; in the unmade bed a book of Eluard's poems promised fragile sweetness in the body of this Amazon charged with busting the balls of warriors in transit to the carnage of the front.

'What do you drink, Blue Eyes?' she asked with a carnivorous smile that made me think of the story of Little Red Riding Hood: All the better to eat you with, my dear, said the Wolf, wearing a nightcap and baring his pointed teeth. All the better to eat you with, all the better to eat you with, all the better to eat you with, my dear. Her mouth grew in my direction—concave, gigantic, bottomless—and her red nails grew until they grazed my skin. Her dog scratched at the kitchen door with sad yelps. I put my glass on a bamboo table and was congratulated by the frozen laughter of a ceramic buddha; the clinking ice cubes reminded me of the bell we had bought for my little girl's crib. (Now my wife was heating the midnight bottle; a cigarette burned blue serenity in a tin ashtray; the comfort of domestic silences circled the painful corners of despair. A whole universe from which I found myself excluded went on imperturbably in my absence, its mincing pace marked by the rapid ticking of the alarm clock, by a tap ceaselessly dripping in the dark.) The girl shoved the Eluard book off the bed (*larmes des yeux les malheurs des malheureux*) and slipped out of her clothes shaking her mane. (In Lisbon, my daughter, with eyes shut, nursed her bottle, and in the lamp-light her ears acquired a rose-coloured transparency.) I took off my trousers, unbuttoned my shirt. The buddha jeered at my pale, distressed thinness. I stretched out on the bed, ashamed at the size of my flaccid penis reduced to a shrivelled piece of tripe amid the auburn hair down there; the stewardess handled it politely with two fingers as if she were at a formal dinner—

I'm not sure whether with surprise or distaste. Get hard, you imbecile, I ordered. (My daughter stopped drinking her bottle to burp and her eyes looked inward, unfocused.) I touched the woman's vulva, and it was moist and warm and tender; I found the hard nerve of her clitoris and she let out a small sigh. For the love of God get hard—I begged looking surreptitiously at my dead cock—don't make me look bad and get hard I begged, for your own good get hard, get hard, fuck, get hard. (My wife changed the nappies with pins in her mouth.)

The woman stopped kissing me, propped herself up on her elbow like a figure in an Etruscan tomb, put her hand on my face and asked, 'What's the matter, Blue Eyes?' I hunched my shoulders, rolled over on my stomach and began to cry.

Even at this hour of the night Lisbon is devoid of mystery. The night transforms houses and buildings into sad family vaults where sour couples are allowed for a few hours to forget their petty quarrels. Around Edurado VII Park homosexuals approach passing cars. At the Palace of Justice, prostitutes stand listlessly in the pale light of the street lamps. Inside, before a serenely disinterested judge, busy palpating a boil on his neck, my marriage ended without glory after several months of rendezvous and estrangements. We separated with relief and remorse, said good-bye in the lift as if we were strangers, and kissed for the last time. I don't know if it has ever happened to you: if by chance you have known the agony of clandestine rendezvous on week-ends in seaside motels with lead-coloured waves crashing against the chipped cement of the porch; if you have embraced a body that you love but you don't love in the way small monkeys hang from their mother's fur; or if you have had to make promises that lack conviction. You see, for a year I stumbled from address to address, from woman to woman, with the frenzy of a blind child groping for what escapes him, and I woke many times alone in hotel rooms with telephones without numbers that connected me to the mistrustful cordiality of desk clerks intrigued by my meagre baggage. I ruined my teeth and my stomach in cheap restaurants where all the food tastes like charcoal. I went to midnight shows, my neck chilled by the cough of the man in the back row, who read the credits out loud to invent a companion for himself. And I discovered one afternoon, sitting on an esplanade in Alges, in the bubbly presence of a bottle of soda water, that I was no longer alive.

In Chiume, Christmas '71, the first Christmas of the war after almost a year in the bush, one year of despair, anxiety, and death in the bush, I woke up in the morning and thought It's Christmas day today. I looked outside and nothing had changed in the camp: the same tents, the same circle of vehicles next to the barbed wire, the same dilapidated abandoned building that a bazooka grenade had destroyed, the same slow men tripping in the sand or squatting silently on the broken-down steps of the mess hall like beggars in front of a church. I woke up in the morning and thought, 'Today is Christmas'. I saw the dark clouds in the sky over the Quando River. The heat dripped from my shoulders in thick sticky beads of sweat and I said to myself, 'This can't be, there is something wrong here.'

A few days before a company of parachutists had left in a column protected by South African helicopters that had arrived for an extravagant and pointless operation in the Luchaze territory. And every night the pilots—enormous, blond, arrogant—got noisily drunk, breaking glasses and bottles and singing songs out of tune in Afrikaans. They were commanded by a David Niven type, apparently off his diet, who, with the demeanour of an obsequious nurse, contemplated his subordinates vomiting beer, holding each other up, and said: 'If you worry you die, if you don't worry you die. So why worry?'

The officers in our group observed the pandemonium of belches and broken glass, moving their lips with silent reproaches. The captain, possessed by the spirit of a *Better Homes and Gardens* housewife, fluttered anxiously around the china that was still intact. Lieutenant Eleuterio, wrinkled as a foetus, listened to Beethoven in a corner. The Catanguese snuck off the black compound in search of a rat barbecue. And I, leaning against the window frame, watched the elliptical flight of the bats around the light bulbs, not hearing anything, not thinking anything, not wanting anything, sure that my life would end in the barbed-wire space in which I found myself, under a low sky, talking in the shade with the chief about his sewing machine and listening to stories of crocodiles in happier times.

The brutal impertinence of the South Africans, who regarded us as if we were barely tolerable mulattoes, sparked a flame in me that had already been fuelled by the savagery of the secret police and the abject patriotic speeches on the radio. The Lisbon politicians appeared to me as criminal puppets or imbeciles, simultaneously defending interests that were not mine and preparing for their own defeat. The troops were aware that neither these men nor their sons would ever see action; they knew where the men rotting in the bush were coming from. Every afternoon we listened clandestinely to the MPLA broadcasts; we fed our wives and children on miserable salaries; in Lisbon there were too many cripples limping around the Military Hospital grounds in the evenings, and every stump was a shout of revolt against the incredible absurdity of bullets in Angola. Later, we learned about the hostility of the Angolan whites: the farmers and industrialists secluded in their pretentious residences full of fake antiques, from which they sauntered to pick up Brazilian prostitutes in the cabarets on the Island, and consume bottles of local champagne.

'If you weren't here, we'd clear the blacks out in a minute.'

Pricks, I thought, drinking Cuba Libres at the bar, sweaty fat slobs, rich shits, slave traffickers. But I envied them the giggles of their women, their embraces, the smell of cheap perfume coming from their armpits and groins at the slightest movement, the Queen Maria bed in which they would get laid early in the morning amid tarnished mirrors, rubber trees, and Ming miniature dogs.

It was Christmas in Chiume and nothing had changed. No one from my family was there with me. My grandfather's house—with its garden and statues, the lake and the greenhouse into which the dining-room extended—remained anchored in Benfica, behind the brick-coloured gate and the driveway filled with the cars of visitors: they are arriving for lunch, the old servants of my youth are serving the soup, and shortly my grandmother will tell a grandson to ask the staff to come for their carefully wrapped presents (socks, underwear, sweaters, long johns). Sitting on my bunk, in front of the green-yellow vastness of the plain and the thunder along the River Quando, I recalled my ancient aunts in their enormous apartments on the Alexandre Herculando and the Barata Salgueiro, submerged in an eternal dusk in which wine glasses and soup tureens sparkled: Aunt

Mimi, Aunt Bilu, a sick gentleman babbling in his armchair, old fellows who parted their hair from behind the ear to hide their baldness, upright pianos, a portrait signed by Portugal's last king, biscuit tins with hunting scenes on the lid, Uncle Eloi winding the clocks in the hall, and the suddenly delicate fingers of the grounds-keeper tending a flower. I had jumped without transition from that solemn community to the war—I thought, buttoning up my camouflage uniform—to being forced to confront a death which had nothing in common with the antiseptic death of hospital patients for which I had been prepared. Their agony had only intensified my assurance that I was alive. Now I was offered the vertigo of my own end in the end of those who ate with me, slept with me, talked with me, lay with me in the trenches during the cross-fire of attacks. Silhouettes and voices arose from the black compound, approaching me: my uncles, my brothers, my cousins, my grandmother's chauffeur (affected and very delicate), the old men with the parts behind the ear, the grounds-keeper, the sick old gentleman in the arm chair—uniformed, exhausted, dirty, their weapons over their shoulders—all were now walking towards the infirmary, carrying me in a piece of canvas between two sticks, my limp body with a bayonet in my bloody thigh. I recognized myself as in an excessively faithful mirror, and examined my shut eyes, my pale mouth, the blond turf of my beard on my chin, the mark left on my finger by the wedding band I had lost. My family, standing still, waited at the door of the first-aid station, waited in suspense for me to revive myself; the transmissions corporal shouted orders to the helicopter to take me to Benfica in time for coffee and liqueurs. No sound came through the rubber plugs of the stethoscope I held against my chest. The medic handed me the adrenaline syringe and I opened my shirt and stuck the needle into my heart.

Here we are. No, I don't think I've had too much to drink. I always fumble with the lock, maybe because I find it difficult to accept the fact that this is my building and that the terrace up there in the dark is part of my apartment. I feel like a dog who sniffs its own urine on the tree it has pissed on, and sometimes, surprised and incredulous, I stand here for a few minutes, between the letter-boxes and the lift, searching in vain for some sign of myself; a footprint, a smell, a piece of clothing. You can't imagine how I envy the tranquil security of my neighbours, the decisiveness with which they open their door, the cordiality of their smiles. I always suspect that they are going to kick me out, that when I walk into my apartment I will find someone else's furniture instead of my own, unfamiliar books on the shelves, a child somewhere in the hall, a man installed on my couch looking up at me, baffled but indignant.

We are never where we are, don't believe it, not even now, as we ride in this small lift as you, serious and quiet, obliquely encourage my goatish impulses. At this moment you, my friend, are probably nude on the beach last August in the company of one of those intelligent, ugly creatures who are easy to like because, on the one hand they don't compete with you, and on the other, they save you from having to go alone to the film series at the Gulbenkian Foundation, often attended by lucid myopics and imperious sociologists; at this moment I might be in Angola as I was eight years ago, saying good-bye to the chieftain-tailor, standing next to his sewing machine now covered with rust and corroded by the sand. We are going to leave Chiume for the north. The convoy is waiting for us. And I am standing at the centre of the black compound, nauseated by the odour of manioc drying on the roofs of the huts.

The story of Portuguese Africa—as told by lycée history books, politicians, and chaplains—was really nothing more than a provincial drama unfolding in immeasurable vastness; housing projects devoured by the grass and the underbrush; a great desolate silence. The lands at the end of the earth were governed by alcoholic, greedy commanders shivering from malaria in their empty houses, reigning over a passive people sitting at the entrance to their huts with vegetal indifference. President Tomas looked at us with the idiotic, glassy stare of a stuffed bear, while his militia dozed off at sentinel posts guarding useless barbed wire.* But there was the almost immaterial beauty of the Ninda or Cessa eucalyptus, imprisoning the dense nights in their branches. There was the angry majesty of the Chalala forest resisting the bombs. And there were the tatooed women giving birth to children who would be, I hoped, greater than those around us and would not squat, defeated, in front of their huts, passing a gourd pipe to one another.

_____

*Rodrigues Tomas was President of Portugal from 1958.

313

The East? Yes, in a certain way I am still there, sitting next to the driver in one of the trucks in the convoy bouncing along on the sand roads on the way to Malanje. 'No one who comes here goes back the same,' I explained to the captain of the wire-framed glasses, delicately moving pieces on the chessboard. When the gangrened thigh of an MPLA guerrilla captured at Mussuma was amputated, the soldiers had their picture taken with it as if it were a trophy. The war has turned us into animals, you see, cruel, stupid animals taught only to kill. Just before we arrived in Luso, we were stopped by someone who, having been sent out ahead in a jeep, was meant to tell us that the General did not want us to spend the night in the city, did not want us to expose our wounds in the mess hall.

'We are not rabid dogs,' shouted the lieutenant, not caring that he was addressing the envoy of the zone command. 'Tell that bastard that we are not rabid dogs.'

Another lieutenant threatened to destroy the mess hall with the bazookas. 'Let's blow up the fuckers, Lieutenant, sir, there won't be one bastard left to drive us nuts.'

'One year in the ass-hole of the world doesn't give us the right to sleep in beds at night,' the operations officer observed.

The lieutenant banged the bonnet of the jeep with his fist, 'Tell the general to stick it up his ass.'

'We were not rabid dogs when we got here,' I said to the lieutenant who was pacing back and forth with furious indignation. 'We weren't rabid dogs before the censored letters, the attacks, the ambushes, the mines, the shortages of food, tobacco, soda, matches, water, coffins, before a Berliet became more valuable than a man and before a man was only worth three lines in the newspaper: "He died in combat in a province of Angola." We were not rabid dogs but we were as nothing to the State that shit on us and used us like laboratory rats—the same State that now is afraid of us, so afraid of our presence, of the unpredictability of our reactions and of the guilt we elicit that it goes the other way if it sees us from a distance. It avoids us. It avoids facing a vanquished army in the name of cynical ideals nobody believes in, an army defeated while defending the wealth of the three or four families that support the regime.'

The lieutenant turned to me, touched me on the arm and begged, 'Doctor, inject me with a disease before I explode from all the shit inside me.'

My company went through Malanje like a shot, and we set up camp in Marimba, where mango trees grew atop a hill in yet another encirclement of barbed wire, and where little black boys from neighbouring villages would come and peer at us.

There we waited, waited for months, waited for mines, waited for malaria, waited for our improbable return to our families and friends at the airport or at the docks, waited for mail, waited for the PIDE jeep that made weekly trips to check with informers at the border to come back, bringing three or four prisoners who would dig their own graves, curl up inside them, squeeze their eyes shut, and go limp after being shot through the head.

'A ticket to Luanda,' the PIDE agent remarked calmly, enjoying the euphemism, as he put his gun back in its holster. 'You can't trust these bastards.'

That night the agent cut his ass on the broken toilet seat, and I sewed up his behind without anaesthesia in the cubicle of the first-aid station under the satisfied observation of the medic, avenging, if only in a trifling way, the silent Angolan prisoners whose panic had manifested itself in sheets of sweat, and who had stared at us with eyes as hard and blank as those of naked corpses in the hospital morgue.

In the North, for lack of whiskey, we drank the sulphuric brews provided by the administrator—a fat Indian who received officers with the amiable pomposity of a monarch, and after dinner, we ceremoniously visited his house for a game of bingo. Dona Aurea, the administrator's wife, distributed the cards and the chick peas, and pulled wooden numbers out of a bag. Her husband, on the other side of the room, invited the school teacher to dance tangos cranked out by the record player. She was a thin little creature, with clavicles as pronounced as Brezhnev's eyebrows, and her interminable menstruations afflicted her with colic and anaemia. She looked at us through tired eyes that suggested fainting spells and addition tables. Lightning from the Cambo River illuminated the windows. A mulatto, owner of the only shop around, dozed with a tooth-pick in his mouth.

Outside, the African guarding the generator with a musket from the days of the Spanish conquest snored under the cement roof. Bats the size of partridges flew around the lamps. Pale fires could be seen in the dense shadows of the black settlements: Chief Macau, Chief

315

Pedro Macau, Chief Marimba. After the war began the Mo-Holos and the Bundi-Bangalas—the primitive inhabitants of the Baixa do Cassanje—had been killed or exiled to the Congo. Their villages were repopulated with Gingas from the area around Luanda, who were more obedient and accommodating because their chief had rotted for twenty years in the colonial prisons, falsely accused of some crime. Forced to wear the embarrassing uniform of a carnival emperor, a tin crown encrusted with glass diamonds, ridiculed by the Salazar corporate state in front of his people, the king wandered among the members of his tribe like the mentally ill in a psychiatric ward. The elders of the tribe observed him with incredulity and displeasure. Nevertheless, Chief Bimbe and Chief Caputo, from the other side of the border, continued the fight, and you could see the MPLA bases in the Congo from Marimbanguengo, tiny but burgeoning constructions.

You can't imagine the absurdity of this bingo game in the middle of nowhere, the dusty tangos, the pathetic toilettes of the women, the men's flattery, the European water colours on the walls. While those condemned by the PIDE coiled like retracted tentacles in their holes, soldiers trembled with malaria on their bunks. In Luanda, in air-conditioned quarters, generals invented the war in which we were dying in and off which they lived. The African night unfolded into a majestic infinity of stars. The Bailundo tribesmen, purchased in Nova Lisboa, suffered in the black compounds with an agonizing homesickness. And I wrote home saying that Everything is fine, in hopes that they would appreciate the uselessness of the suffering, the sadism, the separation, the uselessness of tenderness and longing, hoping they would appreciate what I could not very well write down on paper, the Shit shit shit shit shit of the medic after the ambush—remember, the one in the East—the sand lots of the Luchazes, where the corporal's corpse rotted in my room under the sheets. And I sat on the steps of the first-aid station as I am sitting with you here in this room, watching the boats on the river and our reflections in the window.

Let me rest my head on your knees for a while and close my eyes, the same eyes with which I saw the African guard stick ice cubes up this guy's ass and I didn't protest because fear, you see, restrained me from even the slightest gesture of revolt. My egotistical desire was to return to Portugal intact and quickly. I wanted to return and forget, to go back to work at the hospital and my writing and my family and the cinema on Saturday and my friends. I wanted to disembark on the Conde De Obidos rock and declare to myself, It was all a lie and I've woken up. And still, you understand, on nights like this, when the alcohol accentuates my feeling of solitude, the memory of my cowardice and conformity eight years ago haunts me. How do I say it? A kind of remorse drives me to crouch in a corner of my apartment like a hunted beast, pallid, ashamed, afraid, waiting for the dawn.

Morning won't come. It's useless to wait for the glare of the roof-tops, for light to flicker through the blinds. We are condemned, you and I, to an endless night, a labyrinth of anguish obliquely illuminated by the turbid clarity of Scotch.

Meanwhile, maybe we could try to make love, and indulge in pagan gymnastics. My bed doesn't creak; nothing will disturb our mechanical caresses. We have gone through too much to run the idiotic risk of falling in love. Time has conferred on us the wisdom of scepticism. We lose the frank simplicity of youth after our second suicide attempt, when we wake up on a hospital bed under the reproving look of a doctor and distrust humanity as much as ourselves, because we have got to know the sour egoism of our character, hidden under a deceiving veneer. It's not that I don't believe in you. My distrust is in myself: my need to sabotage the pleasant everyday moments, pulverizing them with acid irony until they turn into the awful pabulum of my habitual bitterness. What would happen to us if we were really happy? Have you noticed how we cannot stand sincere, unconditional affection? These people, the Camilo Torreses, the Guevaras, the Allendes, we hurry to kill them because their combative love disturbs us. We search them out with bazookas perched on our shoulders, angry in the jungles of Bolivia. We bombard their palaces. We replace them with cruel, slimy characters more like ourselves.

Between us sexual relations would be a soft violation: the defeat of two wet exhausted bodies lying on a mattress, checking the time on the clock on the night table, waiting to dress silently, wash our faces, comb our hair, and leave under cover of darkness. But if I were to tell you that I love you, you would answer me, in the most serious tone in the world, that you haven't felt so passionate about a man since you were eighteen. You would insist that something different and strange was happening to you, that all of a sudden you have a catfish urge never to leave me. We would end up laughing into our respective glasses at the innocence of our innocuous lies. But suppose we were to divest ourselves of our malice for a minute, and were, instead, sincere? Suppose that while stroking your hand I were touching a vulnerable and fragile girl, chewing gum under a poster of James Dean, blond archangel whose brief trajectory abruptly ended in a heap of smoking scrap iron. Suppose that your nipples were to harden from real pleasure, that your thighs were to quiver, that you wanted me in you? Don't worry. It's too late. Our excessive lucidity pre-empts the stupid, hot impulses of passion. My thin hair and your wrinkles, are our defences.

We are in a position, therefore, to go to the bed and make insipid love.

I told her I'd be right back, Sofia, and I came here to sit in front of mirror where I shave every morning to talk to you. I miss your smile, your hands caressing my body, your feet tickling mine. I miss the smell of your hair. I need your body next to mine, your black thighs, your hot mysterious laughter that the PIDE, the government, the CETEC tractor operators, the administrator's greed, and the sadistic and perverse fury of the whites were incapable of silencing.

I met you in Gago Coutinho on a Saturday morning, when the washerwomen came to the barbed wire to deliver the soldiers' starched clothing, and they waited, on the slope of the hill, next to the guard-gate, talking in their native language that I hardly understood, but in which I heard Charlie Parker's swing when he's not shouting his hatred for the ridiculous and cruel world of the whites. Holding the clean clothes wrapped in colourful bundles, they allowed the soldiers to graze their hands over their bellies, their backs, their breasts, under the hot, stationary sun of Angola, while they jeered among themselves at the pathetic desire of the whites, their clumsiness and their haste.

On Saturday mornings the old people gathered around a gourd of tobacco in the centre of the black compound exhaling through their nostrils and their mouths billows of brown smoke, masking their hatred for the occupying forces with vegetal indifference. They were the old men of Nengo, Lusse, and Luate; the old men of Cessa and Mussuma; the old men of Launguina and Lucusse, of Narriquinha and Chalala; the proud old Luchazes, lords of the Lands at the End of the Earth, who had come many centuries ago from Ethiopia in successive migrations. They had expelled the Hotentots and the Kamessekeles to inhabit this land of sand and cold nights. Free old men were put behind barbed wire and turned into ragged slaves by the primitive rifles of the black bodyguard and the furious lizard-like faces of the secret police and the rancour of the colonial state that treated them like a subhuman race.

The old men gathered in the centre of the black compound. The wild dogs barked at the scrawny chickens in the settlements. The commander shrugged his shoulders in his armoured office—he too was a slave behind barbed wire, a slave of the proud perpetrators of the war who, sticking coloured pins into their maps in Luanda, killed us off one by one—and I looked at you, Sofia, sitting on the slope among your women who laughed and made fun of the soldiers pawing them: the Luchaze women spreading their indifferent thighs for the whites in the huts cursed by the silence of the solemn children in the corners playing games with pieces of sugar cane.

I met you on a Saturday morning, and your uninhibited laughter touched me.

I was sick of the war, sick of the obstinate evil of the war and of listening, in bed, to the protestations of my dead companions persecuting me in my sleep, begging me not to let them rot in their lead coffins. I was sick of being a larva among larvae in the mourning chamber of the mess hall. I was sick of the old captain's chess games and of the lieutenants' depressing jokes, sick of working, night after night, in the infirmary, up to my elbows in the viscous, hot blood of the wounded. I was sick, Sofia, and my entire body ached for the serenity that a man can find only in the body of a woman.

The sergeant medic led you over by the arm to a corner of the compound facing the road to Luso, where I had stayed to look at you. In the distance there was a verdigris expanse of forest that the CETEC machines were stupidly destroying, trunk by trunk, and the medic asked me in a sad voice, timidly, afraid of himself, 'Do you need a washerwoman, Doctor?'

I didn't, Sofia, because the orderlies took care of my shirts and towels and shorts and socks, but I needed you.

I was sick of the war, Sofia, sick of seeing the wounded arriving from the sand road on makeshift canvas stretchers, the wounded whose mouths opened and closed with indecipherable and tortured appeals. I was sick of bending over dying soldiers in an improvised operating room. I was tired of stepping outside to smoke cigarettes before daybreak, to see a curved sky with unknown stars. Standing at the door of the operating room—the camp dogs greedy for the carnage of my wounded companions, sniffing at my clothes, licking blood off my pants and my arms—I was filled with hate, for the people who lied to us and oppressed us, humiliated and killed us in Angola: the serious and dignified gentlemen in Lisbon, the politicians, the magistrates, the police, the informers, the bishops, the people who, with hymns and speeches, sent us off in battleships to die in Africa.

After dinner on the evening of the day when I first met you, Sofia, I fled from the old captain's chess game and from the lieutenants' poker, and I walked through the guard-gate in the direction of the chaos of the black compound below, where the smell of manioc rose like moisture from a tomb.

I could have sworn you were waiting for me, Sofia, inside the thick adobe walls, because the wooden door opened, without my touching it, into a darkness darker than the night. There was only sound—breathing, whispers, and the soft cackle of sleeping hens—as you led me through the dark. And I imagined your triumphant laughter, the laughter of a free woman whom no secret police, no soldier, no African guard could ever silence.

I could have sworn that the hollow in the straw mattress was the shape of my body, as if you had been waiting for me forever; that your vagina was perfectly fitted to my penis; and that the little mulatto boy, sleeping soundly in the cane crib has features resembling mine before the bitterness and the suffering of the war changed me into a disillusioned, cynical creature, proceeding mechanically through love-making with the indifferent gestures of people dining alone in a restaurant.

You were waiting for me, Sofia; you lit an oil wick in a bottle, and the flickers of light revealed, intermittently: tins on shelves, a clothes basket, the closed window, and an old woman sitting in a corner smoking a cane pipe in absolute quiet. You were waiting for me, and we exchanged not a single word, because you understood my anguish, the indignation that my cowardice provoked in me, my submissive acceptance of the violence and the war that the gentlemen in Lisbon had imposed on me. You understood my desperate caresses and my fearful tenderness, and your arms made their way slowly down my back, slowly up and down the length of my cold flanks, until you rested my head on your shoulder.

Your house smelled hot and healthy, delicate and invincible; and, coming from the camp, twisted, as I was, by homesickness and fear, I felt I was re-enacting my childhood with you.

I have always been a loner, Sofia, while I was in school, at the lycée, the university, the hospital, while I was married; a loner with books I read too many times, with my pretentious and vulgar poems; alone with my anxiety about writing, my fear that I wasn't good enough, that I wasn't able to translate into words what I felt like screaming into people's ears: I am here; notice me because I'm here; listen to me even in my silence and understand. But it's impossible to understand what is not said. People look at you. They don't comprehend. They walk away. I was always alone, Sofia, even in the war, especially in the war, because the camaraderie of war is a fellowship of false generosity resulting from a destiny suffered together but not really shared. Even in the abandoned mission, sitting with the lieutenant in the back seat of the jeep under the acacias, listening to the insects and the birds and the deafening silence of Africa, I was alone. Alone in the infirmary with the wounded who moaned and cried and called for me nights on end, doubled over with fear and pain. What an idiotic war, Sofia. What an idiotic war in a miraculous place which makes you feel that you could sprout with the sunflowers and where the children are ushered into the world with the thrust of a geyser, steaming and triumphant.

Sofia, we lost each other. When I got to your house and the door didn't open, I knocked. I circled the adobe, listening, and heard nothing, no breathing, not even the cackling of the hens through the cracks in the mud, through the grass on the roof. I knocked again and the old woman smoking her pipe opened the door a little and stared at me vacantly. I approached her, peered inside. The oil wick

illuminated the deserted bed, the limey folds of the sheets, the rusty tins on the shelf. The old woman took the pipe out of her mouth, spat a wad as dark as a rain cloud at my thigh. Her lips looked like the concentric folds of an anus; the pipe belched a smoke signal, and she said:
'The PIDE boss took her.'

She may have been your mother or your grandmother but there was no apparent displeasure or alarm in her voice. If there was, I didn't notice it, astonished as I was to hear her talk, as I would have been if a chair or a table had suddenly begun to speak.

The next day, on my way to the civilian hospital, I stopped by the PIDE barracks where the prisoners gathered the agents' crops under the fierce vigilance of an armed jailor, overseeing emaciated men and women, almost naked, their heads shaved, swollen by kicks and punches, bending over the earth in limp attitudes. I stopped at the PIDE barracks, Sofia. I walked through the gate trembling with fear and disgust, and I inquired about you, addressing the chief of the brigade who, standing beside the Land Rover, was giving instructions to two pale creatures armed with pistols who were taking careful notes on pads of lined paper that students use at the lycée. The bastard chuckled with contentment like a friar at a banquet.

'A nice piece of ass, hah? She worked for the guerrillas. Headquarters, get it? So, first, we gave her orders to be nice to all the boys, and then we sent her to Luanda.'

I have to go back inside now, Sofia. It's almost morning. The whiskey is making me twitch, nervously, in disenchanted anticipation of the lucidity of dawn. I leave this bathroom as I left the PIDE barracks, where the prisoners gathered the agents' crops, bending over the earth in laconic attitudes without the courage to shout their indignation or to revolt, like me during twenty-seven months of hell. I am going out to the hall, Sofia; I'm turning off the light. And I'm getting ready to smile again like the chief of the brigade, the son of a bitch. I'll chuckle like a friar at a banquet, the son of a bitch standing beside the Land Rover, displaying his buck teeth with the satisfaction of a hyena. Because, Sofia, I have turned into a creature who laughs at himself and at others with the envious, cruel laughter of the dead.

Translated from the Portuguese by Elizabeth Lowe

CONTRIBUTORS

Daniel Kon is a journalist in Buenos Aires. **Andrew Graham-Yooll** was born in Argentina and moved to England in 1976. He is on the staff of the *Guardian*, and is the author of twelve books, the most recent of which are *Forgotten Colony* (about the British in Argentina) and *Portrait of an Exile*. **Jeremy Seabrook**'s books include *What Went Wrong, Unemployment*, and the autobiography *Mother and Child*. **Trevor Blackwell** is currently researching working-class education. **Boaz Evron** is a columnist for the Israeli daily newspaper *Yedioth Aharonot*. **Jurek Becker** was born in Poland in 1937, and spent the first years of his childhood in the German concentration camp at Lodz. He is the author of a number of novels, including *Sleepless Days*, which, like 'The Wall', has been translated into English by Leila Vennewitz. He lives in West Berlin. **Gregor von Rezzori** was born in the Bukovina, studied at the University of Vienna, and, after World War Two, settled in Germany as a writer and radio broadcaster. 'Memoirs of an Anti-Semite' is the title of *A Novel of Five Stories* to be published by Pan Books in autumn 1983. **The Transcripts of Eichmann** is from *Eichmann Interrogated*, a selection from the 3,547 page interrogation that preceded the Eichmann trial in 1961 and that will be published by the Bodley Head in the spring. **Peter Weiss**'s works include *Marat Sade* and *Oratorio in Eleven Cantos on the Auschwitz Trial*. He was about to receive West Germany's highest literary award, the Büchner Prize, when he died in May 1982. **Milan Kundera**'s books were banned in his native Czechoslovakia shortly after the Russian invasion of Prague in 1968. Since 1975 he has lived in France. His books include *The Joke, The Farewell Party*, and *The Book of Laughter and Forgetting*. **Ariel Dorfman**'s first book published in English—*How to Read Donald Duck*—was confiscated by New York customs authorities and then banned in the United States. A version of 'How to Read the Comics' will be included in his forthcoming essay collection *The Empire's Old Clothes: What the Lone Ranger,Babar, the Reader's Digest,and other False Friends do to our Minds*, which will be published by Pantheon Books of the Random House Corporation. **Uwe Johnson** has lived in West Germany, the United States, and, since 1974, England, where he has settled on the northwest corner of the Isle of Sheppey. His most recent book in English is *Anniversaries*. He was awarded the Büchner Prize in 1971. **Nadime Gordimer**, the author of nineteen books, lives in France and South Africa. She was the joint-winner of the Booker Prize in 1974. **Antonio Lobo Antunes** was born in Lisbon in 1942. He is the author of three novels, and has written extensively (in Portuguese) on Lewis Carroll. 'South of Nowhere' is his first work published in English.

Correction: Jorge Ibarguengoitia is not, as previously stated, from Spain. He was born in Mexico and is currently living in France.

EASTERN ARTS ASSOCIATION

The Regional Arts Association for the East of England: Norfolk, Suffolk, Cambridgeshire, Bedfordshire, Essex and Hertfordshire

Support for Literature

Visiting Writers Scheme:

The largest scheme in the country for visiting writers in schools and community workshops.

Creative Writing Courses:

Up to 20 courses a year at residential colleges in the region.

Festivals:

The Cambridge Poetry Festival and Essex Festival of Contemporary Literature.

Support for Literary Groups and Societies.

Writing Fellowships in Community and University

Including the University of East Anglia Fellowship.

Small Press Distribution Scheme

At St Mary Arts Centre, Colchester.
First Scheme of its kind.

Financial Assistance for Literary Magazines

Including GRANTA.

Literature Officer (Laurence Staig)
Eastern Arts Association
8/9 Bridge Street, Cambridge CB2 1UA
Cambridge (0223) 67707

Oxford University Press

Short Stories from the Second World War
Chosen by Dan Davin

Dan Davin has brought together stories from all the wartime services, and from the home front, to create a fictional counterpart to life in time of war. Some of the authors—Graham Green, V. S. Pritchett, H. E. Bates, and Kingsley Amis, for example—are well known. Others will be mainly remembered only by those who recall the little magazines of the time. But they all share the capacity to depict individuals at moments of danger and stress, and the collection is a very moving one.   £9.50

James Joyce
Richard Ellmann

'Most welcome of the publications promised this year is a new edition from Oxford University Press of Richard Ellmann's authoritative and consistently entertaining biography.' *Sunday Times*. 1982 is the centenary of Joyce's birth, and Richard Ellmann has thoroughly revised and expanded his classic biography to incorporate the wealth of new material that has come to light in the twenty-two years since it was first published. Second edition illustrated £20

The Flower Master
Medbh McGuckian

'*The Flower Master* is her first full-length volume, but it contains a highly accomplished body of work . . . If they baffle at first sight, these poems disclose their virtues after due acquaintance and contain enough incidental beauty to make the pursuit a delightful one. *The Flower Master* has brought something strikingly new to English verse and should not be missed.' Christopher Reid in the *Sunday Times*.   £3.95

Collected Poems of Ivor Gurney
Chosen and edited by P. J. Kavanagh

Many critics regard Ivor Gurney as one of the most interesting and original poets of the first half of this century. The appearance in 1976 of a large collection of manuscript originals has enabled P. J. Kavanagh to prepare what is virtually a new edition, the first major collection of Gurney's work to be published. It includes over 300 poems, of which more than a hundred have not previously been collected.   £12

**Edited by
Malcolm Bradbury and
Christopher Bigsby**

Contemporary Writers

Over the past twenty years or so, it has
become clear that a decisive change has
taken place in the spirit and character
both of contemporary writing and
criticism. This series of books is designed
to examine the work of leading novelists,
dramatists and poets who have helped to
shape and define the nature of
contemporary experience and who have
contributed to what can now be seen as a
remarkable period of creativity on an
international scale.

Many of these books will be written by
people who are themselves writers as
well as critics. They are designed to
introduce the work of major figures in a
lucid and engaged manner and to relate
them to the emerging styles, tendencies
and forms of a new age.

Saul Bellow
by Malcolm Bradbury

Thomas Pynchon
by Tony Tanner

John Fowles
by Peter J Conradi

Seamus Heaney
by Blake Morrison

Joe Orton
by C W E Bigsby

Kurt Vonnegut
by Jerome Klinkowitz

Philip Larkin
by Andrew Motion

Philip Roth
by Hermione Lee

Donald Barthelme
by Maurice Couturier
and Régis Durand

METHUEN
11 New Fetter Lane, London EC4P 4EE

ALL PAPERBACK
AT £1.95

Fiction this Autumn

PAUL THEROUX
The London Embassy

Stories of Anglo-American intimacies narrated by the American consul who first made his appearance in THE CONSUL'S FILE.
October £7.95

WILLIAM BOYD
An Ice-Cream War

After his ebullient first novel, A GOOD MAN IN AFRICA, winner of the Whitbread Literary Award and the Somerset Maugham Award, William Boyd strikes a deeper vein in the story of a bizarre and little known East African war.
September £7.95

GERALD HANLEY
Noble Descents

After a break of ten years, the author of THE CONSUL AT SUNSET and THE JOURNEY HOMEWARD returns with a remarkable novel of India set during the early years of Independence.
October £8.95

RACHEL BILLINGTON
Occasion of Sin

A highly intelligent contemporary love story which explores the dilemmas faced by a happily married woman when she finds herself passionately in love with a younger man.
September £7.95

SHAKESPEARE STORIES
Edited by Giles Gordon

A collection of short stories inspired by Shakespeare, contributed by twenty writers ranging from Kingsley Amis and Robert Nye to Salman Rushdie and Angela Carter.
October £7.95

from Hamish Hamilton

Elliott Mossman [Editor]
THE CORRESPONDENCE OF BORIS PASTERNAK AND OLGA FREIDENBERG 1910-1954

"No, not a novel: life in twentieth-century Russia. Two marvellous characters; a marvellous book."
D. M. Thomas, **Observer**

"This collection of letters exchanged between Nobel prize-winner Boris Pasternak and his cousin Olga Freidenberg may well turn out to be the most dynamic, revealing and fascinating personal document to come out of the Soviet Union . . . I cannot think of a book which so illuminates the experience of what it was *and* still is like to be an artist or scholar in the Soviet Union." *Kay Dick*, **Standard**

"This is an absorbing book, and the translation by Elliott Mossman and Margaret Wettlin is excellent."
Kyril Fitzlyon, **Sunday Telegraph**

"This remarkable exchange of letters."
Henry Gifford, **Guardian**
£15.00

Dan Jacobson
THE STORY OF THE STORIES

"To read this book is to enjoy the company of an erudite, original and stimulating mind."
Chaim Bermant, **Daily Telegraph**

"Mr Jacobson's fascinating and finely written essay . . . a rich book, and one to re-read and think about."
Conor Cruise O'Brien, **Observer**

"A sensitive and scrupulous inquiry into a most important aspect of this book of books." *John Ryle*, **New Society**

"Jacobson tackles these paradoxes with a fine sense of parallelisms, a sharp ear for echoes, for events transformed into metaphors, for nuances which theologians have missed." *Martin Jarrett-Kerr*, **Guardian**
£8.95

Secker & Warburg

BACK TO THE LAND

The Pastoral Impulse in Victorian England from 1880 to 1914

JAN MARSH

By 1880 when industrialization had spread so far as to be irreversible and the rural population was rapidly declining, the back-to-the-land movement began to pervade all areas of life and thought.

This is the first study of that widespread alternative movement in Victorian England which is echoed uncannily in the forces and feelings of the 1970s and the 1980s.

Price: £12.95   Hardback
Available from all good bookshops

Quartet Books Limited   A member of the Namara Group
27/29 Goodge Street, London W1P 1FD   Tel: 01-636 3992